M000204348

# PUNDITS FROM PAKISTAN

Rahul Bhattacharya was born in 1979, and was part of a St. Xavier's College team that comfortably failed to carry forward the legacy of Gavaskar and Ashok Mankad. He began writing on cricket in 2000. He lives in Bombay, where he is contributing editor at *Wisden Asia Cricket*. He covered this tour for the *Guardian* and *Wisden*.

RAHUL BHATTACHARYA

# PUNDITS FROM PAKISTAN

*On tour with India, 2003-04*

PICADOR

First published in Great Britain 2005 by Picador
an imprint of Pan Macmillan Ltd
Pan Macmillan, 20 New Wharf Road, London N1 9RR
Basingstoke and Oxford
Associated companies throughout the world
www.panmacmillan.com

ISBN 0 330 43979 0

9 7 5 3 2 4 6 8

Printed and bound in India by
Replika Press Pvt. Ltd. Kundli 131028

# Contents

# Prologue

ON 14 DECEMBER 2003, long after the Indian cricketers had repaired to their hotel rooms following a famous recovery at the Adelaide Oval, there was an assassination attempt on General Pervez Musharraf, the president of Pakistan, when a bomb went off beneath a bridge in Rawalpindi seconds after the last car in his convoy passed over the spot. Eleven days later, there was another bid on the General's life, the third now in eighteen months, when two explosive-laden vehicles assaulted his motorcade 250 yards from that same spot, shattering the windshield of his car, killing sixteen, injuring fifty, and setting off alarm bells in Melbourne, where the Indians were readying themselves for the Boxing Day Test. That night every member of the Indian squad signed a letter addressed to the cricket board expressing his reservations over the proposed tour to Pakistan two months hence. This letter was never sent. Instead it was leaked to a journalist, who would bring it to the attention of not just the cricket board but the entire country.

It was here that the necessary, protracted, and often farcical debate over India's revival tour to Pakistan got underway.

But for a while the storm didn't gather. Disregarding the assassination bids on the General, the Indian prime minister, Atal Behari Vajpayee, travelled for a regional summit to Pakistan in the first week of the new year. Almost concurrently, in Kolkata, Jagmohan Dalmiya, president of the Indian board, announced that the Indians would undertake a tour of three Tests and five one-day internationals to Pakistan starting 1 March. The Pakistan Cricket Board (PCB) learnt of this from television. 'Vajpayee has, in fact, opened the innings,' gushed Shaharyar Khan, the retired foreign secretary, cousin of Indian cricket's most revered captain, M.A.K. Pataudi, and now chairman of the PCB. The subcontinent was bathed in a kind of glow. The governments were talking, cultural exchanges were growing more frequent, there was ceasefire in Kashmir and, at long last, cricket could be played. There was the real feeling that things could be achieved.

And then the obstacles began to mount. In the middle of January, as they succumbed in the one-dayers in Australia, the Indian cricketers revealed that not a thing had been done to assuage their concerns. 'There seems to be more talk of television revenues rather than security which is disturbing,' one team member was quoted as saying. By the end of the month there emerged from Pakistan the scandalous results of a four-month long inquiry which indicted Abdul Qadeer Khan, the revered father of its nuclear programme, for pilfering weapon technologies for the global black-market. And it had been two years ago, almost to the week, that the Delhi Police had leaked the purported plans of a terrorist group with alleged Pakistan links to kidnap Sachin Tendulkar and Sourav Ganguly.

And so a montage of mental associations: assassination bids on the president, abduction plans for star cricketers, nukes in who knows whose hands.

Even then, all was deemed to be on track when, on 9 February, the Indian board dispatched a three-man delegation to Pakistan on a reconnaissance mission headed by Yashovardhan Azad, Inspector General of Police (VIP security), who had handled the Vajpayee recce the previous month. For a week the delegation criss-crossed Pakistan and was presented everywhere with plans:

plans for the airports, plans for the hotels, plans for the grounds, plans for the journeys between the airports and the hotels, plans for the journeys between the hotels and the grounds. The General, well aware of the wonders a safe event of this magnitude could do for the international image of Pakistan, assured it of the highest level of security: the one enjoyed by him, though perhaps that was not saying much given his recent adventures.

Meanwhile, in India, greater wheels were in spin. The home ministry, under Lal Krishna Advani, Vajpayee's hawkish deputy in the coalition government and its largest component, the right-wing Bharatiya Janata Party (BJP), was in favour of shelving the tour till after the general elections, which had been brought forward by several months, and were eventually slated to begin on 20 April. It sensed – but not the people, as the polls would show – this heady ephemeral buzz, a 'feel-good factor' sweeping through the nation, and what might a possible cricket loss to Pakistan on the eve of polls do to that? And would such friendly overtures towards Pakistan before elections make the party look too soft in the eyes of the voters? The shamelessness boggled.

Postponing the series would pose another problem. It would mean having to play in May, in the most hellishly searing innards of summer, where cricketers and spectators alike would have fallen like flies. And beyond the summer were a chain of commitments for both teams, extending into the early months of the following year. So then there was talk in India of splitting the tour into two, holding only the Tests – 'less excitable for the masses' – before the elections. We were getting into truly absurd territory.

The PCB reiterated that scratching the tour would be a serious blow to the rapprochement between the countries, but really their desperation was more rooted in their financial plight. They had sunk into a quagmire in the aftermath of 9/11, when, in

9

what was the heart of the cricket season, the General, amid violent opposition at home, declared logistic and military support to America in its war in Afghanistan. New Zealand would cancel their tour out of security concerns. As would their replacement, Sri Lanka. In early 2002, West Indies were met at a neutral venue, which provided only a percentage of earnings from a home series. And when New Zealand were finally persuaded to make their visit, a bomb blew up outside the team hotel at Karachi hours before the start of the second Test, killing fourteen and leading to instant abandonment of the tour. And so back one step again, with Australia agreeing to play out their Tests only at neutral venues. South Africa arrived in late 2003, but only under the pressure of a lawsuit, and then too for a shortened tour at handpicked venues.

In the two and a half years since 9/11 only Bangladesh, the feeblest commercial attraction of all, had completed a full tour of Pakistan. And the biggest draw, India, had not toured, owing to wretched political conditions – increased Pakistan-supported militancy in Kashmir, the Babri Masjid demolition by Hindu fundamentalists in Ayodhya, the war in Kargil – since 1989, except for a rushed set of three one-dayers in 1997. The monetary consequences of another no-show – the PCB had sold this series for USD 21 million, comfortably the most lucrative deal in their history – were hard to contemplate, let alone endure. Their only consolation remained the International Cricket Council's (ICC) policy on cancelled tours, which could compel the Indian board to cough up a fine running into millions of dollars.

As India vacillated and debated, and the home ministry planted story after story to gauge public sentiment, Pakistan's government officials, cricket officials, former cricket players, current cricket players, newspaper men and public, all urged them to purge their minds of doubt and just come. Nobody was left uninterviewed, not even a spokesperson for a terrorist group, who claimed to be unaware that there was a tour on the cards at all – but quickly added that the Indian cricketers would be 'our guests and it is our responsibility to give them full honour and respect.'

The most instructive call came from Wasim Akram, captain when Pakistan had shrugged aside similar security concerns, political pressures, and pointed warnings from the Shiv Sena, a Bombay-based party of bigots and thugs, to play out a magnificent series in 1998-99, a tour, like this one would be, made after a gap of over a decade. To the vandalising of the cricket pitch in Delhi, to the throwing of pigs' heads outside the stadium at Chennai, to the ransacking of the board's head-office in Bombay, to threats of releasing snakes into the crowd should the tour proceed, to statements such as 'Hindus should rise up against the [visiting] Pakistan cricket team' from the Sena's venomous leader, Bal Thackeray, Akram's response had been calm and eloquent: 'We are going there to better the relations between the two countries, and I hope the Indian Government will not allow a handful of people to deprive cricket lovers of some action and tension packed cricket.'

Finally, ending a week of utter confusion, it was on 14 February, also Valentine's Day, an occasion reviled by the Sena and the Hindu nationalists as a Western import, and precisely two months from the day the Indian cricketers had signed the letter in Adelaide, that Prime Minister Vajpayee took the game by the scruff of the neck and announced that the tour would proceed. Even if Vajpayee's choice of date had not been by design, it was fitting. He had been foreign minister in the Janata Dal government when India made the resumption tour in 1978-79; and it was he who had reversed India's stance on bilateral cricket with Pakistan in October 2003.

Seven days after the Vajpayee announcement, the itinerary was approved. The PCB, somewhat indebted to Vajpayee's gesture, were obliged to make two compromises, of limiting the matches at Karachi and Peshawar to one-dayers, and to day games only, and the second, a meaningless Indian insistence really, of scheduling the one-dayers before the Tests.

It was the tightest itinerary conceivable; the tickle of a feather and it would have simply burst. It was a thirty-nine-day schedule, starting 10 March, finishing 17 April, and containing twenty-one possible days of cricket in between. Factoring for two practice days before each Test, one before each one-dayer and seven travelling days, there remained not a single genuinely free day all tour. A warm-up one-dayer was pencilled in, but no first-class one. Excluding one-off Test tours, the only precedent for this in Indian history was the 1984-85 tour to Pakistan, eventually abandoned unfinished owing to the assassination of the Indian prime minister, Indira Gandhi. On the last tour undertaken by undivided India, to England in 1946, the team played twenty-six first-class matches to three Tests.

Not that the Indian players were complaining. At the fag end of an intense season – six Tests and seventeen one-dayers in the past four months – practice games, they felt, would be encumbrances more than anything.

I certainly did feel deprived, not because of any especial interest in covering side games, but because I thought them essential to the rhythm of a tour: time to breathe, to sniff around, to work at larger stories, to wander about, imbibe. I was convinced there was no book inside this itinerary.

By the end of February everything seemed in order, but there would be one last twist. In the proposed Memorandum of Understanding – the document sealing the tour on paper – the Indian board pushed for a clause that would allow them to instantly walk out of the tour, no questions asked, even at the merest incident of stone-throwing. Coming after all the convoluted deliberations, this was testing Pakistani patience to breaking point. A cricket reporter with *The News* fired off a polemic pointing to India's inglorious history, and hence their hypocrisy, when it came to spectator behaviour, before concluding: 'There is a famous saying that never try to take so much advantage of your host that he eventually kicks you out of the house. The same thing applies to the Indians, they have done enough squeezing and pressurizing and if they believe that they would be playing in front of terrorists, criminals or illiterates in Pakistan it is best if they don't come.'

Despite the overheating, I could not help but enjoy the general spirit of the article. Enough, after a point. Fastidiousness was one thing; high-handedness another. India could not have it all, least of all that which they could never give. The Indian board was made to see this by the PCB, the MoU was tempered down, and less than two weeks before its eventual start the final technical hurdle before the Indian Test tour to Pakistan, the sixth in history, was surmounted, and not even the horrendous carnage of Shias in the western town of Quetta on 2 March, Ashura, the holy tenth day of Muharram, which led to the escalation of sectarian violence throughout Pakistan, could sow any further doubt.

BUT THE MOOT question remained. Was this really a good idea?

Any argument could be turned inside out and thrown back. Some held that the risk was simply not worth it: an attack on the team by motivated parties, god forbid, something like the massacre of Israeli athletes by Palestinian terrorists at the 1972 Munich Olympics, would in a stroke destroy the peace process and set off a series of calamities. Some reasoned that *not* touring would be the real sabotage of the peace process, preventing, as it would, the rare opportunity of thousands of people meeting thousands of people across the border and watching a game: if not this, what hope of bigger things?

And some argued that it was precisely because of the danger posed by thousands of people meeting thousands of people and watching a game that the tour must not proceed. And here we must stray beyond current realpolitik, into still cloudier territory.

What is the point of sport? What, indeed? A grand scheme to keep the masses distracted from revolution, it has been suggested. A grand scheme to keep the masses in a state of competitive frenzy and hence in perpetual readiness for war, it has been suggested. Some even contend that it is a simple pleasure.

And whatever be its point, what is its effect? Divisive, irredeemably divisive, according to George Orwell, the British literary giant of the early twentieth century.

Orwell, in what became a much-cited essay, published under the ironic title, 'The Sporting Spirit', but identified always by the catchphrase inside – 'war minus the shooting' – was not the only person to hold this opinion of organised sport, nor was he the first. But, owing to a combination of the man's eminence, the absolute, unhesitant, lucid cold-fury of his tone, and the rich variety of life experience he brought to his writing, his articulation is the one that has lived on in popular consciousness. Undesirable as it is to have to try and précis his thoughts, it will not amount to distortion to present Orwell's contention of sporting contest as 'mimic warfare', as 'an unfailing cause of ill-will', 'bound up with hatred, jealousy, boastfulness, disregard of all rules and sadistic pleasure in witnessing violence', and which leads to 'orgies of hatred', when one considers, especially, the 'rise of nationalism – the lunatic modern habit of identifying oneself with large power units and seeing everything in terms of competitive prestige.'

Orwell's essay, published in December 1945, was a response to a tour of Britain by a Russian football club shortly after the countries had fought as allies in the Second World War; a tour which, with its petty brawls and controversies, he believed only served to worsen the deteriorating Anglo-Soviet relations if anything.

Nothing in Orwell's argument has been inapplicable to the Indian situation. The most successful domestic tournament India ever staged was one played along communal lines: Parsis, Europeans, soon the Hindus, then the Muslims, and eventually the Christians, Buddhists and Jews under the banner 'Rest', slugging it out before rapturous crowds. So wildly popular was this cricketing carnival, that is, so popular and so wild, that the Pentangular was eventually abandoned after 1945 by the will of the Congress party, who had the blessings of Gandhi in arguing that the tournament served as a mass vehicle of communal animosity and identity-indoctrination, militating against the very idea of the conceived republic of India. And after the independent republic was created, there has been the razor-edged alliance between sport and nation, doubly sharp in this case because the contest between countries is also perceived by some as a contest between faiths.

Having to concede to the Orwellian notion puts the liberal sports lover in a terrible predicament. For even the most unbiased aesthete must confess that the thrill of sport, in whatever quantity, is gladiatorial.

The disquiet is apparent in the explorations of Ramachandra Guha and Mike Marqusee, two social historians who over the last fifteen years have provided cricket with some of its most valuable literature. In his colossal *A Corner of a Foreign Field,* Guha wends his way through the highways and bylanes of colonial and post-colonial Indian history, through the howling gales and the tempests of the Triangulars and Quadrangulars and Pentangulars, through the currents and undercurrents of India v Pakistan, and at every step of the way he must contend with the question: cricket and race conflict, cricket and class conflict, cricket and communal conflict, cricket and caste conflict, cricket and national conflict. Marqusee, in his compelling journey through the subcontinental World Cup in 1996 – titled, in fact, *War Minus the Shooting* – considers the Orwellian theme in the context of a corporatised sport in a globalised world, a hectic, invidious space, he finds, scrutinising always through a prism calibrated due left, of multimillion-dollar identity mongering and identity exploitation.

Neither author dwells overmuch on his dilemma, but we are allowed several glimpses. Their evidence, their experience, compels them to go along with Orwell some of the way, a lot of the way, at some points almost all the way. But they cannot adopt his formidable stance. They cannot bring themselves to it. Cricket has touched them too intimately to be so callous. And Orwell's certainty is so unflinching that even if all that he has written were true, it could not possibly have been the whole truth. They are able to recognise that sport is not a one-dimensional force.

Indeed, Orwell was so bold as to question the very act of playing and following sport that is representational: 'as soon as the question of prestige arises, as soon as you feel that you and some larger unit will be disgraced if you lose, the most savage combative instincts are aroused.' He does not, 'of course, suggest that sport is one of the main causes of international rivalry; big-scale sport is itself, I think, merely another effect of the causes that have produced nationalism.' But since this affiliation with a larger group, particularly, by his reckoning, in the 'modern' world, cannot simply be wished away, he is in effect questioning the act of playing and following sport at all. It is a most severe proposition. And a most unfair one.

For, to ask the question, 'why play sport', is in my view analogous to asking the question, 'why live life' – if we can see life as a fundamentally useless interlude in the infinity of time spent consumed by the means to survive and get ahead amid the tugs and pulls of millions of other such lives. If competition and competitive prestige is at the heart of sport, then it is also – with the world being finite as it is, with human nature being what it is – then it is also at the heart of all living.

Yet we recognise, don't we, that life, despite its inherent cruelties, its numbing everyday brutalities, still glistens moist with a numberless other hues?

Sport is able to sum up life, able to strip it bare and put it under a drama-filled magnifying glass. And through this magnifying glass we are able to see ourselves, vividly; able to see, like they sometimes say of the arts, our condition. And whereas the arts have the option of describing their own universe, or isolating the conditions and proceeding thereon, sport, like the real world, must work largely under a specified code of laws and obligations, the first objective of which is to get ahead for oneself, a process that must require the partnership of some, and be at the expense of some.

If the magnifying glass is a frightening prospect it is because it is so revealing of our condition, and if it is an uplifting prospect it is so for the same reason. Nothing which is not in us falls inside its perimeter. And everything that is in us does; every human aspiration, every human prejudice, every human strength, every human frailty, every human beauty, all of it so naked, all of it in collision.

And being so, the interaction of sport with the world is bound to be a loaded thing. It can narrow the mind, as Orwell has illustrated: the shame heaped upon the losing group, the demonising of the opponent group, the violence of spectators: in 1969, riots after a football match between Honduras and El Salvador escalated into war between the countries. And it can broaden it, as articulated by C.L.R. James, whose beautiful meditation on cricket and the

Caribbean condition and much else besides, *Beyond a Boundary*, finishes with a quarter million Australians flooding the streets of Melbourne at the end of the magic cricket summer of 1960-61 to wave farewell to the West Indian touring party, the first such to have been led by a black man, a man, who would not, at the time, be granted citizenship to their country because of his colour; and therein with the remarkable, remarkable conclusion: 'Clearing their way with bat and ball, West Indians at that moment had made a public entry into the comity of nations.'

And so I remained strongly pro tour, on the selfish grounds of being able to travel to Pakistan, on the practical grounds that it would be a step forward in the dialogue between the countries, and in the hope that coming, particularly, as it did in the current climate, our magnifying glass would be able to show up something, something... something basically *good*. How frozen could we remain by fear? Could we so easily stop playing? Could we so easily stop living?

Now, having unloaded all that from my chest, now to step across that line...

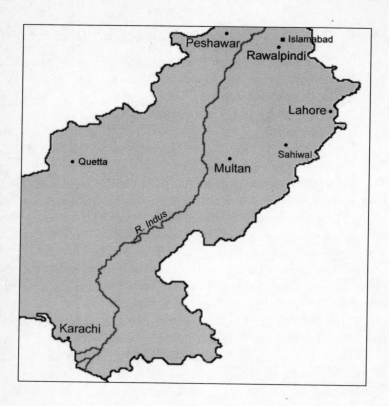

| 10 March | Arrival | Lahore |
| 11 March | v Pak A | Lahore |
| 13 March | First ODI | Karachi |
| 16 March | Second ODI | Rawalpindi |
| 19 March | Third ODI | Peshawar |
| 21 March | Fourth ODI | Lahore |
| 24 March | Fifth ODI | Lahore |
| 28 March-1 April | First Test | Multan |
| 5-9 April | Second Test | Lahore |
| 13-17 April | Third Test | Rawalpindi |
| 17 April | Departure | Islamabad |

# 1. *Dawat*

THE MAN at the counter was familiar with the inquiry. He pointed back out the door of Mandvi Post Office, to a shrouded row of stalls. The stalls curved all around the hairpin bend on which the post office stood, eating into the concrete shadows of the flyover above Mohammad Ali Road.

Quintessential Bombay stalls: stalls of typists, form-fillers, photocopy-operators, stationery sellers: nuts-and-bolts of personal enterprise. On the third attempt, we located the correct one, stall no. 9, run by Yakoob Memon and his sons, a green tin box, 3 feet deep, 4 feet wide, 5 feet high.

The order was placed. The son removed it from under a pile of A4 sheets on a shelf embedded in the back of the stall. It was a rectangular form, broader than longer, with its six jointed leaves coloured four different colours. Forty rupees each.

'Anywhere else you can get this in Bombay?'

'Must be some more stalls.'

'Where?'

'Don't know.'

'Who will know?'

'Don't know.'

A flush of success and subterfuge, for the moment overwhelming the smoke, grime, noise and interminable chaos of Mandvi.

The form I filled by hand with exaggerated care that evening but several others engaged the typists perched on stools in a

21

diplomatic boulevard in New Delhi one week later.

Terrific fights broke out on this boulevard over the first weekend of March. A doctor who had skipped his morning visit to the clinic heaped shame upon the journalists who wangled their way to the window. The journalists flung back the shame, arguing that the counter had been reserved for them. The foolscap paper declaring the reservation had been stuck in between the two windows.

In the adjacent queue, a more vital battle raged. 'Just because you are ladies does not mean you can do what you want,' a man cleared his throat and hollered. 'Don't you know how to speak to laydees?' he was rebuked by the lady. 'Just because you have long hair does not mean you are ladies,' the man retorted with a twist. 'Doesn't he know how to speak to laydees?' the lady asked the cameras which had scuttled across to imbibe these scenes.

These were only the cricket windows. Up the road, outside the general window, families sprawled on the footpath with bedding as if for months now. Further up, in the mid-morning haze, the typists accepted another form, perked up their spectacles, and clickety-clacked away, expressionless. Upstream still, just beyond the makeshift metal road-blocks, the cigarette guy and the tea guy, parked together, made brisk trade. Lining all this were the impenetrable iron gates and the high cream walls of the High Commission, iced by sparkling blue domes.

The one thing that kept everybody apart and everybody together on the diplomatic boulevard over the first weekend of March was that nobody knew anything for certain. What grounds for acceptance? What grounds for rejection? Who knew? What if it doesn't come through before the flight? Who to ask? How?

My own tensions waxed and waned but I became adept at biding my time. I lay down on the pavement below the neem tree and watched the sun gleam off the ceramic mosaic on the domes. I used the cellphone for fresh attempts at the Snake II record, and to seek refuge in the comforting routine of dialling the minister of press inside who would never answer. The one time he answered it was so unsettling that I forgot who I had dialled and he swiftly hung up.

The journalists, their flights booked, grew insecure and frustrated and united as one to demand a meeting with the minister of press. But when the minister acquiesced to a meeting at a furtive gate around on the other side of the fort to issue a noncommittal placation, I found that my name was not on the list at all. This was serious, and it earned me the privilege of getting behind the gates and walls and beneath the sparkling domes.

I spent five hours in the minister's office wondering what the hell was happening outside just as I'd spent the previous eight hours wondering what the hell was happening inside. I was fidgety-nervous, speaking at inappropriate moments, making wrong statements, touching things I wasn't meant to touch, and was once reprimanded by the severe young assistant for lifting up the phone without permission.

I learnt to sit quietly and observe. The BBC called the minister for a soundbyte and the minister informed them that a hundred journalist visas had already been issued. Really?

Slowly, I began feeling at home, and as the evening wore on, the minister and I, without saying it to one another, were secretly pleased at how another day of life had been endured by delving into the futility of process, and we ended up discussing the *zabardast* nature of the bond between a mother and a son. With this I felt the minister and I had reached a deeper level, and when he dropped me off at a tandoori place late at night, I was secure in the knowledge that the visa would come through the next day; but, of course, it did not.

Saturday passed with wait-and-watch apprehension, Sunday, Holi, with bhang thandai and more tension, and it was two hours and forty minutes before the flight on Monday that the stamped passport was squeezed back out the fortress through the window, whereupon the waiting taxi was whipped mercilessly towards the airport.

Six hours later, still at the airport. No aircraft. The scheduled one was on its way, erroneously, to Kathmandu.

\*

THE CONTINENTAL, as it came to be simply known, stood between a bridge and a KFC; a squat, brick motel that might have been picked clean out from a Nevada highway; only, the red signage was not neon. The foyer was lit dim and the walls layered with lurid orange textured wallpaper, made more inescapable by the mirrors on all sides of every pillar.

My room on the first floor had dark maroon carpeting holding a perpetual dankness. There was no air-conditioning for the moment because there was a still a week to the official start of a/c season; the mattress sagged at the lumbar; there were no shower curtains in the toilet, the water-force was negligible and hot water was on request. Apart from this, a thoroughly agreeable depravity. It was easy to become the room.

The first friends were made at the Dubai Mobile Center, a small shop under the bridge. Under the bridge: just like at Mandvi; and just like at Mandvi, cheek-and-jowl, glass shops, butcher shops, mattress shops, bangle shops, electronic shops, cloth shops; interminable chaos.

I stepped into the Center to make an inquiry about local simcards. The advertisements said connections were available for

24

Rs 499, plus tax: the tax was Rs 1,999. Anjum called himself the chief executive of the Center. Anjum was a hero. His greased black hair fell to the sides of his forehead and behind tapered away into a mullet. His black shirt he kept unbuttoned till the solar plexus. He cudded tobacco and every now and then stylishly flicked open a lid on his counter and spat through into a receptacle below. A photograph with Saeed Anwar revealed he had been an active club cricketer.

There was a buzz in this little room. Anjum's friends concentrated their energy on me on learning I was from across. Ishfaaq, the oldest, told me: 'If you need anything, you call me. If you want to be shown around, you call me. You don't think twice.' As I was about to leave he added: 'And remember. We are good people here. There are bad people too. But mostly, we are good people.'

Back at the Continental, Aslam Ahmed, the manager, a rugby-ball-like man with a twitching Chaplin moustache and a loud and slightly nasal voice introduced me to another Aslam, a policeman, who engulfed me in a bear hug and called out for a bottle of Coke to inaugurate the friendship. 'I will give you *dawat* before you leave,' he announced and then disappeared up the stairs with his keep.

'Farmaiyenge aap?'(Would you indulge?), Aslam, the manager, asked. I nodded. I was to wait in the room; he would arrive soon.

An awards show in Dubai was on TV when Aslam came upstairs with a bottle of Rasputin Vodka, pineapple flavour, a local brew. Amitabh Bachchan, receiving a lifetime honour, had tears in his eyes, and watching him, there were now some in ol' Aslam's. Indian movies had been banned in theatres since 1965 but not one of Amitabh had escaped him. 'Not one.'

Aslam's wife knew that he indulged but not his parents or his children. Our spirits rising, Aslam spoke of his family, his life now and his previous life as a civilian in the Air Force. There was no ashtray around; he pulled up the dustbin, but kept missing it as he ashed, leaving the maroon carpeting like a spent campfire. Flipping channels to a local cable brought to the fore India's remixed hit of the time, 'Kaanta Lagaa' by DJ Doll, and Aslam cranked up the volume and swung in his chair.

By midnight we were famished. Down in the orange reception, we met with Aslam's uncle, Nasir, who reminded me, not just for his name, but for his air of unrepentant wisdom, of Naseeruddin Hodja, the Persian wit in the comic-books.

Outside Asad waited in his white taxi. Upon the word, Asad set off, scorching past cars, burning through tar, blasting through walls, dissolving around bends, leaping over flyovers, till we were no longer grounded and by the time we stopped at Laxmi Chowk the skin on our faces had stretched back, distorted, exhilarated, as if packaged in cellophane.

The night was out in full bloom at Laxmi Chowk. Our brains floating like water lilies, we wound through the lights, the blinding white-bright lights with tiny radii, through the warring sounds of metal on metal, through the mingling, tingling aromas, through the utter life of the night, and settled at a prime table at the stall of Tabussum, who worked the kat-a-kat, known also as tak-a-tak, pounding his pair of *khurpis* on a large flat tava, mashing into a tizzy spices and oil, and kidneys, testicles, livers, and brain, called here not 'bheja', but the more poetic, 'maghaz'.

I was still savouring Tabussum's delights when I felt a pair of hands on my shoulders. Briskly they started running up and down and side to side performing magical manipulations which provoked both awakening and slumber. It was a masseur, acting on Aslam's instructions; I was embarrassed, and requested him to stop; Aslam kept signalling him to go on. There was nothing to do but submit, and it was inside this submission that Aslam declared, garrulously,

'I love India'. 'I love Pakistan,' I replied. He summoned Tabussum. 'I love India,' he was asked to embrace me and say, and he did. 'I love Pakistan,' I embraced him back and said.

It was all terribly grandiose. We must have thought of ourselves as benevolent emperors, able to dole out such a large love on a whim. But this was Punjab; and we must proclaim. And we were in the moment and we were true to the moment.

All around the kat-a-kats thundered in the Lahore late-night, and in between the warring sounds, the white-bright lights, the tingling aromas, the utter life of the night, I felt fully that I was here, that it meant something to be here, and I felt a surge of happiness, a new thrill, an alive joy, the cusp of discovery, and the strains of a wistful nostalgia, borne out by no personal attachments, no personal memories, no personal reference points, a second-hand kind of nostalgia... wistfulness I suppose more than nostalgia, and one which was then very hard to shake off.

*

THE MORNING AFTER. The plastic mug in the toilet of the Continental resembled a teapot, full of curves and designs and a long spout. What chance the lingering cranial stabs of Mr Rasputin before such poetry first thing in the morning?

Mundanity returned. A day spent organising currency, a phone card, an Internet connection, collecting press accreditation and acquainting oneself with local English-language newspapers, at Rs 12 and 13, more expensive than a pack of cigarettes or biscuits.

I was an object of some curiosity. Some said I was the first Indian they had met. Some asked what religion I followed. When I answered none really, they felt they'd frightened me and would begin apologising, so to avoid the trouble I just started saying

Hinduism. Everyone talked about Bollywood, not so much the movies but actor gossip.

The following afternoon, Wednesday, 10 March, the Indian cricket team were to land in Pakistan.

Perhaps I had romanticised it too much. I had wanted to be on this side for the arrival, the extraordinary emotional historic arrival. Instead I found a great array of security personnel, two young girls with a chart, and one man from Sialkot.

It was a hot, dry, cactus kind of day. I asked the driver if he might switch on the air-conditioner. Gruffly he said it did not work. Soon he learnt I was Indian. At once he switched on the a/c. He felt ashamed. He did not charge me extra for the a/c.

The pampering would not cease over the coming weeks. Friends and family in India had advised before leaving that better to be inconspicuous and try to pass of as Pakistani; by the end of it Pakistanis were seriously contemplating posing as Indians and reaping the rewards. I had not been made to feel so welcome anywhere in the world.

The first indication of the security web that lay not just round this corner but the next six weeks came when the taxi was halted at two places well before the terminal, for a boot and undercarriage scan. And at the terminal, a variety of security units made themselves conspicuous.

Catching the eye first were the all-black Elite Force, their sporty logoed caps and t-shirts at odds with their thumping boots, their silver buckles on leather belts, the semi-automatic pistols hitched on to their waists, the rifles in their hands. What appeared from a distance to be a phoenix on the front of their t-shirts was two pistols in profile facing away from one another; the No Fear tagline on the back had been nicked from an Australian surfwear company. The Elite Force, I was told by a journalist on security affairs, was a unit of the Punjab Police set up in 1998 to combat growing sectarian terrorism in the state.

The other slick lot appeared to be the Tiger Force, many of them with 250cc Honda motorcycles in tow. The Tigers, I was told, were conceived as the Elites of the Sindh Police, and largely employed in urban areas, and thus the bikes. On closer inspection there also emerged a Mujahid Force. This was a paramilitary unit derived from the civilian population as well as the armed forces, and usually assigned to protect national security installations.

As the tour went along, two more units would make their presence felt at the grounds. Deputed at Lahore and Peshawar were the grandly titled, grandly attired, Frontier Constabulary, a force of tribal men from the regions by the Afghan border trained by the army, deputed to patrol the western boundary. At Karachi there would be the Pakistan Rangers (Sindh), another paramilitary force whose primary function is border patrolling.

Out and about at the moment were also a number of airport security staff, all of them carrying weapons, and a smattering of plainclothesmen. Altogether, the men were in their hundreds. The Indians were in many safe hands. And they were travelling with two security men of their own.

I had reached too early. Despite the guns and jeeps and bikes, it was an afternoon of drift, detachment. The Allama Iqbal Airport possessed an unhurried, almost lofty, air, as befitting a structure named after a poet. It was a new facility, elegant, modern, fresh, spacious. There were barely any lookers-on. The only persons, other than the security and the mediamen and the PCB officials, present with the express purpose of receiving the Indian team were the two delightfully shy little girls. They had been brought there by their mother, a Patna resident before marriage. The girls, dressed identically, had come with a bouquet of flowers each, and a white chart. 'Main apne Hindustani mamaji ka swagatam karti hoon' (I welcome my Indian uncles), the message on the chart said. The script was Devanagari. The girls had made the chart themselves, the mother said, following her directions.

In the eyes of the growing crew of media corps on this vacant afternoon, the sisters and their mother became the atmosphere. The girls were asked to pose for photo after photo and the mother chatted with journalist after journalist. Soon, the Indians would be here.

The cricketers had endured a long morning of protocol in Delhi. Hair combed and boots polished and togged in national blazers and ties, they had been marched to 7 Race Course Road to meet with Prime Minister Vajpayee. Schoolchildren had held up placards and flags to wave them to the lawns inside, and on the lawns a police band made symphonic renditions of Hindi movie songs before the PM requested 'Hum Honge Kaamiyaab' ('We Shall Overcome'). Ladoos and fruit juices were served, and finally Vajpayee bid the ambassadors farewell with the message, 'Khel hi nahin, dil bhi jeetiye' (Win not only matches, but hearts too).

A newspaper sponsoring a send-off event presented them with a good-luck card signed by fans. They might have considered carrying it along for inspiration had the thing been smaller than 22,500 sq ft. Still, the card must have been more reassuring than the pronouncement from Kapil Dev, who had spent time with the squad at the preparatory camp in Kolkata: 'It may be a goodwill series for some,' he had said, 'but for the boys, it's life and death.' India's flair is not for understatement.

The players did not arrive at the appointed hour. Their take-off had been pegged back by thirty minutes. This was a ruse, to throw off any time-activated bombs. Ruse after such ruse and arrangement after arrangement had been devised for the next month and a half.

There were to be multiple options for each land-route the team took, with decoy motorcades sometimes sent out on the false one. All stadiums and hotels would be searched for explosives by sniffer dogs. A helicopter would monitor activity on high-rise buildings around the National Stadium at Karachi. At Karachi and Peshawar, safe houses had been identified should the situation come to it. Already confined to a bubble, would the next step for the Indian cricketer entail living in a bunker? The players were provided a USD 500,000 insurance cover against a terrorist attack, twice the usual amount.

The dry-hot noon grew long on the flat outskirts of Lahore. There was talk about Pakistan's successful testing the previous day of the missile Shaheen II, which, at 2,500 km, had most of India in its range. The Indian government had been informed of the test in advance, as a courtesy. The television sets beamed pictures from Karachi, where Pakistan's best XI were trouncing the second-stringers in a warm-up match. The media contingent steadily kept growing, the little girls continued to strain themselves shyly, and, by now, sensing all the activity, a decent gathering of bystanders had developed.

I had immersed myself in the Karachi game when I felt a sudden rush. Cameramen and photographers bustled to get to the upper tier of the terminal. The bystanders were trying to follow. All but one stairwell and elevator had been put out of limits, so a fervent scramble ensued. I managed to squeeze my way up.

Another ruse: the Indians were to exit from the arrival lounge. The arrangements below, the security, the vehicles, the coach, were all a decoy. Thrice the number of everything awaited upstairs.

Things happened rapidly now. Shutters began going off everywhere as the players emerged, through layers of human chains formed by the commandos, led by a smiling Sourav Ganguly, captain of India. In brisk strides, the squad covered the 30 metres out from the doorway of the terminal to the coach, some like Rahul Dravid and the physio, Andrew Leipus, filming, some like Mohammad Kaif playfully engaging the cameras, some like Sachin Tendulkar inscrutable behind tinted glares. As they zipped past, one by one, the only thing that struck me was the youngness of the bunch, the fresh-facedness of Irfan Pathan and Laxmipathy Balaji and Parthiv Patel and Ramesh Powar and Yuvraj Singh. Would they be up to these weeks?

In a trice, with the lensmen tripping over one another, the coach took off, with a horn which sounded like the last exhale of a slain giant. I looked around; it did not seem like the girls had made it upstairs. Their poster would return home unseen by the Indians. And it was now that I ran into the man from Sialkot, who'd just raced up, breathless. 'Chali gayee Indian team?' (The Indian team has gone?), he asked, a little confused. He'd travelled, he said, four hours by train for a glimpse.

Down in the distance, the motorcade powered on in formation, the bullet-proof coach led by a jeep and a stagger of bikes, flanked by bikes, and brought up on the rear by a set of jeeps and a fire-engine. It picked up pace and grew smaller and smaller till it pulled away from the airport site, turned right at the yellow-green fields across the road, and headed, purposefully, towards the city of Lahore.

ENTERING THE LUXURIOUS spick white premises of the Pearl Continental entailed, at the main gate, the boot and undercarriage scan, and past that, at the portico, the three-step check which over the next six weeks, at the grounds, at the team hotels and at the airports, would become like a bodily function: metal detector, body frisk, bag inspection. There was no point grumbling: this was India's condition for touring.

There were, reportedly, 250 security guards manning the hotel – that is, about fifteen per player. No access was available, naturally, to the players' floors; and no other guest was permitted to occupy a room on those floors. Any envelopes addressed to the team, it was said, were to be scanned by a bomb-disposal unit. All food for them was to be prepared under the strictest supervision. Still, it did come as a shock when one of the commandos encircling the table in the lobby coffee-shop where Ganguly sat briefly with a few journalists asked that the tea be tasted before it pass the lips of the captain. A journalist obliged. Yes, we know our place in the world, we lot.

And there were a lot of us. Already the Pearl Continental looked geared more for a rally than a press conference. Many were still not here.

On my first tour with India, to the Caribbean in 2002, there were eleven print journalists, one photographer, and one television channel, the one that produced the series. For this tour, over 120 accreditations were handed out to Indian journalists alone. These included correspondents and photographers and cameramen for six news agencies, close to forty newspapers and magazines in six languages, three websites, eleven TV channels and All India Radio.

And there was significant interest from outside India. The major newspapers from the Gulf sent out a man. Several British broadsheets commissioned reporters rather than rely on agencies, with the *Guardian* dispatching their chief sportswriter for the Indian arrival and the first one-dayer. Surprise cameos were made by the American magazines *GQ* and *Sports Illustrated*, and the newspaper *San Francisco Chronicle*; *The New York Times* commissioned a piece for its hallowed editorial pages, very likely the first time cricket ever featured there. A Chinese agency reporter popped in and out at some point. I'm not sure what became of them, but applications were received also from Germany's *Deutsche Wello* and Norway's *Daily Aftenposten*. The BBC team was one larger than the Indian cricket squad – sixteen – and represented five of its arms: Radio Five Live, Radio Five Live Sports Extra, the World Service, the Asian Network, and the language services; material was also supplied to Radio 1 and the forty-nine local stations. For the final one-dayer, and all three Tests thereafter, they ran ball-by-ball radio commentary, the first time they had ever done so for a series not involving England. Cricinfo.com set up an Internet audio commentary team, which streamed out to users in dozens of countries. Accounting for the Pakistani journalists – those covering the entire tour, as well as the local ones at each of the eight matches at the five venues – and editors and influential media figures, the PCB were to make out a total of about *five hundred* media accreditations for the series. Did I mention there was an application from India's *Cable Quest* magazine?

So, media and security: two tour themes established well before a ball was bowled. In some ways, the media circus was the more stifling, wearying for both the players and the media and, I'm sure, for the consumer. Journalists worked with the resignation that no story would be truly unique, and still with double the usual insecurity for the competition was so large. The players, thankfully for them but not the reporters, were required to be approached through the media liaisons or team managers. There was little scope for spontaneous, informal interaction. However, for many Pakistani cricketers, past and present, the tour provided a rare opportunity to cash in, and they struck handsome deals for columns or exclusive comments to, mostly Indian, publications and TV channels.

Where, apart from the occasional picture and a short story on the front-page on the important days, Pakistan's English press covered the series in their sports pages, following the Indian

English-language dailies, it was easy to think there was no world outside this cricket tour. *The Times of India*, on a few days – the good days for India – ran not a *single* front-page story outside of the tour. Their slug for the series, typically, was tasteless wordplay: 'Pakraman' (an amalgam of Pakistan and *akraman*, the Hindi word for attack). This put them on the same footing as Bal Thackeray's paper, *Samna*, which opted for 'Cricket War' transliterated into Marathi. *The Indian Express* got it about right with 'The Great Game', direct, warm and uplifting on the surface, yet suggesting contest, with its allusion to the strategic rivalry between the British and the Soviets in Central Asia and the Frontier in the 1800s. The weekly magazine *India Today* unwittingly captured another aspect of the series: the sponsored pages had dictated that their slug simply be 'Samsung India-Pakistan Showdown'. The hype was probably best reflected in *The Hindustan Times*' 'Fever Pitch'. I can only imagine how the twenty-four hour news channels went at it.

At four o'clock in the afternoon, in a capacious chandeliered hall, with about a hundred of the media in attendance, the first of countless press conferences of the tour got underway.

Ganguly was compelled to shoulder arms to the very first question, a loaded 'Who do you blame for India not having played a Test series in Pakistan for fourteen years?' But he would not disappoint for long. Asked what he made of Javed Miandad's statement that goodwill was more important than winning, he shot back, 'I don't really agree with this goodwill issue – it's a cricket match and both teams are competing to win.' Asked, for the third time in five minutes how India hoped to deal with Shoaib Akhtar, the Rawalpindi Express, he replied with a smile: 'Pull the chain and stop it halfway.'

Two headlines in the pocket, the congregation breathed easy and tucked into a handsome tea buffet before setting up shop.

The tour had begun. It would hurtle on, inexorably, for the next thirty-nine days.

The following evening I flew to Karachi. I was received by Osman Samiuddin, a journalist who was doing impressive work on Pakistan cricket for *Wisden Asia Cricket* and Cricinfo. I would stay with the Samiuddins in Karachi, and would feel a part of their home in my time there. Osman would acquaint me with Saad Sayeed, another young cricket writer, on the *Herald* magazine. For most of the tour I would room with one of Osman or Saad, and both would become close friends.

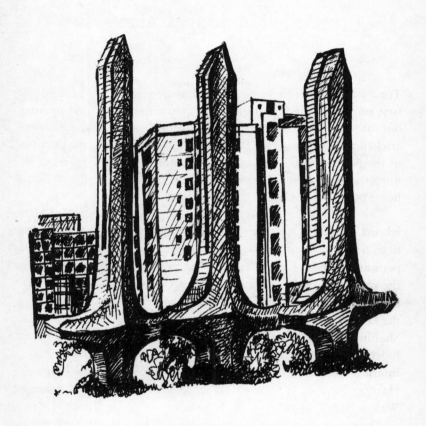

# 2. The longest day

THE PATHS OF EVENTS leading up to and winding all around the first one-dayer were so terrifically distracting, each one opening out into its own labyrinth, that my initial sighting of the Pakistan cricketers, kneeling down, praying, at a mosque inside the premises of the National Stadium at Karachi while the dust blew from the immense sandy parking lot and clung to the skin in the liquid heat, provided an image of almost surreal calm.

The first player to catch my attention was Inzamam-ul-Haq, who, I was told, was the tableeghi torchbearer in the team now that Saeed Anwar had retired, Saqlain Mushtaq was not a permanent fixture and Mushtaq Ahmed was almost always on the outer. Slowly the rest of the players came into view, in ones and twos, the strutting Shoaib Akhtar and the noble Younis Khan, the laidback Moin Khan and the grave Yasir Hameed, the mopey Shabbir Ahmed and the bright-eyed Mohammad Sami, a bunch more approachable than the cricketers of any other major international team. The old boys were about too, the manager, Haroon Rashid, the coach, Javed Miandad, the chief selector, Wasim Bari.

Things move circularly in Pakistan cricket. The beauty is that there is still no foreknowing them. Precisely a year ago, after bombing out of the World Cup in the first round, the usual cull had been conducted. The captain, Waqar Younis, was sacked. (Nobody realised at the time, but the loss against India at Centurion was to be the last time either Waqar or Wasim would bowl for Pakistan.) The coach, Richard Pybus, was fired. Wasim Bari, the chief selector, resigned. Inzamam, who had averaged 3.16 in the tournament, was axed from the squad, along with seven others. Rashid Latif was given his second stint as captain with the promise of a one-year tenure. Miandad was cajoled back for his third stint as coach. The position of chief selector went to Aamir Sohail, the legendarily brash opener of the 1990s who, among other things, was once said to have soaked a pitch in oil in response to being dropped from his domestic team.

Now, a year on from the doomed World Cup everything was different and everything was the same. Let alone being captain, Latif was no longer in the squad, having been temporarily suspended by the ICC for an on-field misdemeanour, following which he fell out over a number of issues with the PCB, and now antagonised them from the outside with frequent threats to reveal once and for all the whole sordid truth about match-fixing and other assorted muck. Inzamam did not just make his comeback, but a mere three matches into that comeback was crowned captain. And Sohail, who blithely picked and announced teams without so much as mentioning it to the other selectors or the coach – and then proceeded to lambast that very team in his role as television commentator – had been made to quit. (Though Sohail himself rubbished such notions on his website, claiming that he had only stepped away to seek sterner challenges now that he had quickly resurrected Pakistan cricket as per brief.) Replacing Sohail, yes, was Bari again. In other words, Miandad was the only survivor from the post-World Cup carve-up.

Viewing the Pakistan think-tank through the eyes of their media was an entertaining exercise. Inzamam was regarded as not specifically bright or inspiring – but it was generally agreed that there was no alternative. Miandad was considered behind the times – but there was common recognition of his genius cricket brain. Bari was viewed as the trouble-free man in the middle of tumult – yet predictable, too predictable: one writer described him as 'amorphous'; another welcomed his third coming, like 'a breath of stale air'.

Endearing, sleepy giant Inzy; provocative, hustling Javed; staid, amorphous Bari: Pakistan's high command for the series did indeed make a fetching trio.

India's duo of Sourav Ganguly and John Wright provided a no less beguiling contrast; yet, ever since they met three and a half years ago, they had come to represent a quite opposite quality to the Pakistani condition: continuity. Certainly they had built the most achieving team in Indian history, which fell well short of the heights reached by the most achieving teams in Pakistani history, but still. No, India's leadership on this tour was on firm ground. Their problems at present were smaller, though not by much. Such as their record in crunch one-day matches, which had gained such a susceptibility that the mystery of it had become awesome. And the bowling was prone to the harshest of lashings.

Take, for instance, the warm-up game they had just played in Lahore. The young turks of Pakistan A – only one player was older than twenty-three – had whipped them witless. Virender Sehwag had smashed the first ball of the tour for four, Sachin Tendulkar and Rahul Dravid had built expert innings thereafter, but the total of 335 came to nought as Imran Nazir, suavely menacing in his new Rhett Butler moustache, and the captain, Taufeeq Umar, swagger-blasted their way to a first-wicket stand of 127 runs from 8.3 overs. Zaheer Khan's first over had gone for 17, Irfan Pathan's for 24, and Murali Kartik's for 23. The youngsters sailed home with four overs to spare.

Wright, though, had come to terms with the nature of the beast. 'The consoling feature,' he reminded the press mischievously, 'is that at the start of the World Cup we lost to a Natal Selection, and then we went on to reach the final.' He might have mentioned, also, the build-up to the Australian tour a few months ago, consisting of a near-loss in a home Test series against New Zealand, a loss in the one-day tri-series which followed, and two under-par showings in the tour games leading up to the first Test. Then they became the first visiting team in fifteen years to take a series lead in Australia, and the only one in three years to depart with the series drawn. So yes, for Indian supporters, this latest capitulation provided much perverse comfort.

There was still no sign of the Indians at the National Stadium. Yet another ruse: the flight had been deliberately delayed. When it did land, it was at the old airport terminal, now used mostly for cargo flights. They were to spend just the one night in Karachi, flying out the same evening that the game ended. About 7,000 security personnel were to be deployed in and around the stadium on match-day. At least half that number appeared to be on duty on this day.

The National Stadium was typical of the subcontinental metropolis; big, concrete, devoid of brightness or delicacy. But it could boast a rich history of cricket matches, the richest in the land. So it hurt locals that since the visit by England in late 2000, there had been only three internationals here, two of them against Bangladesh.

Accordingly, the anticipation in the city was palpable. The province of Sindh had declared a holiday for the match (Saturday is usually a half-day). The municipality had granted permission to two cinema houses to project the match live. The tickets for the match itself had been sold out. Alas, it had been rather ugly.

The previous Saturday, the PCB had announced, was to be the day of ticket sale. Thousands of fans, some of whom had travelled from interior Sindh, had queued up since dawn. At 9 a.m. they learnt that the counters would not be opened at all that day. The fans hurled abuses at the police, the police got violent with the fans, and there ensued scuffles which, according to news reports, 'lasted for several hours', while one PCB employee had his motorcycle flung aside, and another had his car banged in. Finally, the crowd was baton-charged away. The tickets would be sold the following day.

When sales did begin the next day they did so ninety minutes late and from only three booths for a total of about 23,000 tickets (20 per cent of the tickets were kept aside for Internet sale, mainly to facilitate Indian purchase). Being a Sunday, no other sales points in the city could be utilised. Barely had the counters opened than a rumour began circulating through the burning queues that the tickets had all been sold, and with policemen barging into the line to buy tickets in bulk, another agitation took flight. Fans flung stones and flower pots and chairs and police retaliated once more with violence. By noon the show was scrapped.

Two days, two melees, and a handful of tickets sold. Rameez Raja, the CEO of the PCB, tried to soothe all by explaining that 'in a city of 140 million such minor incidents take place due to over-demand'. The jury was out on whether he meant 'country of 140 million' or 'city of 14 million', whether he had simply been misquoted or whether the strain was indeed getting too much. In any event, the fans needed to come out for a third successive day. The tickets were gobbled up in a matter of hours.

But the fracas had vindicated the local association, the Karachi City Cricket Association (KCCA), which had been given no responsibility for the ticket sales. Indeed, they, or any other local association, had been assigned no responsibility at all for this series, going against the grain of cricket administration worldwide. Besides the point that local delegation had some administrative benefits, an international match was also a moment in the sun for the associations, their raison d'etre. But for this series, as Shaharyar was to often repeat, the orders were coming in from the highest levels of government. And where was the time to delegate? Even after pressure from the governor of Sindh, the KCCA had found themselves with just a token one-man representation on the match-administration committee. The tussle between the centre and the states would be felt often.

India, meanwhile, were not staging any matches but still needed something to fight about, so they zeroed in on the issue of television broadcast. The rights-holders were Ten Sports, of the Taj TV bouquet, owned by the Sharjah cricket sultan, Abdul Rehman Bukhatir. In a familiar pre-series scenario, the channel haggled with cable operators over monies and the cable operators threatened a blackout. This was the minor battle. The bigger one began when the government realised that its 'India Shining' election campaign would fall a bit flat if it was unable to bring live India-Pakistan cricket to every television home in the country – an estimated 85 million, only about half of which were hitched on to cable TV – via the free state-channel. Doordarshan thus negotiated at the last minute with Ten Sports. No agreement could be reached till a day before the match, when, lo, everything on all fronts was sorted out because everybody stood to lose. Ten Sports would provide the feed to Doordarshan free of cost, but with its logo and its commercials. As it turned out, Doordarshan, for the first match, failed to carry the Ten Sports logo, slyly sold its own commercial space and coolly beamed the broadcast to areas outside India, a set of moves bound to lead to the Supreme Court, which it did.

And the commercial spaces were going at tizzy rates: anywhere between Rs 2.5 and 4 lakh for a ten-second slot, as opposed to the 1 lakh usual for India matches. At the ground, the jump in the rates for the 20 ft x 3 ft boundary boards was even greater; and so strong was the demand for these banners from Indian and multinational companies that the PCB were compelled to reserve a quota for Pakistani companies.

The total ad-spend by Indian corporates on the series was estimated to be a gargantuan Rs 300 crore, that is, close to USD 70 million, about a three-fold increase on the average spend on an India bilateral series. Samsung, the electronic consumer goods company, had purchased the title rights at USD 4 million, about twice the going rate. The co-sponsors, the motorcycle manufacturers, Hero Honda, had forked out USD 1.5 million, entitling them to virtually all the rights as the main sponsors but not that of using their name ahead of the series. Besides all this, unfathomable, unspeakable amounts would change hands in betting; suffice it to say the bourse at Karachi was anticipating a sluggish fortnight due to diversion of funds to cricket gambling.

And it was before Samsung's logo-tattooed screens, which, after a while, seemed like they were attached to the rears of every player, that the captains and the coaches addressed the press. Miandad denied ever having said 'your Irfan Pathans are in every galli and mohalla of Pakistan – we don't even bother to look at them', as he was quoted having done a few weeks earlier. But I swear I saw the same words almost in his signed newspaper column this morning!

Every other question was about pressure. How much pressure is there (answer in Pascals please)? Is there more pressure than a usual India-Pakistan match? Is there more pressure because the one-dayers are before the Tests? Is there more pressure because the match is at Karachi? Is there leftover pressure from the World Cup match? Is there leftover pressure from the 1999 series? Is there political pressure? Is their security pressure? Is there goodwill pressure? How to deal with such pressure? But, hang on, is pressure really a bad thing?

Michael Parkinson, the English television host, once suggested that every sports dressing room in the world ought to have up on its walls the following quote by his friend and hero, the dazzling, hair-in-the-wind Australian all-rounder, Keith Miller, who had served as an air-bomber during the Second World War. 'Pressure?' Miller had remarked, 'I'll tell you what pressure is. Pressure is a Messerschmitt up your arse. Playing cricket is not.' But the only banner up in the dressing rooms at the National Stadium and at every other venue for the series was the one announcing the hotline telephone number for the ICC Anti-Corruption and Security Unit. All kinds of Messerschmitts in this world, I suppose, raring to get up all kinds of arses.

\*

ABOUT AN HOUR after we'd been introduced, Saad took me to meet Arif Abbasi. We met him in the study of his lovely bungalow at PECHS, an affluent, old Karachi housing colony full of bougainvilleas and electronic surveillance systems. It was a well-balanced study, the carpets, the paintings, the antique furniture, the wood panels, the rows of books, some of them leather-bound, providing gravity, but the bright cushion thrown on the floor and the television compensating for any dreariness.

I had come to see Arif for a few yarns on Pakistan cricket administration. At the time he quit the PCB eight years ago Arif had been the longest-serving official in its history. He'd been secretary, treasurer, CEO (three times), and, 'when for three years I went around studying pitches I became the best groundsman in the country.' Twice he had served as managing director of the state airline, PIA, by virtue of which he had also been the head of the Pakistan Hockey Federation. He'd been involved in organising two subcontinental World Cups, in 1987 and 1996. By his own reckoning, he was the protégé of Air Marshal Nur Khan, considered the third of the powerful Pakistani administrators, after Justice Cornelius, a founder member of the board, in the 1950s, and Abdul Hafeez Kardar, the all-India player who became the first captain of Pakistan, in the 1960s and 70s.

Arif was a short man, with very thin legs. His face, his voice and his demeanour exuded a friendly kind of dynamism. While listening, he had the habit of flicking his front teeth with his forefinger, prepared at any point to break into a guffaw or a broadside, often both together. There is a story he likes to tell. A bewildered English official at Lord's once asked him how on earth he had pierced the tight-bummed gate security, succeeding where Sunil Gavaskar among others had not. '*Supreme* confidence,' was the reply. That much was easy to see.

Arif's association with the board, he said, began around 1978. Those were hectic times. India had travelled to Pakistan after twenty-four years, a period in which the countries fought two wars. The series had prompted the Pakistan board to become the first to reconcile with their star cricketers – Mushtaq Mohammad, Imran Khan, Majid Khan, Zaheer Abbas and Asif Iqbal – on Kerry Packer's rebel circuit.

'You were involved in the Packer reconciliation?' I asked.

'Look, I called them up and told them: "you make our boys available to us, and we make our boys available to you." Everybody had their balls in an uproar. Everybody had to come around.'

Indeed, speaking to Arif it became hard to escape the point that world cricket would have had it tough without Pakistan's administration, rather the one he had been involved with.

'We were the first team to introduce the concept of a professional manager. Neutral umpires? We campaigned for that for years and years and then started doing it anyway years before the world followed. The ball-boys, you know, those kids at the boundary, we introduced that. Sunil Gavaskar thanked me for that idea. When they were using two white balls, one from each end, in one-day cricket? Well, that was my idea.'

'So this board,' he added, 'this ad-hoc board, as it lurches from muddle to muddle, better recognise the legacy it has to carry forward.'

'Ad-hocism,' he thundered, 'ad-hocism is the bane of this country, and it is the bane of this cricket board. Our last three boards, including this one, have all been ad-hoc boards. Look, the board is a registered company with the Stocks and Exchange Commission of Pakistan. Its shareholders are the thirty-three members of the general council. The council has not met for years. What is in place now is, basically, an illegal body. Already the state associations are taking them to court...'

I knew Arif was a critic of the current administration, but even then I was slightly taken aback by the candid passion with which he laid into them.

'Now, for the first time, they haven't involved the local associations in the organisation of the matches. I mean, can you believe that. Look at the mess they ended up with during the ticket sales. Did you see it on TV? Disgraceful. Eighth March, Women's Day, and women are getting thulped on their heads with sticks.

'The warning signs have been coming for a few years now. One match was delayed because there was nobody to operate the sightscreen. Another one because there were no white balls available. Another one because the super-sopper was not accessible – the bloody chowkidar had taken off for the day with the keys! Yes, these were all international matches.

'They're planning to have 33,000 at the ground for the match. You know how many I got in for the World Cup? 45,000. The ground is meant for spectators, not for police. The biggest myth is that Karachi is unsafe for cricket. Look, there were two attempts on the president's life in Rawalpindi. I think we could have easily had a Test here...'

I would have liked to have agreed with Arif on these last two points, but I couldn't. First, extra security or not, I was glad there was no overselling of tickets, a chief cause of spectator unrest. Second, I was inclined to think that it was in Karachi's own interests to stage a safe, high-profile one-dayer in order to assuage the world's fears and be welcomed back into the Test fold. They would get all the necessary attention – historic-tour-starter and all – but without the headaches that an eight-day long stay by the Indians would entail. Indeed, a blast in an empty office building as a result of an internal dispute in which nobody was injured had cost them a match against South Africa the previous year. And there is barely a peaceful week in Karachi. A week before the Indians arrived, a local parliamentarian had been murdered, leading to riots where four people were killed and over a hundred arrested. And less than forty-eight hours after the Indians departed, a vanful of explosives was defused outside the US consulate. With paranoia running so high now could Karachi, or indeed Pakistan, afford the risk? Could the PCB?

There was another thing about Arif which caught my interest. He had casually slipped into conversation a couple of times that he was an Oxonian. While the first two decades of independence found the Indians and Pakistanis with an equal Oxbridge representation – Abbas Ali Baig and Tiger Pataudi for India, Kardar and Javed Burki for Pakistan – the two who carried the tradition into the 1980s were both Pakistanis, the cousins Imran Khan and Majid Khan (whose father, the all-India cricketer Dr

Jahangir Khan, was, like Majid, a Cambridge Blue). All four of Kardar, Burki, Imran and Majid captained the country, whereas only Pataudi did India. In the 1980s, Imran and Majid, along with the Raja brothers, Wasim and Rameez, sons of a high-ranking Punjab bureaucrat, and who studied respectively at Durham University and Lahore's Aitchison College – 'the Eton of the East' – constituted the image of the urbane, Anglicised Pakistani. Whereas Pataudi and Baig never took up serious roles in the Indian administration, Kardar, Burki and Majid Khan all served as chairman or CEO of the board at some point, as, of course, did Arif. The current CEO was Rameez – and the man he had replaced was Chisty Mujahid, better known as a commentator, and himself a post-graduate in law from Cambridge. Justice Cornelius, too, was a Cambridge man. As was Shaharyar. The top Indian administrators, on the other hand, tended to be homegrown politicians or industrialists. This reflected, more than anything, the marginalisation of the politician in Pakistan. And it suggested – if I may be allowed a moment of absolute cynicism towards administrators – that where the Indians hid behind 'democracy' (i.e. vote-bank politics) and a unique 'honorary' altruism (i.e. part-time amateurism) to play out their power games, in Pakistan cricket was apparently still a matter of Anglicised cultivation, with the lines drawn accordingly.

The antithesis to the Oxbridge image in Pakistan cricket was Javed Miandad, the type who took glee in riling the English during county matches by sauntering up to them, turning around, and breaking wind. It was thus not at all a surprise to see his splendidly one-eyed autobiography – he's always right, but it's so much fun! – closing with a proper lambasting under the subhead, 'The Oxbridge Complex': 'There has been a tendency in Pakistan cricket in which players with an Oxford or Cambridge background have been overvalued, and players far removed from such a background have been undervalued. It is an injustice that was part of our cricket from the earliest days, and was kept alive well into my playing years... In recent times the Oxbridge Complex in Pakistan cricket continues to exert its influence, albeit in a different form. The modern version exists in the value placed on the ability to speak English.'

When I asked Arif about the class gulfs in Pakistan cricket he let out a booming laugh.

'Basically, everybody is illiterate, so it's not a problem. You remember Zahid Fazal? Yes, the chap who got stretchered off on 98 against India at Sharjah. I had to literally force him out of his shalwar kameez and into his whites. Heck of a job it was trying to do that, I can tell you.' He laughed again.

'No, but let me say that when it comes down to it, cricket is *the* great leveller in Pakistani society. Look, there are only two things in my opinion which run right through this country, through all regions, through all sections, through everything – one is Urdu, and the other is cricket.'

It was ironic he should refer to Urdu that way for it has been one of the moot points in the various ethnic separatist movements in Pakistan.

'When all is said and done, everybody is cut down to the same size on that cricket field. It's a terrific leveller. What say, Inti?'

Inti tended to agree. Inti was Intikhab Alam, the distinguished leg-spinning all-rounder and former captain whose perfectly round face was familiar to younger generations as that of the coach or manager of the Pakistan team. Inti had just dropped by for a chat. He and Arif went back a long way.

Now, with Inti in the house, the conversation became more free-flow cricketing. Inti reminisced about the discontinued Super Wills Cup, where for a couple of years at the turn of the 1980s the domestic one-day champions of the countries met each other for one-off matches. 'We should revive that straightaway – but in proper first-class format, the Ranji winners versus the Quaid winners.' He spoke of the proliferation of bent-arm bowlers in the international game. 'The off-spinners now don't even have a pivot in their delivery stride, so tell me how they can bowl without their elbow straightening?'

This second strand somehow led to the late Sylvester Clarke, the huge, frighteningly quick West Indian bowler whose square-on action sometimes gave the impression that he was throwing, but nobody could quite tell. Twenty-three years ago Clarke had left his mark on Pakistanis – one Pakistani in particular. Enraged by the barrage of oranges and apples directed at him by the spectators at Multan, he picked up a brick and hurled it into the crowd. It hit a young man on the head. The young man, unfortunately, happened to be the leader of an influential students' union. Big Clarke, with his captain, Big Lloyd, was then compelled to make a hospital-visit with a box of chocolates.

Arif guffawed at the memory and related another tale. When Clarke was signed as a relative unknown by Surrey in the late 1970s, Raman Subba Row, the former England opener and senior administrator at the county, set off to receive him. Hours after the flight landed, hours after the last passenger had cleared, still no sign of Clarke. Subba Row roamed the terminals till he chanced upon an immense black man lying across five seats like Cleopatra.

'Excuse me?' he asked.

Now Sylvester Theophilus Clarke was given to making slow baritone pronouncements.

'You-are-excused.'

'Would you happen to know if there is a West Indian gentleman by the name of Sylvester Clarke anywhere here?'

'I-am-He.'

Subba Row introduced himself. Clarke handed him his luggage

– a plastic bag with a couple of t-shirts – and together the two walked away. As far as airport tales go, not quite Tony Greig asking Don Bradman if he happened to have any connection with cricket, but it had its charm.

We took Arif's leave. He was to dine in a few hours with his Asian powerbroker buddies – Jagmohan Dalmiya, partner-in-crime during the 1996 World Cup, and Ehsan Mani, the chairman of the ICC ('my man in London').

'Ooh,' I joked with him, 'cricket will never be the same again.' He seemed to enjoy the thought. He doubted he'd come to the ground the next day. But he was there. This was bigger than his battle with the board.

And Inti, a few months on, would not only find that his suggestion of the cross-border first-class match had been agreed on by both boards, but would also be appointed coach of Punjab: the Indian Punjab, the land of his birth, the first time a foreigner, if he could be called that, had ever been made coach of an Indian domestic team. Who would have thought?

\*

OSMAN AND I rose early and arrived at the National Stadium ninety minutes before the match was to begin. Long, single-file columns from all directions converged like tentacles towards the arena. There was calm in the ranks, the first good sign.

The PCB had spread the word well through advertisements in the newspapers. Please reach two hours before the match begins. Please do not come if you do not hold a ticket. Please do not bring with you – too long to list here. Maps had been provided to indicate the traffic flow and the parking arrangements. Chortled Omar Kureishi, the veteran commentator, in his column: 'In normal circumstances one would have written that all roads will lead to the National Stadium for the Karachi ODI. Precisely the opposite will be true. All roads will be closed.'

There was already a sense that few cricket matches have had this much riding on them. 'It is not the question of win or lose, the good performance should be appreciated. We must show that we are a disciplined nation,' the General beseeched from Islamabad. The governor of Sindh issued a similar exhortation; so did its chief of police. The match previewer on *The News* could not be bothered with such formalities: 'All the talk about peace and goodwill will go for a six on Saturday when traditional rivals Pakistan and India face off...'

India's last three visits to the National Stadium had been tinged with hostility, whether or not this hostility had been meant specifically towards them as Indians. The 1989-90 series had kicked off here, and on the opening day of the Test, a spectator ran on to the pitch and scuffled with the captain, Krish Srikkanth. This was no tomfoolery; it was manhandling. When the Indians returned to the venue for a one-dayer, the match had to be abandoned after Manoj Prabhakar had claimed three wickets in his opening spell. It had started with a walk-off following stone-throwing by the crowd, but the players soon returned. Then, says *Wisden*, 'As missiles more deadly than stones kept coming, they walked off again. With a full-scale battle between the police and the students resulting in the use of teargas and gun shots outside the National Stadium being heard, the abandonment of the match was a formality.' The only time the Indians had played at Karachi thereafter was during the whistlestop one-day tour in 1997-98; it was, also, the only venue out of the three where there was any crowd trouble. Five Indian fielders were struck by missiles, which led to a walk-off, and the match was eventually curtailed because of lost time. What would Karachi have to say for itself this time?

Inside, past the layers of security, the green was alive with the buzz of first rites. The teams practised cheerfully, jauntily, men who knew they were being lapped up. The cameramen assumed their positions; Ten Sports had planned a twenty-three-camera coverage, another record. Commentators, wired-up, strode the turf like lions. Radio and TV journalists got about and conducted spot interviews. Up in the press box, agency reporters set up their desks with that steely glint in their eyes. Feature writers breathed in the air and smiled panoramically. The smoggy cool of the morning slowly shed.

The two times I had watched India play Pakistan were both at neutral venues, a reflection of the way things were in the 1990s; besides, Mr Thackeray had put paid to any hope of a match in Bombay. The first occasion was at Manchester's Old Trafford in the 1999 World Cup, played while the countries fought a war in Kargil. The second was at the following World Cup, in South Africa, and came at the back of a year of military eyeballing, which, we were warned, could lead to war that could turn nuclear.

Both were gripping, tense affairs, the second the more spectacular. The first I had watched from the stands, the second mostly from the press enclosure, which was in the open. But that could not be the only reason that the first had felt more vicious. There had been an instance of flag-burning at Old Trafford, and three arrests and nine ejections. At the end, there was a mini-stampede when supporters of both teams spilled on to the field. Venkatesh Prasad reluctantly found himself hoisted up on the shoulders of fans. Nobody invaded the field at Centurion. Indeed, apart from the booing of Waqar Younis at the presentation by Pakistani supporters, the atmosphere seemed one of genuine enjoyment. But back in Gujarat, the brittle post-Godhra calm was broken by communal clashes. Shops were vandalised, vehicles were torched. One teenager was shot as police opened fire. In Bangalore, one person was killed in a boiler explosion when workers at a dairy, desperate to watch the match, had increased the heater levels to hasten production.

The National Stadium is a large ground. Having toured here in 1989-90, Tendulkar remembered it being bigger then. Perhaps this was an illusion of space created by the uncovered stands of those days. Now, while the shade was no doubt welcomed by spectators, the constructions also served to block much of the cross-ground sea breeze which aided swing and provided relief to fielders. Presumably sponsors then were also less insistent on bringing the boundary in.

The stands were only about half full at the time of the toss. Yet, an avalanche of sound accompanied Sourav Ganguly and Inzamam-ul-Haq to the centre. Its force trebled when Inzamam was first to be invited to the microphone. But in the commentator's box, jaws dropped. Imran Khan had just spent ten minutes expounding, Imran-style, the importance of winning the toss on this ironed-out brown pitch – he was working on the natural assumption that the captain would bat. He was to spend much of the day coming to terms with the decision.

I had felt a similar sock in the stomach watching Ganguly insert the Australians in the World Cup final a year ago. Then, Ganguly had sought to use the juice in the pitch after a morning drizzle, or rather, deny the Australian fast bowlers that advantage; here, Inzamam was banking on the raw power of his pace attack for a first strike, hoping also that the 9.30 a.m. start meant there would be some moisture on the surface. He would have probably also been swayed by the fact that six of Pakistan's seven losses in the last fifteen games had come while batting first. Against this was the risk of allowing a dazzling batting line-up run away with the game.

Pakistan had a first-choice XI at their disposal, apart from

Shabbir Ahmed, the tall seamer, who'd cut his finger at practice. India, on the other hand were missing from their squad entirely their two best spinners – Anil Kumble, to a shoulder strain, and Harbhajan Singh, to a finger injury – as well as the medium-pacer Ajit Agarkar, to a shin injury. V.V.S. Laxman could not make the XI because of a knee niggle.

The record books, not that it means much, favoured Pakistan. Out of the eighty-two completed one-dayers between the teams, they had won fifty-two. Out of the thirteen completed matches in Pakistan, they had won ten. Of the last twenty encounters anywhere, they had won fourteen. The bookies made them favourites.

WHEN THE MOMENT came I found myself, hands quivering, knees knocking, in a little BBC booth out on the gallery. I had never been on radio before; this was a (sixty-second) debut at the deep end. As I stuttered and strove to make valuable points, Shaharyar, the silken former diplomat, swung by and sold the moment in effusive melodies.

Below, the blue figures of Sachin and Sehwag emerged, Sachin going through his slow neck rotations, Sehwag vigorously swinging his bat to loosen his shoulders. Almost simultaneously the two looked up into the sun to accustom themselves to the glare.

Not that the glare had left them for the past few weeks. Wherever they went, they were reminded of the 95 mph bombardments awaiting them. Sehwag had prepared, as was usual for him, against a barrage of net bowlers on a shortened pitch at his Delhi club. Sachin had been revving up the bowling machine at the Middle Income Group Club, a stone's throw from his old childhood home.

The Pakistanis were already out on the field, their camouflaging two-tone green jerseys on grass adding to the sense of ambush created by the circling helicopter and the noise, the tremendous noise.

Inzamam arranged his field, a regular one, the two catchers in the slips and the two stoppers out at third man and fine leg. Shoaib kicked off from afar, from far far afar, the sightscreen almost, and as he steamed in to Sehwag, a rush of adrenalin surged through the stadium.

The first ball was a wide down leg. Shoaib turned to stare at the umpire and the cameras, and tossed his hair back: look, this was not *my* doing. The third ball was again a wide, gathering such a life after beating Sehwag's wild swish that when the keeper failed to gather it the impression was of a dropped catch. Accordingly, an 'oooh...' went out. The single on the fumble brought to the fore the confrontation spinmeisters had been flogging. Shoaib versus Sachin: the headline for the tour, the image for the tour. 'Believe the hype', urged the cover of the monthly political and cultural magazine, *The Herald*, juxtaposing action shots of the two; in thirty-seven years, this was only their third cricket cover.

The last time these two had met sparks had flown. Sachin's sequence of three strokes – a cut for six, a swirl for four, a dead-bat-block for four – in the course of an eighteen-run first over became one of the highlights of that World Cup or any other. Later in that innings, Shoaib had him caught off a delivery that burst into his ribs off a length.

First ball now Shoaib opened up Tendulkar and whizzed it past his edge – line and length and bounce, and pace, pace, pace – to set off a medley of hoots, howls, whistles and roars in the stadium. Sachin left the next one alone, a no-ball; and one ball later he got his own back, employing the most nuanced give of the wrists for a flick behind square, not meeting force with force as he had done with the six at Centurion, but merely diverting it. Shoaib sent down another no-ball, and then Sachin took a single to third man. Sehwag drilled the final delivery of the over into cover. Shoaib Malik dropped the catch.

Two wides, two no-balls, two past the edge, one four, one dropped catch in a ten-ball, ten-run first over: looking back, there could have been a no more apt start to this series.

From this end, Mohammad Sami, the most naturally athletic fast bowler since Michael Holding, marked out his twinkling run. This was the first time I had watched Shoaib and Sami bowl in tandem. It was easy, I found, to get engrossed in their motions. The two Ss were not the two Ws, not at all, but the thrill of their speedy contrast was not much less exhilarating. Shoaib pounded in from 40 yards, bosom heaving, thighs bulging, nostrils dilating, a bawdiness beyond redemption. Sami flitted in from fifteen paces, powered by nothing but the wind dusted up by his arms and hair. Saad had mentioned something amusing to me. Word was that the eunuchs of Karachi had become *fida* over Sami. It was that slim frame, virile yet effeminate; the soft cascading hair, now tinted red; that pouty glare, those crinkled eyes, that *matak-matak kamar... Hai!*

Sami's first over was harmless, for either team. But the drama from Shoaib's end did not let up. Sachin turned him to square leg where Younis Khan held a nifty catch on the forward dive. Another no-ball; another oooh. Rubbing it in, Sachin, on the last ball of the over, went for the hook, went for it like he rarely goes for it nowadays, a full-blooded roundabout down-to-up hook. It caught the top-edge, and carried high, high, high, just over the man at fine-leg. The first six of the series. Sachin, off Shoaib.

The early overs roller-coastered on at a hectic pace. Sachin brought up India's 40 in the fifth over with a block that sped away for four; Sehwag the 50 in the sixth with a slash and a flick and a single. Then Sachin popped a catch behind square on the off, upon which Shoaib pointed at his man, then at himself, and wheeled away into the arms of his converging team-mates. A fantastic explosion of sound erupted from the bowels of the stadium. But with 69 having come from nine overs – 16 of them in extras – the opening partnership had been a success. Job done, Shoaib was pulled out of the attack.

In came Rana Naved-ul-Hasan, a nippy, prematurely balding seamer with a powerful rock-back delivery stride. This was only the third international of Naved's career, and by a distance the most significant. Even then Inzamam could not have anticipated him conceding 21 runs from his first two balls. The two balls were, in fact, seven deliveries. Five were no-balls and four were smashed to itty bits by Sehwag. Then with a peaceful dab into the off, Sehwag brought up his nineteenth one-day fifty: thirteen of these had come at better than a run-a-ball. Firestarter.

India were on a roll. Naved took the well-intentioned step of greeting Ganguly, the no. 3, with a bouncer. Only Ganguly was *so* expecting it that he hoisted it over midwicket for six. It was his first scoring shot. At the other end Sami made way for Razzaq; Sehwag laid out for him the same red carpet he had for Naved, driving him through cover, glancing him past short fine-leg, and pulling him, shudderingly, wide of mid-on. Eighteen runs.

Faced again with Naved, Sehwag blasted him greedily over long-on for six, and on the next ball he retreated to outside leg stump, looking to launch one vaguely in the direction of Bombay. Naved countered it with a slow yorker. Bowled. But an irresistible innings: 79 from 57 balls. India, as far into the innings as the fourteenth over were bouncing along at a run rate of 10. And Sehwag became the first man to leave his mark on the tour.

I looked around the stands. There was noise, a lot of it, but it had yet to find a definition: no chants, no songs, no waves, no rhythmic clapping or stamping of feet or banging of paper rolls.

It was a thick random energy. There were not many flags in; the biggest was a joint one, a hand extending out of the tricolour and shaking hands with another emerging from the star-and-crescent. Another carried the message, 'One blood'. There weren't many Indians. Samsung had flown in one group; otherwise only a smattering.

Dravid joined Ganguly, and captain and deputy nurtured Firestarter's flames. Dravid found his centre by taking two perfect straight-driven boundaries off Razzaq, a sight so soothing in middle-overs one-day cricket. Ganguly, whenever he got bogged down, went aerial. He flicked Naved to bring up India's 200, in the twenty-fifth over, and then shimmied down to Shoaib Malik and lofted him for four. Eye-catchingly, he pulled Naved for another six over wide long-on, with an almost vertical bat. Next ball he aimed for the shot again and, like Sehwag, perished right after the six, as a top-edge fountained straight up and fell into Naved's hands. Ganguly stood still for thirty seconds at the crease. He was too competitive to brush aside a squandered chance – and he wanted the world to know. 'I knew I'd missed out on a hundred,' he was to rue later.

The innings was entrusted now to Dravid, who had emerged as the one man in the world who could be trusted with any situation. He accepted with customary poise; urgent, but still mindful of the fate befalling Tolstoy's peasant, who ran all day for land but died at sundown. Yuvraj came and went but in Kaif Dravid found the necessary busybody. In the steaming noon noise the two ran up a hundred in even time. And the extras kept coming. India were building a very large mountain indeed. The noise did not ebb.

Entering his 90s, Dravid drove Shoaib repeatedly through the covers. When he reached 99, in the forty-eighth over, Shoaib rolled out another slower delivery, his fourth in five balls. Dravid tried to work it to leg and played on to his stumps. There was something of a gasp from the spectators. Could it really be that the Pakistanis were mourning Dravid's dismissal one short of a century? Saad was in the stands at this stage, and he found, to his surprise, this to be the case. A standing ovation followed.

Kaif whipped up 46 with only four boundaries, three of them in a single hopelessly leg-side over from Razzaq. The innings ended in a whirl of straight, fast bowling from Sami and Shoaib against India's tail-end swishes. Yet they finished on 349, their highest against Pakistan, their fifth highest against anyone, and the thirteenth highest by anyone ever.

Pakistan's second twenty-five overs had cost 148 runs compared to the 201 from the first. They had conceded 38 extras, 30 of them in no-balls and wides; that is, they had bowled fifty-five overs. Sami had leaked 74 in ten overs, Naved 73, Shoaib 55 and Razzaq 83 in just nine. The most economical bowler had been Shoaib Malik. It was an irony waiting to happen: after weeks of talking pace like fire, the lone spinner in the XI would do the most efficient job.

And to win, Pakistan now needed to score more runs in the second innings, by a distance, than any team had done in the 2,111 one-day internationals played till date.

IT FELL UPON Laxmipathy Balaji to begin India's defence, a considerable turnaround for this unassuming twenty-two-year-old seam bowler with a charming proclivity for changing his action. Fifteen months ago he was handed a one-day debut against West Indies, got thrashed for 44 runs in four overs and was dropped for a year. Upon being picked again, in Australia a few months ago, he endured ten games without an injury, a massive feat for an Indian bowler at the time, and returned the best economy rate among his team-mates.

## The longest day

Opening for Pakistan were Yasir Hameed and Imran Farhat, the young right-left pair who earlier this season had made a name for themselves with a world-record four successive century partnerships. So from the clash of the titans which heralded the first innings, we were now to witness the collision of the neophytes.

Farhat set Pakistan's innings to life with a series of wristy flicks and guides, but the batting in the early exchanges remained patchy, and so did the bowling, till all of a sudden both openers fell; Yasir bowled on the walk by Balaji for 7, Farhat, who took more strike, nicking Zaheer to the keeper, on 24.

And so, Inzamam-ul-Haq and Yousuf Youhana found themselves together in the space of two runs and eight deliveries. It was 34 for 2 in the eighth over. Pakistan needed 316 more in forty-two overs, at, already, 7.5 an over. This was a staggering ask. This had not been done before.

Defending his first ball off the front foot, Inzamam gave the impression that he had been at the crease forever. Because he plays the ball so late, because his movements are so swallowed by his bulk, he is able to suggest that batting just happens to him. I imagine it must be daunting for the bowler. He left, for the time being, the scoring to Youhana, Pakistan's most luminous strokemaker.

Straightaway Youhana set about the bowling, driving and flicking and cutting, letting his bat wave like a ribbon in the wind. In between these he attempted the most horrendous slogs for which he was rebuked by his captain, and on the last ball before the first drinks interval he was almost toppled on to his stumps, stunned by Nehra's 90 mph bouncer, which then screamed away over the keeper's head for four byes.

Pakistan's situation at that break, at sixteen overs, was desperate. The required rate was already past 8. Hope had not fully deserted the arena. But let's just say there was an acceptance of probability.

Whether or not it was planned, first thing after drinks Inzamam launched Murali Kartik's left-arm spin straight back for six. Soon after, Youhana picked up the medium-pace of Ganguly with a sharp curl at the tip of his swing, a lizard pouching its prey, to send it one bounce into the long-off boundary. Four balls later he repeated the stroke: this time it carried all the way. Something in these three shots sent out a signal to India. Not merely, 'we have heart and we will fight'. No, something more coldly frightening: 'look, we are good, so very good that your mountain could mean nothing'.

I think it was about now that the noise in the crowd arranged itself into properly deafening rhythms that were then never to cease. The slow-fast bursts of hand on hand, of feet on floor, of rolled-up paper on railing, of 33,000 pairs of lungs... Ganguly would remark that his players could not hear each other.

The boundaries began to flow. With another six, a huge one off Kartik, and a single thereafter, Youhana brought up his fifty, from fifty-three balls. Inzamam, more invisibly, followed with his own, from forty-eight. Their 100-run partnership had taken fifteen overs. But the required rate still hovered at 8. In the twenty-fifth over, Ganguly turned to Sachin's allsorts.

Youhana leant back and once more made his rapacious inside-out loft, for six. And in Sachin's next over, he did it again. It was simply astounding to see this most difficult of strokes being executed again and again with such nonchalance. The Indians were gobsmacked.

Pariah kites, dozens of them, swooped theatrically in the sticky warm afternoon breeze. Below them, Ganguly chewed on his nails and planned his next move.

He gave Sehwag a go. Youhana went for the inside-out again, but against Sehwag this was harder: there was more loop on the ball, and it was turning into him. He got under it, he got inside it, but he did not get a full hold of it. Irfan, substituting, held the catch at the boundary.

This was a stunning hand, 73 from 68 balls, and four sixes. Pakistan were 169 for 3 in the twenty-eighth over. Still 181 runs to go. At 8.2.

Inzamam absorbed the blow and moved on. He cut Tendulkar behind point for four, then he cut him in front of point for four, and then Younis Khan, the new man, drilled a low full-toss through the covers for a third four in the over, the twenty-ninth.

Ganguly removed Tendulkar and brought back Kartik to partner Sehwag. Inzamam and Younis milked. A single here, a single there... and the rate climbed, beyond 8.5 now.

This was a call to action. Younis put his full strength behind a low slog against Sehwag that carried over the ropes. From the other end, Inzamam waltzed outside the leg stump to fetch Kartik's over-the-wicket stuff for another six. Even so, at the end of the thirty-fifth over, the required rate climbed, for the first time on the day, past 9. What to do? This was a fight against quicksand.

In the rising run-rate, in the rising tension, in the rising sound, in the rising hopelessness, Inzamam unfurled such inspired, resonating strokeplay, that it bore comparison with that first burst of youth, at the 1992 World Cup semi-final, where as a virtual unknown in the eyes of the world he made possible an impossible victory. But this was not the diffident youngster who had requested he be dropped before the match. This was now the leader. Twelve years on, he was bigger, broader, curiously less hunched over the bat, he wore a beard, and even a helmet. The grimace was exactly the same.

Genius stroke blurred into genius stroke as Inzamam swung Kartik behind square leg for four, chipped Sehwag past midwicket like a man toying with a 7-iron, and, once it became clear that spin was not working against him, smacked Zaheer's full-toss to long-on to reach hundred, his ninth in one-day cricket. Because of a scoreboard malfunction and Inzamam's own measured reaction, not everybody realised it. Nehra came on for Sehwag and pitched on a length; Inzamam stood tall and pulled him away and did not take a step forward because he knew from the first where he would hit it. Zaheer tried the leg-stump yorker and Inzamam crouched into it and glanced it for four. Nehra put another one back of a length, and Inzamam, this the pièce de résistance, disdained it to behind square, waved it away really, as one might a fly.

A quite incredible aura soaked the ground. In the stretched-out, energy-filled minutes, breathless cricket in slow motion, as Inzamam stroked, as the sun poured, as the runs rained, as the kites circled, as the noise thundered, India and Pakistan in the heat of cricket and no malice in sight, there went a rush to the head that anything was possible. I have rarely felt a power like it at a cricket match; or, for that matter, anywhere.

Ganguly was under the cosh. Pakistan still needed to go at 9 an over, but now, suddenly, for only eight more overs. Spin had not worked and pace had not worked and part-timers had not worked. A shroud of blue collected at the wicket as the captain contemplated his options. He tossed the ball to Kartik.

With the first ball of his third spell, attacking from round the wicket, laden with accessories, shades on eyes, elbow guard on left arm, watch on left wrist, beads on right wrist, beads around neck, cool Kartik removed Inzamam, whose intended tickle was too literally one. Dravid held a superb catch under pressure. What is the sound of 33,000 hearts wilting?

Inzamam was given a hero's ovation into the pavilion, for his had been the innings of a hero; 122 from 102 balls, speaks for itself; and from that situation and on this occasion. Pakistan needed 72 from 47 balls, with six wickets in hand. It was difficult to see it being done. It had never, after all, been done before.

Razzaq joined Younis, who had raced along to 38 in good time. Ganguly enforced the double-change by bringing on Balaji alongside Kartik. Younis flayed him over the off side, then Razzaq did. In between they scampered singles and a two. Twelve runs from over forty-four.

Razzaq now began launching his virtuoso explosions as he does when all seems buried, yanking his left foot out of the way and running Kartik fine to third man, then yanking his left foot out of the way and blazing him back along the carpet to take Pakistan past 300. Kartik fired one fast and full to Younis and hit the base of his stumps. 305 for 5; 45 needed from five overs, five wickets in hand.

Moin Khan emerged, the cheekiest scamperer limited-overs cricket has known, the hustler of hustlers, the possessor of a sweep shot with an arc from long-off to long stop – and that just against pace.

Balaji continued from the other end and Razzaq hit the roof. No, really. He coiled up, splayed that front-foot out towards square leg, gathered himself, and let rip the almightiest of almighty swings. The ball clunked off the asbestos ceiling behind long-on and fell into the crowd.

By the end of over forty-six, Pakistan needed 34 runs from 24. Suddenly it looked ludicrously simple. How had it come to this?

Kartik's quota was finished. Ganguly needed to decide between Zaheer, who had two overs remaining, and Nehra, who had one, or else take a gamble with Sachin or Sehwag, both of whom had risen to these situations in the past. He chose Zaheer.

Zaheer responded with two leg-side wides. And then he summoned a turning slower ball, a properly turning one, which defeated Razzaq's step-away glide, and pegged back off stump. Twenty-eight required from twenty. Malik stepped out, but this was no no. 8. Five months ago against South Africa he had smashed 82 not out from 41 balls with six sixes. Straightaway he glanced to midwicket and Moin urged him back for the third.

Down to the final three overs. Twenty-four needed. Still advantage Pakistan. Balaji bowled a fine over, full and straight, yet – dot, one, two, one, two, one – seven helter-skelter runs.

Seventeen required from the final two overs, Zaheer to bowl. Moin shimmied down and swatted to long-off, Kaif made the throw, Zaheer made a miserable attempt at collection, and a two was converted into three. In the balcony Miandad clapped vigorously, not only because his team had inched closer, but because he knew better than anyone that it is upon these psychological fluctuations that a match of cricket is played. Fourteen needed from eleven: a cakewalk. Four more giddy sprinting runs from the next three balls, and down to 10 from 8. Malik aimed for the one that would, in all but name, seal the deal. Elbow high, he flowed into a straight loft. He got height on it, a lot of height. A volcanic pandemonium spewed out of the stadium, tens of thousands sensing the kill. The roar ebbed as two blue figures were spotted running *in* from the boundary rather than pushing back. Both blue figures were outstanding fieldsmen: from long-on Hemang Badani, from long-off Mohammad Kaif. The ball was to the on of straight, and now beginning to drop from higher than the highest flags on the grandstand. The roar gathered again, with the thrilling anticipation of both sprinting figures missing it, or, now it suddenly seemed, colliding. Closer to the ball, Badani slowed his run as he prepared to slide into the collection; meanwhile Kaif hastened his, preparing to dive headlong. Inside the suspended roar, amid visions of broken bones and splattered blood, Badani recoiled and staggered into a fall, a horse shot on the run; Kaif, in mid-stride, kept an eye on the ball, an eye on his team-mate, thrust his leading knee out of the path of Badani's face, extended himself along the ground, held the catch, and slid into a spectacular follow-through. He was up in a trice with the ball in his hand and a shout on his face. The crowd hushed. In the silence, India's huddle was muted. This was not the hour to let go.

In the Pakistan dressing room, the question must have raged: who to send out? Sami played with a straight bat but was possibly too turgid. Naved was a newbie but averaged 25 in first-class. Shoaib was erratic but capable of deciding the game with a couple of snaps of the biceps: a year ago at the World Cup he had smashed 43 from 16 balls against England.

Naved got the nod, and when he reached the centre, umpire Simon Taufel asked him to take strike. This was contentious. Moin claimed to have crossed during the catch. But Taufel, on referring it to the third umpire, Asad Rauf, had been told that Naved ought to be facing. Later reports were to suggest that Rauf's decision was based on the misconception that the wicket had fallen on the last ball of the over when in fact there was still one to go. Was this true?

Naved managed a single. Nine required from the final over. Crucially, Naved on strike.

In the booming cauldron, Ganguly summoned colleagues and grappled with his final and most wrenching bowling change of the afternoon. His options were Nehra, Sachin and Sehwag. He had said before the tour that he did not believe in history. He proved it now by remaining unswayed by Sachin's last-over heroics at the Hero Cup twelve years ago. He tossed the ball to Nehra, thin, pitter-pattering Nehra.

Nehra went over the wicket. The four compulsory fielders in the ring were three to the off and the captain at midwicket.

Right. Nine from six. Nehra fires it on a length, following Naved's withdrawal to leg. A swing and a miss. Nine from five.

Naved adjusts his crotch guard, rehearses his swat and takes stance. Again Nehra zeroes in on leg stump, this time fuller. A desperate shovel to mid-off. Single. Eight from four, Moin on strike, hustling down the crease and towards square-leg as Nehra runs in. A near-identical delivery, but a touch more legside, a touch fuller and, at 83.5 mph, a touch quicker. Straight through Moin. Dot. From the pavilion, Miandad gestures wildly. He wants Moin to hang back, make room and slice fine. Inzamam and Razzaq have already fallen to the stroke. And what if the ball is full? Worth risking? Nehra, for the third time in succession, bowls the same ball. Moin connects to midwicket. It is destined for a double, Moin completes half the second, but Sachin, learning from an instance two overs previously, has pulled himself slightly inside from the ropes. A smooth and precise pick-up-and-throw. Seven from two, Naved on strike. Nerveless Nehra again, swift, full, middle-and-off, Naved hits, hits well, but a single, no more, to cover.

And with that we were down to it. Six from the last ball. What irony! Miandad, purveyor of the single most famous stroke in Pakistan's history, perhaps even India's history, shouted out and gesticulated avidly from the dressing room. He wanted to do it himself, he was itching to do it himself, he would give anything to do it himself. But Moin had to do it. Before India was the opportunity to lay to rest a ghost, to draw a line.

Ganguly made a tinker with the field, sensibly calling up fine-leg into the circle to install extra protection at cow corner.

Nehra hared in with his short steps, curved as a bow but piercing like an arrow through the thick, quite unbelievable layers of noise. Whether it was a yorker gone wrong or whether Nehra indeed planned it that way, as he was to claim later, it will never be known, but the most momentous delivery of his life came out as a rapid groin-high full-toss. It started leg, angling, swinging even a touch, away into middle, rushing Moin, who nevertheless appeared for a split second positioned to deposit it as per requirement. But it was quicker than he expected, and it was higher than he expected, and as he leant back and lashed, his right hand slipped off the handle and the ball slid off the face and looped lamely in the air – O Moin! What have you done! – and into the hands of Zaheer Khan at mid-off who whooped a triple whoop which rang starkly in the naked silence of the arena.

Then, after a few seconds of recovery, as the Indians clustered together in triumph, applause poured forth from every direction, and it poured and it poured and it poured in absolute loud unison. It poured till the hair stood on end, till one felt at one with it, *of* it really. No one spoke in these moments, the most moving of moments, a people reaching out to another.

The mind went back to the beautiful occasion at Chennai in 1999, when Wasim Akram led his team for a victory lap to a standing ovation after a startling win in a stunning Test. The Indians did not make the lap at Karachi. Indeed, the applause at Karachi had been far more spontaneous than at Chennai. But the Indians passed up the chance to participate in a rare, special bond. Instead, Ganguly bristled up to the press conference, planted a question about an ICC law on over-rates through the Calcutta journalists, then proceeded to rail against that rule, which was not new as he claimed, but a year old, and, on balance, an improvement to the one it had replaced. Anyhow, what an irrelevance! This is not to say that the occasion was soured, far from it; but it was disappointing that he had not felt the moment in the same way as the watching thousands, the millions on television. Perhaps it spoke of his unyielding resolve to treat this as 'just another series' lest his team lose focus. Perhaps he is just not the sentimental kind.

Meanwhile, Pakistan's hardened warriors down the ages were

astonished. 'I did not show it, but I must admit I was concerned as to how this day would go,' said Imran. 'But this, this was something unique. I haven't seen anything like it in Pakistan.' Echoed Rameez, 'I mean, I never thought I would see a day when Indian and Pakistani flags were stitched together for a cricket match.' 'The greatest thing that's happened for a long time in Pakistani cricket,' added Mushtaq Mohammad.

Moin was just befuddled: 'We know what this match meant to the two nations,' he would say later. 'But somehow I remain unconnected – it's a puzzle.'

Stirred by this triumph of Asian solidarity, on the back of which he had risen to become the most influential cricket administrator of the time, Dalmiya proclaimed: 'This is the best crowd I have ever seen... the next time we visit Pakistan, we will open the tour with a Test in Karachi.'

Within the political parties of India, hectic appropriation followed. Priyanka and Rahul Gandhi, who were given filmstar treatment by Pakistan's public while attending the match as state guests, spent time in the Indian dressing room; soon SMSes beeped to mobile phones in India: '*Bharat ko jitne ki sahi aas thi*, Rahul *aur* Priyanka team *ke paas the*!' The sender was 'Congress', though the party later claimed it to be a hoax. The BJP retaliated with its own SMS: '*Khel bhi jeeta, dil bhi jeeta. Shabash* India!'; Vajpayee got on to the phone to Ganguly.

Packing up late in the evening, an exhaustion and a heady tingling persisted side by side; and above all the satisfaction that here was a match of cricket and an occasion of cricket transcending one another. By the time we finished, the sandy parking lot was empty and bathed in darkness. Somebody had broken into Osman's red Suzuki Mehran. There wasn't much to take. So the thief had made off with the registration papers.

This was the longest day.

# The longest day

*India 349 for 7 in 50 overs (Dravid 99, Sehwag 79, Naved 3-73, Shoaib 2-55) beat Pakistan 344 for 8 in 50 overs (Inzamam 122, Youhana 73, Zaheer 3-66, Kartik 2-74) by 5 runs*

\*

*Ripping the belly cleanly, the knife moved in a straight line down the midriff, in the process slashing the cord which held the man's pyjamas in place. The man with the knife took one look and exclaimed regretfully, 'Oh no!... Mishtake.'*

WHEN ALL ELSE FAILS, one resorts to irony, and Saadat Hasan Manto did frequently. In this prose miniature set at Partition, a man goes about his routine of murdering by faith, and realises his error only when he finds a circumcision, or its absence, we do not know which. Manto's target here as elsewhere, I like to think, was not so much murder, but religion itself, that strange allegiance system which has constantly driven the world mad beyond belief.

And so it was with a mix of irony and apology, for this would be in a sense a bow before that allegiance system, that I sought to meet Danish Kaneria, the young cricketer who had attained fame not only for his leg-spinning prowess, substantial and growing, but as the second Hindu cricketer to have played for Pakistan; the first had been Danish's maternal uncle, Anil Dalpat, who kept wicket briefly in the 1980s.

Following the exodus at Partition, the Hindus in Pakistan had dwindled, according to the 1998 census, the last to be published, to 1.4 per cent. Applying that to the current estimated population of 150 million, the figure worked out to a little more than two million. The large majority of these two million Hindus, up to 90 per cent, was said to live in Sindh, many of them in poverty in the rural interiors, and a sizeable number in Karachi.

73

The Kanerias had a flat in central Karachi's Rimpa Sunbeam Apartments, which had a feel no different to Bombay's myriad little apartment colonies. But outside the gates the graffitied walls corridored a street that was far too broad for central Bombay. It was perfect for cricket. There was still no activity on this Sunday; at noon, perhaps it was too early.

On either side of the Kaneria door was a freshly-laid *rangoli* design. From above hung a *toran* of swastikas, a symbol, regardless of the savage Nazi appropriation, of good luck in Hinduism. Danish's elder brother, Vicky, welcomed us in – *Mid Day's* Ehtesham Hasan and Santosh Harhare, and me. The mother, Babita, and the father, Prabha Shanker, rose from the sofa to greet us. Soon Danish emerged from the bedroom, tall, fit, gangly, in a full-sleeved jersey and jeans.

The Kanerias are Rajputs from Surat in Gujarat. They have been in Karachi since the early 1900s and did not relocate at Partition. They do not eat beef, and like many in Karachi, speak Gujarati. Babita is especially thrilled to exchange a few sentences in Gujarati with an Indian. She has never been to India. It is her ambition. She wants *darshan* at Sai Baba's shrine at Shirdi. She is wondering if a trip to the four Himalayan *dhams* may be feasible. Behind a curtain on the far side of the hall, the Kanerias keep a small mandir of their *kul devi* (family deity). Rings of incense keep curling up above the level of the curtain, and then the fan scatters them.

The Kanerias have been fielding Indian journalists and know what will be asked.

'Frankly, we're really comfortable in Pakistan. It's never been an issue ever. We lead a normal life, like we would anywhere. We have our temples. We go to the Shiv mandir, on Saturdays we go to the Hanuman mandir. We celebrate navratri for fifteen days, play dandia; we play Holi; we celebrate Diwali, burst crackers all night. We don't find anything missing from our lives.'

Much has been written about the plight of the religious minorities of Pakistan. Yet, at this moment it was hard not to sense the triumphant smile on the face of Jinnah, whose speech at the creation of an Islamic nation had included the words: 'You are free; you are free to go to your temples, you are free to go to your mosques or to any other place of worship in this State of Pakistan.'

Danish brought out his bride, Dharmita, shining in gold jewellery and a bright-red sari. Theirs was a love marriage, not still a month old. 'They covered it live on a local channel,' Danish said proudly. 'We got married on 15 February – the same day as V.V.S. Laxman.' With this piece of information, his innocent reply to a later query about the mental approach while bowling to this intimidating Indian batting line-up – 'Woh Laxman hai, toh main bhi Danish hoon' (If he is Laxman, then even I am Danish) – assumed a whole new resonance.

Danish had a warm and informal air. Just as Inzamam prefixed his sentences with '*yeh hai ki*', so Danish suffixed his with '*theek hai na*'. For fun he threw in some Bambaiya *tapori* picked up from the movies: '*bole toh*' and the like. His greeting was assalam aleikum and his god-willing was inshallah. Danish is a Persian name; it means wisdom.

I enjoyed watching Danish bowl. It was not about flight or turn, for he employed modest amounts of both, though he had a big heart and a nifty bag of variations. It was more his action, which, essentially, involved building himself up into a tangle, and then extricating himself from it in the nick of time. Most of all I think it was his teeth. The top row was considerable and jutted out a little; while bowling he pulled up his upper lip further still, so the row dazzled all the more. He took on the image of, as they say in Gujarati, a *luchcha*, a schemer, unleashing his trickeries on batsmen. The image was irresistible in a wrist spinner.

Danish's early cricket was nurtured by his uncle, Cawas Mullah – a Parsi, thereby providing all-roundedness to the story. In his teens, he says, he was fat, and shorter than average, which meant that flight came naturally to him. Adolescence arrived with its sudden onslaught of height, a development which has crushed many a precocious spinner in the bud. Danish was not elbowed out; he worked around it, adding a dash of Anil Kumble to Abdul Qadir, his idol. As it stood, Danish had an impressive record, with five-fors against South Africa and New Zealand, apart from three against Bangladesh, in his first sixteen Tests.

Babita brought around tea and snacks. I asked Danish if he ever felt like an outsider, especially now, when there was so much talk of a religious awakening in the team. 'I've never felt that way – they've treated me like a yaar, a brother, a son, better than that.'

And before leaving I brought myself to ask the Kanerias who they supported when India played Pakistan, the subcontinental version of the Tebbit Test – after Norman Tebbit, the British MP who demanded ethnic minorities prove their commitment to the nation by supporting the England cricket team in a match against the land of their forebears. This was ridiculous. An individual ought to be free to support who he wants, no questions asked. Who is anyone to sift through and rate somebody else's allegiance? Indeed, why should it be expected that there be an allegiance at all? Yet, I knew that statements of the kind made by Fazal Mahmood (in his autobiography, *From Dusk to Dawn*) and Iqbal Qasim (in *Pride and Passion*), who have spoken about the support they received from Indian Muslims during their Indian tours of 1954-55 and 1986-87, were perfect weapons in the hands of snakes like Bal Thackeray. If it ever came to it, I could imagine the same being thrown in the face of the Kanerias. Above all, I was curious, perhaps perversely so.

'Pakistan,' they all replied.

KARACHI IS RECENT. A fishing village till the mid-1800s, when the Raj deigned to recognise its potential as a port town, it held less than half a million people at the time it was instituted the first capital of Pakistan. It has burgeoned on, colossally, to become the fifth most populous city on the planet. People still stream into Karachi from every part of Pakistan, at the rate of, it is said, 3,000 a day.

Karachi is not only volume. It now has the most hard-edged reputation of any South Asian city. It was born out of conflict, the child of Partition, and conflict has been its leitmotif; between the Sindhi-speaking local and Urdu-speaking Indian migrant, between the Sunni Muslim and the Shia Muslim, between the mullah and the one looking further west. In the darkest days of the mid-late 1990s, it was said that 200 people were killed on the streets of Karachi every month.

Karachi's reputation precedes it, overwhelms it. Karachi of the mind's eye is drugs and madness and guns and bombs. Its promise is a touch of the bizarre. On his first visit to the city of his ancestors, the British author Hanif Kureishi wrote: 'In a flat high above Karachi, an eighteen-year-old kid strung out on heroin danced cheerfully around the room in front of me pointing to his erection, which he referred to as his Imran Khan, the name of the handsome Pakistan cricket captain.' Indians know Karachi as the city of the underworld lord, Dawood Ibrahim. The world knows it as the city of Daniel Pearl's slaughter. In a study of 130 cities around the world, the Intelligence Unit of the *Economist* ranked Karachi as second from last. The French writer Bernard-Henri Lévy infamously condemned it as 'a black hole'. Is it a wonder at all then that when I mentioned to Sourav Ganguly, during an interview at the end of the tour, that I would be spending a few days in Karachi before returning, his response was a disturbed '*Karachi*? Why *Karachi*?'

The idea of Karachi is such a ruinous burden that it is easy to overlook that it is still a mass of people who eat and drink and breathe and sleep and laugh and joke and work and play and get on with life. Indeed, it is inside these getting-on-with of lives that lie energies that become indefinable, indescribable addictions; and Karachi's addiction has proven to be irresistible, at this moment, by about 15 million.

But a reputation is a reputation, and it is all a traveller has for a starting point.

In the few days I spent in Karachi I felt no trepidation. I was struck, however, by the elaborate security and surveillance measures at the residences; at how guards on bicycles would make rounds at night, piercing the dark with their sirens, to keep awake chowkidars and to sow doubt in the minds of any burglars.

On a Sunday evening, the day after the game, I was taken around the city by Murtaza and Shahrezad. Shahrezad is Osman's sister; Sonny, as Murtaza is better known, her husband. Along with us were their two beautiful baby daughters, who they had named Maya and Priya, not to make a statement but simply because they liked the names. On the stereo played ambient, mildly intoxicating local bar music from the 1950s and 60s, before prohibition had kicked in. It was a mix of old-movie, jazz and cabaret. *Roma Shabana* the compilation was titled, after a Karachi nightclub of the era.

Sonny is an editorial writer for *Dawn,* Pakistan's highest circulating English daily, and a repository of knowledge. Patiently he answered the questions of a first-time visitor. We started with the security.

'You know, the only culture shock I got on my first visit to India was the absence of such security measures, even at the airports.

'You must understand that terrorism has been very much a

78

part of our urban life since the Russian invasion of Afghanistan in 1979. We're used to being frisked at entrances to offices, to banks, to even mosques. At the recent cricket matches here, the city has been in a state of siege, the same measures as at the India-Pakistan match, maybe with fewer personnel deployed. Schools and colleges were called off for the day, roads within a kilometre of the stadium were blockaded. Music concerts regularly have that type of strict security arrangement. When Musharraf or the PM visits, the city's main artery, the 22 km road from the airport to the heart of Karachi, is shut to traffic, with people stranded for hours. It's a fact of life here.'

'How non-violent was the country before the Afghan conflict?' I asked.

'Totally, I would say. Nobody carried firearms; security guards were non-existent; our houses didn't have burglar alarms or iron grills; car thefts were unheard of. Everything changed with the American-funded jihad against the Soviets. There was an influx of foreign, mainly Arab, warriors – volunteers – with their petro-dollars. They opened up seminaries and lured the locals with their wealth to wage jihad in Afghanistan. Afghanistan's emerging Taliban leadership looked to these seminaries. Many of them indeed were the product of these seminaries. And with the money, the firearms, the military training, also came drugs – we're talking about something like five million Afghan refugees, over three million of them officially acknowledged, and many among them poppy growers and heroin processors. Practically overnight, the crime graph shot up. This is not to say that the refugees were criminals; but their arrival here unleashed forces – money, drugs, firearms and religious fanaticism.

'The seminaries that trained the jihadis were all puritan Sunni, the Saudi variety. With so much money and firearms available they first set out to wage jihad against the Shias, the minority in

Pakistan. Iran in turn funded and armed the Shias. The Shia-Sunni conflicts escalated. Basically, terrorism had arrived. And we're still dealing with the remnants...'

We drove by the monuments at Clifton's intersections. These were monuments not of people, nor were they abstractions; they were swords; tall, clean, harsh structures, Do Talwaar, and Teen Talwaar, the first an emblem of Zulfikar Ali Bhutto's Pakistan People's Party, the second appropriating that emblem to represent Jinnah's motto of Unity, Faith and Discipline; but both perhaps symbolic also of a conceived democracy which has spent half its life under the rule of the sword.

I asked Sonny about the military rule.

Musharraf had suspended Pakistan in a catch-22. His dictatorship offered more civil liberties than many elected governments did. Unlike the previous General who ruled Pakistan, Zia-ul-Haq, Musharraf had no Islamist agenda: indeed, his hero was another General, Kemal Ataturk, the early-twentieth-century leader who abolished the Caliphate and formed Turkey as a secular democracy; and it was Turkey that Musharraf looked to as the model of a progressive Muslim country. Musharraf went after the terrorists. Musharraf did not ask the women to hide behind the veil or the men to grow beards. Musharraf did not clamp down on music shows or theatre, and he did not perpetrate liquor crackdowns; he himself was said to fancy his whiskey. He allowed the press to function independently, more, in fact, than the last civilian government; and Sonny reckoned that Pakistan's English press was far more critical of the establishment than was India's. My impression from the few non-Muslims I encountered in Pakistan was that they felt secure under Musharraf. And while I was there, it was reported that one survey, admittedly American, found that 86 per cent of Pakistanis rated him 'favourably'. But, for all that, a military dictatorship.

'My stance is clear on this,' said Sonny. 'The job of the army is security, not governance. Musharraf basically represents an institution which has long abandoned its professional role of safeguarding the country's physical frontiers. It has concentrated instead on building an empire. It has inherited the prestige and social attitudes of the colonial rulers. Many in the army behave like kala sahibs, who have complete disdain for the "bloody civilians". They have ventured into profit-making commercial enterprises, owning large industrial units set up under extremely lenient conditions, often at the cost of other public and private sector businesses. Their overland cargo service, National Logistic Cell, has deprived the state railways of its cargo earnings. They own private airlines, oil refineries, mills and factories churning out consumer products, a large commercial bank, you name it. They are the single largest land-developers in the country, appropriating prime commercial land in the best of big-city neighbourhoods and selling it at inflated prices to civilians.'

'But,' I asked, 'what about this perception in the public that the country is secure under Musharraf, economically stable, liberal?'

'See, the army is the most powerful interest as well as pressure group in the country. When a political government comes to power the army acts as a pressure group to the point of rendering it ineffective. For it is only in the public discrediting of the political process that the army comes out shining. And when they seize power, there's apparent consistency in government policies because no other state institution has been left intact, least of all politicians and the political processes which can challenge them. But every time this happens, every time there is a military intervention, it pushes the country back many decades as far as viable, lasting, democratic governance is concerned. The stability they provide does not mean long-term stability for the country or its political future.

'If anything, the army is now more emboldened and acts with more impunity than ever before. Curtailing civil liberties has become a thing of the past. Now they just let the people bark to their heart's content! The army under Zia radicalised society to wage jihad in Afghanistan; under Musharraf it is cleaning up its own act by de-jihadising – but remember that both were done at the behest of the US; both were done at the army's desire to stay on the right side of Washington in order to retain its privileged status.'

Winding through south Karachi's colonial district, Sonny and I came to the agreement that equating Karachi to Bombay, as people did so seamlessly, was lazy analogising. The similarities were striking: their humble origin as fishing hamlets, their expansion into port towns; their astonishing growth in the twentieth century; their position as the biggest, most cosmopolitan cities in their countries and as commercial capitals; their concentration of Gujarati businessmen, and their sizeable community of Parsis; their sticky weather and their unappetising beaches; their newness, as reflected in their colonial rather than Mughal monuments. But Karachi was not characterised by Bombay's most singular feature, the lack of space. All living in Bombay was derived from this quality. Any comparison not fulfilling this criterion was at once tenuous. Karachi sprawled, massively, into boroughs. Bombay gasped along straight lines. There were more, many more, bungalows in Karachi's Defence than the whole of Bombay.

We drove by the bandar, the port. I would return here to go 'crabbing', a reputed Karachi activity which involved being ferried out a few kilometres on a little barge, catching crab yourself, having it cooked on board, and eating it under the stars, amid the tingling black ripples of the sea. We did eat the crabs, and they were sumptuous. But stars were few to see. And there were more parked barges on the sea than ripples. And the crabs nowadays were so scarce that they were caught in advance by the cooks. In this was Bombay: a city that has grown far too much for its own simple pleasures.

We visited the Quaid-e-Azam mazaar, the tomb of The Supreme Leader, Mohammad Ali Jinnah, a large marble structure elevated on a plinth, not delicate, nor ornate, but stark, attention-drawing, surrounded by green lawns on which a Sunday evening family-picnic mood prevailed. As a child Shahrezad thought that Quaid-e-Azam was a proper noun, that it was the name of God. The visual image of this god was Jinnah sitting upright, on his knees, with the Qur'an spread before him.

Late in the breezy Karachi evening, with *Roma Shabana* into its third run, with Maya getting just a little cranky now after two hours on the road, Sonny told me his story from Partition. When the time came, his grandfather, an army canteen contractor, made preparations to move the family to Lahore from Saharanpur. They were to be transported with their belongings in a military truck to the airfield. The driver was Sikh, born and raised in the house. Out of a foreboding, the grandmother warned her husband, who shushed her: 'Ghar ka ladka hai' (He is one of us). The truck was ambushed, looted. The grandfather was slain. The grandmother's fingers were broken as rings were taken off them. The four children survived, but not the servants who had thrown themselves on the children to protect them. The grandmother stayed behind, until the man was tried and hung.

# 3. The Express is in town!

I WOKE UP only when the taxi driver rang the house bell, and at 4.30 a.m. the taxi got embedded in a pile of sandy rubble. It was a dire situation, the direness of which I did not absorb fully because of sleep. We were on top of the mound, a set of wheels stuck on either side, the undercarriage lodged in the sand like a pregnant turtle. Having got into this position, there was now no going forward and no going back. The driver revved with abandon but that only spluttered dust and made us both cough. Anxious minutes passed. Suddenly six hefty angels in shalwar kameez appeared from a bend in the darkness and pushed us over.

At 7.30 a.m. we were in Islamabad and wheeling our trolleys sympathetically past the group of passengers who had received their bags zipped open and the photographer whose cartridges had gone missing. Outside, a man with beady grey eyes outwrestled a dozen others to transport us to the hotel.

Hotel Park Lane had a turquoise staircase leading up to the reception. Rooms here cost Rs 300 per head. Further, it involved no travelling cost or time since it was across the stadium. It was the deal of all deals. It also meant a desi toilet with no shower curtain and no hot water; also no air-conditioner, a dysfunctional television, a vast industrial standing fan not seen outside godowns, and a fluorescent maroon blanket of thick felt decorated with fluorescent green parrots and Chinese lettering. Breakfast at the Park Lane was a tricky affair; you could order an omelette, but not scrambled or fried egg; you could order toast with jam, but not paratha with jam, for that was a disallowed permutation.

The view from the window revealed Rawalpindi. A grey haze, and miles of hotch-potch flat-top roofs on which dried clothes and spices.

Rawalpindi has a long and layered past, but for the last 150 years it has been known as a garrison town, among the largest in Asia. Forty-five years ago and half an hour away Islamabad was built. Another pointer to the nation: a capital city constructed specifically beside its military headquarters.

Long railway routes connect Rawalpindi, up in the north-east, to all corners of Pakistan. The Tezgam Express chugs down for over a day to Karachi. The Quetta Express does half the same route before turning west into the deserts of Baluchistan. The lored Khyber Mail goes up to Peshawar on the north-west frontier. Yet, the city's best known express, or for that matter, best-known anything now, is one that does not exist at all: the Rawalpindi Express.

Shoaib Akhtar has put Pindi in the pop lexicon of the cricket world. Being what he is, how could he help it? If you regard Wasim, Warne and Lara as of an earlier vintage, Shoaib has been unarguably the most eventful cricketer of his age.

Consider his credentials. He has been banned for ball-tampering. He has been banned for calling a tailender a twat. He has been banned, twice, for chucking. He has been fined for making obscene gestures at spectators in Zimbabwe. He has been admitted to hospital after being hit by a brick thrown by spectators in Bangladesh. He has infuriated his team and administrators by dancing in the discos of South Africa after pulling out of a Test match with an injured knee. He has infuriated his team and administrators by jet-skiing on New Zealand's Lake Wakatipu after pulling out of a one-day match with an injured groin. He has attracted a Public Interest Litigation by slagging off former Pakistani greats. He has attracted a Public Interest Litigation by attending a fashion show on a holy night on the eve of a big match. He has felled top batsmen and held their bleeding bodies in his benevolent arms. He has shattered stumps and toes and spread his wings like an airplane. He has bowled the fastest spells that have ever been bowled. He has fired the most spectacular deliveries that have ever been fired. He has thrilled the world by the very sight of his tassels tearing the wind. He has turned matches with a greater frequency than any other bowler in his time and he has missed as many matches as he has played. He has been born with pancake-flat feet and a motor mouth. He has been able to bend his elbows back by forty-five degrees, and his fingers till they touch his wrist. He has been caricatured endlessly, and he has been endlessly pleased to fulfil such caricatures. 'Basically, mate,' he has declared, running a wet finger through his hair as dozens of women lean out of his sports convertible, 'my life is all about speed.' Here is a Shoaib, when comes such another?

On the eve of the second one-dayer, Shoaib was in even greater demand than usual with the media. Not only was he playing at his home ground, but this would be his hundredth one-day match. In the ninety-nine so far he had demolished opponents at the astounding average and strike rate of 21.81 and 29. Flexing now on the lawns of the Pindi Cricket Stadium, he adhered to his newly acquired position, wherein he offered his team-mates the chance to join him in his conquests: 'I have realised that I'm a match-winner, but I can't do things on my own. I have to take everyone along with me.' Then, summoning his reflective-hero distant gaze for the cameras: 'Started my career right here, right here at Pindi...'

There was no choice in the matter, really. The Pindi afternoon demanded it be dedicated to the Speedy One. And so three journalists set out on his trail.

Shoaib did not play proper cricket till he was about fifteen. One day his elder brother's club team could not make up an XI and Shoaib was reluctantly given a game. Soon he was scorching the Pindi earth, soon he was breaking batsmen's bones, destroying their spirits. By the time Shoaib established himself in the Rawalpindi team, it was time for Sabih Azhar, a bowling all-rounder with a middling record, to call it curtains on his sixteen-year first-class career. Sabih went on to become coach of Rawalpindi and still held the position.

Locating Sabih proved difficult. A series of misinterpreted directions had us skirting the runway of the army airport, driving beneath the bridge on which Musharraf had been assailed by bombs, wandering into an interstellar-pinball-machine-like jam in between a thousand gaudy trucks with a thousand gaudy horns, and finally penetrating the silent depths of a secluded, tree-lined mini-world, so far away from the hustle-bustle of Pindi.

This mini-world turned out to be the mouth of the Khan Research Laboratory, which extended into the forbidden areas beyond. It was here that A.Q. Khan had been working since the 1970s on Pakistan's nuclear weapon technology programme, the secrets of which were recently found to be floating around the world for untold sums of money, much to the red-facedness of Pakistan's establishment. There is a telling little story about A.Q. Khan. Born in Bhopal, he migrated, repulsed by India, six years after Partition. As he was crossing the border a guard snatched away his pen, his favourite pen, which his brother had gifted him on passing an exam. He never forgot this, he said.

The irony of our present location was terrific. Pakistanis had joked before the tour that the only security threat to the Indians was Shoaib Akhtar. And here we were, out to interview one of

Shoaib's early mentors at the very venue whose activities had placed the security of the world in jeopardy.

Khan Research Laboratories, KRL, put up a team in the Patron's tournaments: the collection of banks and government departments which form a parallel structure to the regional one. It was an extraordinary point about Pakistan cricket that, till this season, the 2003-04 season, cricketers received *no* match fee for turning out for their cities or provinces. Only the barest expenses were covered. For decades, thus, it was the patrons, as the banks and departments are called, who kept afloat the domestic game by looking after the cricketers' livelihood; and such a structure also played a significant part in the decentralisation of Pakistan cricket from its traditional power centres, Lahore and Karachi. The trend now seemed to be changing, though, with sponsors coming forth to back the regional teams, while the patrons were increasingly given to employing cricketers only for the duration of the season.

Nothing at the KRL field suggested a nuclear-sponsored patch of turf. It was a most blissful ground. Birds twittered from the trees all around the ground. A dainty white pavilion cottage stood near the entrance. A black sign hung outside a door with Sabih Azhar's name. But the coach was across the pitch, on the balcony of the dressing room, the game at one hand and a mobile phone in the other. The match today was not an interdepartmental one, but an inter-regional one, for the Quaid-e-Azam Trophy.

Sabih welcomed us and called for tea, but our chat never fell into any sort of rhythm. Every few minutes he would be compelled to stop talking and look ahead gravely. Presently, a batsman would trudge up the stairs and disappear into the change-room without making eye contact; soon a pad or a glove would softly thud into the low sliding windows of the dressing room against which we had our backs. Then the conversation would resume.

It was actually a fairly traumatic collapse. Rawalpindi were twenty-something for none as we made our way around the boundary. Fifteen minutes later they were thirty-something for 5. Rawalpindi's opponents were Hyderabad. Though this was the fifth round of the tournament it was only Hyderabad's first match: a player had taken the association to court over his non-selection.

'Very nice boy,' said Sabih in Urdu, about Shoaib, not the player who had taken Hyderabad to court. Sabih had a broad, red face with a tightly trimmed moustache. He spoke in flat, low tones. 'Very decent, very respectful to elders. Nothing at all like what you read about him. That is completely the image that the media has given him.

'Yes, he was always this fast. See, I think it takes one-two matches to know if you have a *fast* bowler on your hands or not. With Shoaib it took even less time. He had those strong legs, he would run in from 30-40 yards. And he was addicted to the bouncer. He won us our first under-19 championship in our history. He took ten wickets in that final. He did a job at KRL, he captained the team. He always worked hard, always took responsibility. I'm telling you he's a victim of media image.

'Yes, always. His run-up was always that long. And according to me he should never change it. When a batsman sees him running in like that, he starts trembling. Half of Shoaib's work is done there. He's hit so many batsmen in local cricket. We have three-four more boys bowling like Shoaib now, almost at that pace. One boy has the exact same action.

'Of course, he is very aggressive while bowling. But, you tell me, don't you think that is the beauty of fast bowling? I think so. People come to see the aggression in fast bowlers. According to me Shoaib Akhtar should remain Shoaib Akhtar.

'No, I don't think he is a chucker. It's not his fault. You meet anyone in his family. Ask his brothers to show you their elbows. They are all deformed. But it speaks volumes for Shoaib, how well he has dealt with that crisis. I'm telling you that boy has a big heart.

'Tendulkar. Tendulkar is the wicket he really wants. The rest are okay for him. They are good batsmen, but he knows he can get them. You know what he says? He says, "Ganguly is scared of me. He runs away to square leg. I can get him anytime." '

And with that healthy provocation for a headline, we took Sabih's leave, freeing him to attend to his team's woes. The following day Rawalpindi's last five rallied to take the score to 452. They won by an innings. It would not matter: matches against Hyderabad, and Quetta, where too a cricketer had taken the association to court, would not be counted.

But our trail was unfinished. And so onward to the erstwhile home of Mohammad Akhtar, to see where our Express grew up. Getting past the security in one little part of Morgah's sprawling Attock Refinery, the oldest crude oil refinery in Pakistan, was not difficult. But getting back out was, for it had dawned upon the guards that they had erroneously allowed in Indians with cameras and notepads. Eventually, the matter was sorted out amid hearty embraces.

Mohammad Akhtar, Shoaib's father, used to be a security supervisor at the refinery. His former quarters, a modest two-roomer, stood in a row of low whitewashed brick structures, each enlivened by an emerald green door. Ten minutes up the road, Shoaib had built a two-storey mansion where the family now lives. Sometimes he still drove by here, on one of his several sports bikes. Nobody had yet moved into the old quarters. The green door was currently under siege from a flutter of chickens.

The quarters stood on a precipice, though not so dramatic as the word suggests. Beyond the precipice sprawled out acres of land in possession of the refinery, dotted with coarse pitches on which Shoaib, we were told by former neighbour Mr Julius Waheed, often played as a youth.

The sun had descended upon the fields and the last of the cricket matches for the day had finished. There was a certain poignancy to the picture before us. It reminded me of the sugarcane wastelands in Berbician Guyana, where the plantations housed bare pitches on which Rohan Kanhai and Basil Butcher and Joe Solomon and Alvin Kallicharan and others would lash their coconut fronds against cork projectiles encased in rags and twine. Port Mourant, the tiniest of sugarcane villages, produced seven Test cricketers. It was tempting to think that there were still a few Expresses to come out of Morgah.

The land beyond the precipice was marked out as part of a proposed biodiversity park, the first one in Pakistan, a joint venture of the Attock Refinery, the Pakistan government and UNESCAP. I'm not sure what this entailed. My only wish was that the pitches don't disappear.

*

THE SCENES OUTSIDE the stadium should have served as a warning. From atop a van a man handed out a sponsor's paper visors. Men of all ages rushed towards the van and leapt up to pouch the freebie. Competition grew intense, and some began scaling the windows to get to the roof. At this the man began throwing punches down at their faces, which encouraged others to climb up and retaliate. Soon it was a free-for-all. The melee was allowed to blossom, because the security guards were across the road, brandishing lathis at ticket-holding spectators who had been misdirected in the first place by the security themselves, or else tossing pressmen among each other for repeated authentication of the same pass.

This could not have jarred more with the smooth match-day at Karachi. The reason, according to *The News*, was that the stadium did not fall under the purview of the PCB, like those at Lahore and Karachi. Indeed, they were compelled to fork out a fee of Rs 12 lakh per day of international cricket to the local government, which owned the ground. And the local administration, it was reported, was gifted at not co-operating. For instance, the PCB arranged to install chairs in some of the stands, but, late in the evening, the local administration threatened to take them away if there was no provision to chain them together. Thus, locks and chains had to be quickly procured, and the task was performed well into the night. Then the PCB were informed that their media accreditations, valid at every other venue, would not be sufficient here; an additional security permit would have to be obtained by all media. Thankfully, this never came to pass.

So it was not a surprise that the travelling media's only sour experience would come at Pindi, during the Test match at the end of the tour. A photographer was arbitrarily halted at a boundary gate by a constable despite possessing the correct pass, which clearly spelt out 'access to all areas except dressing room'. The photographer tried to explain this. The constable slapped him and kicked him in the groin, and nobody intervened. As the TV cameras arrived on the scene to cover the fight, the constable began combing his hair, preparing for his moment. He was suspended for the rest of the Test.

But the ground was kissed by location. For a backdrop it could boast the broad, tall Margalla range, reduced in the haze to a line on the horizon, but on clear afternoons a sight both awesome and soothing. Alas, the stadium did little to reflect this grandeur. The pavilion was a charm-free concrete cube, the colour of faded paan spit. Across it was another cube, paler pink, in which the press box took the form of four cramped rooms distributed over two floors, none of them offering a full view of the field. The ticket-holders did not have it much better. The stench of the toilets was comparable to that at Indian stadiums, which is as bad as it gets. There was a shortage of drinking water (spectators were not permitted to bring their own bottles). The low stands were roofless, inconsiderate given even the temperate climate at Rawalpindi's altitude; fortunately, this was a day-night game. And Ten Sports were rather unhappy with the facilities provided them. The PCB had already acquired land for a new stadium at Islamabad. I suspected the international days of the Pindi Cricket Stadium were numbered.

An evening game also meant that dew and insects would make their presence felt. Insecticide was dispersed like teargas over the field the previous evening to thwart the locusts and moths, but there was no such measure available for the dew, which could conceivably sway the captain's decision at the toss.

And it was Inzamam who won it once more. And on another grassless pitch, he chose to bat, unmindful of having to bowl with a slippery ball in the evening. Pakistan had won eleven of their fourteen matches at the ground, in use since 1992. The Indians had never played here.

There were two changes to Pakistan's XI from Karachi. Shabbir Ahmed was fit and replaced Naved-ul-Hasan, and the dynamo Shahid Afridi came in for Imran Farhat. India, too, made two changes. Laxman, recovered from his knee niggle, reclaimed his position over Hemang Badani; while Murali Kartik sat out for Ramesh Powar, a tubby all-rounder, whose prowess in domestic cricket for Mumbai was neither with bat nor ball, but in situations of strife. Coming in somewhere between no. 8 and no. 10 he would coolly rescue a top-order collapse, and with his lobbing offbreaks he would prise out two wickets just when a game was slipping away. Even so, playing Powar was a risk when the team were anyway one specialist bowler short. India's resources, and Ganguly's marshalling of them, were sure to be stretched.

Ganguly's own availability had been in slight doubt when he did not train the previous day with flu. In his absence, Dravid had addressed the press – and confidently informed them that Ashish Nehra would not be considered for selection because of a swollen ankle. Ganguly had swung by the ground later and told the coterie of Calcutta journalists that no such non-consideration was in place. The press, except for the Calcutta journalists, reported that Nehra would not play. Ten minutes before the toss, Nehra was included in the XI. The Calcutta journalists were smug. Not so the non-Calcutta journalists. Stories about rifts inside the team and selective dispensation of information flew off numerous keyboards.

By 2 p.m., every stand was packed, except for the one reserved by the sponsors, which would remain unpopulated throughout. An estimated 18,000 were in. Another 1,000 or so were perched on the many vantage points around the bowl, including the terrace of Hotel Park Lane.

All 19,000 pairs of eyes were on Afridi because his personality – the wide smile, the bouncy hair, the boyish dives, the large thoughtless strokes – demands so.

Afridi's first scoring shot was a forward prod to Balaji which fetched him four – to fine leg. Soon he tried to blast Balaji through the off and found his outside edge defeated. He then tried to work him to midwicket and instead squirted it through where a second slip ought to have been. But by the time he had reeled off a second pulled four off Zaheer the signs were ominous for India: Afridi had survived till the sixth over and taken his score to 20.

Afridi is all or he is nothing. Lately he had been nothing, going past single digits only five times in his last fifteen innings.

As ever, he had been dividing opinion. One Pakistani reporter described him as a 'three-dimensional heart-throb'. A wit in the press box promptly put into perspective two of those dimensions – '*na* bowling, *na* batting: all-rounder.' Afridi's batting and bowling averages of 25 and 40 certainly lent some credence to the comment.

But there was a purpose to Afridi. For one, he was much needed as a bowling option, because none of Pakistan's other batsmen were capable of a proper spell. The other thing, of course, was that Afridi could set the texture of a game in a flash: there have been many good and several great, but no other one-day batsman in history with even 1,000 runs, let alone the 4,000 that Afridi was approaching, had maintained a career strike-rate greater than 100.

Having got himself a start, Afridi tore into Zaheer, sending him over the midwicket fence with a macho slog, yet raising his rear leg like a teenage girl playing badminton. Buoyed, he went for the shot again, and inside-edged it for four. Then a high slice over point for a third boundary. Zaheer's first four overs had yielded 38 runs.

In the throes of merriness, Afridi thumped Balaji straight back for his second six. Then he charged down and smeared him to midwicket and followed it with a glide to third man to reach his fifty, from thirty-three balls. Pakistan, in the eleventh over, were running hot at 8 an over. Zaheer was switched around to the other end. Afridi tonked him straight and high for four, and then picked him up over mid-on for four more: 5-0-51-0, and surely time to chew the cud at fine leg for a few hours.

All the while, Yasir Hameed had been crafting a precise and elegant innings. There is something stern about Yasir. His features are bony and angular, and he isn't terribly fond of smiling. His short, crisp frame was as if he had been ironed. He batted without curves. Yet, shining through the straight lines and the bones and the angles and the tautness, was a quite exquisite touch, particularly while driving on the off. He led with his elbow, he leant into his strokes. He and Afridi looked good at the moment. They brought up Pakistan's 100 in the thirteenth over.

Ganguly introduced Sehwag. Yasir gently played out his first over but then Afridi intervened and walloped him for two rather high sixes. Ganguly looked to Yuvraj, and Afridi swung at him, and missed, middle stump pegged back: 80 from 58 balls, identical almost to Sehwag at Karachi. Yuvraj proceeded to complete what was only the second maiden of the 119 overs bowled thus far in the series.

The game fell into its one-day rhythms. A series of brisk medium-sized innings from the middle-order thrived alongside Yasir. Youhana casually summoned his ravishing inside-out, and then milked singles against Yuvraj and Powar's lobs, to put on 53 in ten overs with Yasir. Inzamam was just settling in when the General dropped by. He was Patron of the cricket board but had insisted on paying for his tickets – Rs 4,500 for three, we were told – which had pleased Shaharyar and the PCB beyond measure. Inzamam responded to the arrival with a six off Powar: a little more middle on it and it would have crashed through the glass and fallen right at the General's feet.

Yasir departed in a meaningless run-out for 86 in the thirty-fifth over, and the captain again engaged himself in a swift partnership with Younis Khan. Nehra, sure-ankled and accurate in his first spell, returned to the attack. First thing he fired a yorker into Inzamam's off stump. Next he skid one on to Moin's pads, pitching leg, en route to off. Two wickets in two balls and 249 for five in the fortieth over.

This slowed Pakistan, or rather postponed their final fling. Only 29 came from the next five overs. Nehra soon eked out his third wicket, Younis caught behind on the edge. Immediately he held up his left hand and let out a yelp. On the previous delivery he had stopped a straight drive and felt pain. Now he felt it again. He finished his over, the last of his ten, and left the field. It turned out that he had split the webbing between his thumb and forefinger. He was to return home for three weeks.

Razzaq walked out at no. 8 though he really should have at no. 6. Instantly he set about the bowling. Like Adam Gilchrist, Razzaq grips his bat high on the handle, allowing himself to not so much hit the ball as whip it. Zaheer was given a shot at redeeming his figures but Razzaq routinely banished deliveries down the ground. Zaheer finished with none for 72 from seven overs, Razzaq with 31 not out from 18 balls, and Pakistan with 329.

The Indians had now conceded 359, 335, 344 and 329 in their last four limited-overs games, and it brought to mind Miandad's words before the match. Asked if this was the weakest Indian bowling line-up he had seen, he replied: 'Bhai, unke toh bahut dekhe hain hamne…' (Well, from India I've seen quite a few…)

WHETHER IT WAS the push of the hundredth international or a rush of adrenalin under floodlights or the zip of the evening dew or he was simply doing as he always does but now a little more, it cannot be said, but Shoaib really screamed in through the evening haze. He beat Tendulkar's outside edge, he jagged it between his bat and his pad, and he hurried him all the time. Sehwag did the early scoring, carving Shoaib over the slips, clipping Shabbir over midwicket and then meteoring him over cover.

It took till the fifth over for Sachin to find his groove, which he did with a whip over point and a swirl in front of square off Shoaib. He reaffirmed his mastery, standing up on his toes and driving Shabbir on the top of the bounce, a light flick of the wrists guiding the ball to the right of cover when normally he would have hit it square of the man. When he is batting well, Tendulkar's movements are so contained. Every hair is in place.

Shabbir tried a slower ball to Sehwag. Sehwag thrashed it high into the night sky, till it got lost in the lights and then appeared again after scaling the height of the towers and soared higher still before descending inside the boundary and rolling over. He was threatening to get out of hand. Shoaib terminated that possibility and set aflame the evening crowd with a straight, full and very, very fast delivery that cannoned off Sehwag's pad and blew his off stump out of the ground. Laxman arrived but was soon unseated, lbw, by a zinger from Sami: 71 for 2 in the twelfth over. Ganguly should have gone for duck but Shoaib spilled a gentle offering at mid-off. But Ganguly never settled into his innings, and his laboured 15 ended when he curiously jostled down the pitch to work Afridi against the angle of his brisk top-spin and was stumped: 140 for 3 in the twenty-fourth over.

And so Tendulkar was now faced with the task Inzamam had been at Karachi. He had to bat fast, but not only that; he had to bat big, but not only that. He had to do both. He was in less trouble than Inzamam because he had to meet a lower required rate, but he was in more trouble than Inzamam because runs were not coming from the other end.

By and large Tendulkar followed the Gambler's credo that 'you got to know when to hold 'em, know when to fold 'em, know when to walk away, know when to run'. In Dravid, he found a sharp, hard-running ally, and who played a cracking reverse-sweep which may have plucked a string of nostalgia in Tendulkar's heart. Tendulkar used to play it just like that half a decade ago, and then he gave it up. Half a decade ago, Dravid would have scolded himself and performed twenty push-ups if he had attempted the stroke even in a dream.

When he made 51, Tendulkar touched 13,000 runs in one-day international cricket. The nearest pursuant was more than 3,000 behind. And when he reached hundred he became the first Indian to make a one-day century in Pakistan. It was the thirty-seventh of his one-day career. The second in the queue, Ganguly, was on twenty-two.

With Dravid providing cool assistance, Tendulkar now began to up his tempo, getting more and more leg-side. Against the pace bowlers, with men out at deep square leg and deep midwicket, he traded the swirl for the loft to long-on. Against the spinners, he swept increasingly, along the ground, in the air, swept fine, swept square, swept in front of square. India kept meeting their required rate of 7.5.

It was the lofted sweep in front of square that finally did Tendulkar in. He had hit it well. Call it foresight, call it laziness, but Inzamam had persevered with a fielder 10 yards in from the boundary, even though Tendulkar had been skilfully defeating the man. This one was to the left of Razzaq, and he caught it at shoulder height on the run. Tendulkar's 141 had taken him 135 balls. Over a hundred of his runs were to the leg, and so too were all but four of his eighteen boundaries.

How did it stack up against Inzamam's innings at Karachi? It was bereft of the same poignancy of occasion. Inzamam had scored faster, he had been more awesome, but then he had also gotten significant support from Younis and, in particular, Youhana. Tendulkar's was a proper lone hand. In the time he had made his 141, the other batsmen between them totted up 76. Indeed, extras was to finish as the second-highest scorer of the innings.

India needed 85 from 68 balls. They slipped into a descent. Dravid was cleaned by Sami as soon as the ball had been replaced by a drier one; Yuvraj was caught, like Tendulkar, on the lofted sweep. With a thrilling blast, the Express returned to remove two in two, suckering Kaif with a slower ball, trapping Zaheer in front with an inswinger. Mexican waves whorled around the low open Pindi stands.

India had now lost five wickets for 39 runs, the last three for two runs in five balls. A further 46 were needed from 26 balls and there remained only two wickets in hand. The pair at the crease, Powar and Balaji, between them tallied 15 runs in one-day cricket. This game was over. But it was not.

Afridi began the fourth-last over, and Powar creamed him into the midwicket fence. Balaji appeared at the striker's, and his flailing carve trickled without conviction over the rope at point. Two balls later he thumped it in the same direction but with such force that you could hear the crack of the willow even in the ever-growing night noise. Fourteen came from the over.

Shoaib careered in from the other end and zoned in on Balaji's shoulder. Balaji half hooked, half evaded, was late with both, but the ball caught the edge of his bat and shrieked down to the third-man boundary. Four fours had come from the last seven balls; the Indians had come alive.

Shoaib pulled out the slower one again, and Powar biffed it back over his head for another four. Shoaib responded with a wretched beamer. The dew had rendered the ball slippery but it was difficult to give Shoaib the benefit of doubt. He was six when he broke his elder brother's front tooth with a beamer while playing outside the Morgah quarters. Two years ago he was warned for firing one at his pace rival, Brett Lee. He has a hot head and he does not suffer the swings of lower-order batsmen gladly. A tougher umpire may have ordered him off. Powar took another chunky swipe at the last ball of Shoaib's over: edged for four. Poetic justice. Sixteen runs from the over: 16, now, to get from 12.

Balaji was run-out on the first ball of the penultimate over, hitting straight to midwicket and darting. But Powar had crossed ends. Now Sami bowled it full and straight, Powar smacked it into the covers. It should have been four. Inzamam threw his considerable self on to the floor and made a superb save, a save received by the good folks at Pindi with both applause and laughter. Powar still took two. Fourteen from ten. Again Sami pitched it full and again Powar drove into the off, this time unable to gather more than a single.

Thirteen from nine, but on strike was Nehra, anyway famously inept with the bat, and now with a split webbing. Given the injury, given the match situation, surely a tip-and-run was the way to go, but instead Nehra heaved. He closed his eyes and tossed back his head and heaved, and Sami, full and straight as ever, theatrically shattered the stumps. Powar turned around, disappointed, and slammed his bat against his pads. Later he admitted surprise at Nehra's choice of stroke. His valour, and Balaji's, had come to nothing. Not that it was consolation, but both men, particularly Balaji, would find special mention in a tea meeting with the General the following day.

As the match ended, it was hard to argue with the fan who held up the banner, 'India will not win; Pakistan will not win; we will win'. Anything after Karachi was expected to be an anticlimax, but here were 19,000 at the edge of their seats till the end. India and Pakistan were playing without fright, playing with expressiveness.

At the press conference, Inzamam produced his first deadpan funny of the tour, and he would keep them coming. Asked about Pakistan's dire situation with extras, he replied: 'Improvement toh hai. Karachi mein 38, aaj 37' (But there is an improvement. 38 at Karachi, 37 here). Tendulkar found it difficult to summon humour when asked why was it that he failed to win matches for India. 'Go look at the scorecards.'

Outside in the haze a flaming tassel-head was spotted sending down thunderbolt after thunderbolt at a single stump and cussing himself roundly after each such. He may have taken three wickets, he may have nearly hat-tricked, he may have finished on the winning side, he may have completed a century of one-dayers, but the Express, Rawalpindi's Express, the Express of all expresses, wanted more, and he wanted nobody to miss the point.

*Pakistan 329 for 6 in 50 overs (Yasir 86, Afridi 80, Nehra 3-44) beat India 317 in 48.4 overs (Tendulkar 141, Sami 3-41, Shoaib 3-49) by 12 runs*

# 4. There's grass on them thar' frontier

TRAVELLING ON THE Grand Trunk the layers peel away. Our voyage was westward, from Pindi, below the mountains, through the dry plains of Punjab, across the Indus, skirting the lush valleys of lower Swat, and towards the Frontier, the Frontier so endlessly romanticised, the Frontier of ruggedness, of danger, of myth, the gateway to the subcontinent for wave upon wave of conqueror.

Our voyage, our theme-park ride, was up more than two millennia and back slowly down. We stopped at Taksh Shila – Taxila – the most venerated of ancient universities in Indian history textbooks, the cradle of Buddhism a thousand years before Islam arrived in the region, its stupas now serene mounds in the great flatness, of interest to nobody but the few dozen daily tourists at a nearby museum. We journeyed up the road and down to fifteen century AD, halting at Hasan Abdal, its streaky thin lanes bursting with pirated CDs and baby chickens dyed fluorescent before being put up for sale as exotic pets. A set of Sikh families here look after the tranquil cream-golden Panja Sahib gurdwara, visited annually by thousands of pilgrims for its eternal spring of holy water, they say, drawn from a rock by the founder of the faith, Guru Nanak, a rock which still bears the imprints of his hand, his panja. We drove further west and into the next century, past the stunning silhouette of Akbar's Attock Fort, standing mightily upon the confluence of the Dariya-e-Kabul and the Dariya-e-

Sindh, or the Indus, at its narrowest and most treacherous here, the mingling of whose distinct colours was swallowed now by dusk. And beyond Attock, beyond the Indus, we moved into the North West Frontier Province, to the land of the Pashtun, the turbans appearing evermore on men, their noses sharper, their cheeks redder, their eyes greener, their bodies larger, their hair fairer, their lips more chapped, their enunciations more guttural.

BUT THE FRONTIER we drove into was no frontier at all. Topographically, the plains leading up to Peshawar were a natural extension of Punjab. Only further west and south-west of Peshawar did the terrain change, more of a piece with Central Asia; and it was there, those regions, the inscrutable barren mountains, the scent of Afghanistan beyond, which imparted the NWFP its specific allure. The tribal regions, or 'agencies', spread along the Afghan border, were permitted by the Pakistan government, as by the British before them, to largely administer themselves in their ancient, fiercely patriarchal ways, by the consensus of elders or the gun.

A great attachment ran through NWFP for Afghanistan, with whom they shared ethnicity, language, a past – and a cause. There was sympathy for the Taliban regime, which had been destroyed by America in the aftermath of 9/11 with a little help from Musharraf, a kind of reversal of events from a couple of decades previously, when the Americans and Pakistan had nurtured and sustained the anti-Soviet jihad. Indeed, the American invasion had altered the face of Pakistan, galvanising the hardliners. It had led to the merging of six religious parties, otherwise given to fighting among themselves, who rode the wave of anti-Americanism in the last general election to garner an unprecedented representation of almost 20 per cent in the parliament. And they swept to power in NWFP, where they instituted the sharia, which, among other things, meant a ban on musical performances and on music in the buses, on depictions of human faces on murals or posters, and a further clamp-down on whatever daily freedoms there existed for women. Musharraf they considered a traitor, an American tool subverting Islam; 'Musharraf is a dog,' they sloganeered at their rallies.

And in this it was, essentially, that lay the problem of playing at Peshawar. And the sequence of events around the match was to make the whole affair rather delicate.

On 15 March, a day before he stopped by for a spot of cricket diplomacy at Pindi and three days before his scheduled meeting with the US Secretary of State, Colin Powell, Musharraf had been in Peshawar, addressing a large gathering of tribal chiefs. He exhorted them to stop protecting the '500-600 foreign militants', mostly Al Qaeda terrorists, he said, for whom the army had been combing the tribal agency of South Waziristan for weeks now, with little success. There was to be a massive step-up in the military operation. Musharraf wanted their co-operation; not surprisingly, he would receive it only in part measure.

On 18 March, one day before the Peshawar match, as Powell met Musharraf, conferred upon Pakistan the exalted status of a major non-Nato American ally and confirmed a USD 460 million debt write-off, there raged pitched battle in South Waziristan. Thousands of troops moved in, as did fighter jets and helicopters, and they faced stern resistance from the alleged terrorists and their tribal protectors, who occupied dug-in positions in their mud fortresses and caves. By evening the army announced the surrounding of a 'high-value target', conjectured at the time to be Osama Bin Laden's number two at Al Qaeda, Ayman Al Zawahiri. The guerrilla war in South Waziristan would drag on for months and months, leading to thousands of lost lives, of troops, of innocent civilians, and the utter devastation of Wana, the main town in the agency. Though Wana lay some 200 km south-west of it, Peshawar, and the cricket tour, could reasonably feel threatened. For this was a bigger thing.

In her documentary, *Re-inventing the Taliban*, for instance, the film-maker Sharmeen Obaid encountered a shopkeeper in Peshawar who had crossed into Afghanistan to fight the Americans: there were, he said, hundreds like him in that market alone. What if the sympathisers were to prove a point? Leave aside the cricket, what if they were to attack the army installations in Peshawar? That would lead to instant abandonment of the tour. And as it happened, five nights after the Indians left the city, missiles fired out from the outskirts exploded at four locations in Peshawar, one of them at the secretariat, another at the headquarter of the Frontier Corps, another at the Judicial Complex.

Given all this, it was a relief to note that the mood never got severe in Peshawar. The caravan travels inside its own bubble, at its own pace, with its own moods. Besides, it had been more than a week in Pakistan. Everybody had loosened up. Dravid and Kartik had made a visit to Taxila. At Peshawar, the players wandered out shopping for *jutis* and carpets, two of the region's most famous exports.

And Peshawar, in all its tangledness, in all its decrepit glories, evoked a romance willingly nurtured by first-time visitors. Roaming its streets at nights, I was brought back to life at a time when I was feeling stupidly lonely, claustrophobic, underworked. I was suddenly without a room-mate, which also affected my finances for the tour. My magazine deadlines were still a week away. My work on the *Guardian* required short, basic, match reporting and nothing else. And the media circus was terribly suffocating. I wanted to run away from it, but I had become leaden-headed, encumbered.

I jumped into a local bus, a startling colour-burst of a big van, far too low to accommodate most Pathan men, where a stranger insisted that he buy my ticket, and spoke passionately of the hypocrisies of the Punjabis and Sindhis just as the Punjabis had done of the Pathans and Sindhis and the Sindhis had done of the Punjabis and Pathans. The lively Pashto disco suggested the ban on music on the buses was rather easy to sidestep; and in the bus it was also that I sighted the only women I was to see in Peshawar outside of the cricket stadium. I walked about the main Sadar, its garishly tubelit shops flashing replica cricket jerseys and soft-porn CDs of the renowned large women of the NWFP, *Mast Raqsana*, and friends striking majestic poses in short skirts and sequinned tops, with their pillar thighs, their boulder bums, their harvested-cornfield armpits. I ate for eight rupees an oily chapli kabab, the Pashtun steak, at a stall where all eyes focussed on a television set showing a 1980s Hindi movie: Jayaprada was on view, Jeetendra could not have been far behind; Peshawaris take a great pride in saying that theirs was the home of Dilip Kumar, and an even greater pride in saying that it was too of Shahrukh Khan's father. I wandered through the dark streets of Kissa Kahani market, the storyteller's market, the mind imposing on every crumbling building and every black bylane a semi-contrived charm, a pretend danger.

But these were minutes snatched, no more. The many facets of the frontier province demanded deeper exploration. I hoped to be back someday, properly.

\*

'YAAR, THE TOUR is changing.' So whispered a fellow journalist conspiratorially. Gone was the fluff and floss and flimflummery, he meant, and now we were in a grime-nailed contest. He was not referring to the cricket, but the media. Pakistan's press had been immensely provoked by the Indian captain's 'mind games'.

The first of these mind games tickled me pink. It concerned the inclusion of Nehra in the XI at Pindi. It was seen as Ganguly's great ambush, a case of below-the-belt gamesmanship. Commented *The News*: 'Obviously, Nehra was in a position to play the second one-dayer and declaring him unfit a day earlier was just a stunt that aims at playing with the minds of opponents', since Nehra was the 'only bowler of some substance in the Indian side' and 'the right man to play with the nerves of the opponents'. Sneered *The Nation* in a headline: 'Indian trick turns into reality as Nehra is out for a week.'

Secret Weapon Nehra! I wondered what he'd make of it. So gawky and lumbering he was, a ring of apologetic grumbling circling his head, almost audibly. What a way he walked; chest in, head down, shoulders slouched, arms drooping. He did not meander in the outfield so much as lose himself in it. Even in his finest hours he was given to awkwardness. Soon after bundling out England with a haunting spell of seam bowling at Durban in the World Cup, he barfed a banana at the boundary. All this, one assumes, merely made Ganguly's ambush that much more pernicious.

The second mind game, in the world of cricket reporting, was a real mind game, a proper, hairy-chested man of a mind game.

I couldn't believe I had got it wrong the other day, but then several others had too. It concerned Ganguly branding Shoaib a chucker; well, suggesting as much with a wink and a poke. Walking across the dew-laden ground to the press conference the other night at Pindi, the genial Alok Dasgupta, from the Bengali newspaper, *Bartaman*, and I were discussing Shoaib's beamer at Powar. Alok da said he intended to ask Ganguly about it. I assumed that he meant to ask whether Ganguly thought Shoaib had bowled the beamer deliberately or not. And so Ganguly's answer – 'What do you think watching it on TV? I think we all know the answer, don't we?', administered with a smirk – seemed a worthy dig, but in a different context.

Over the next two days, the story gathered much steam. Shoaib's reaction was sought, and this was it: 'Whoever is questioning my action, is questioning the ICC.' *The Times of India* reported Indian team sources as saying that Ganguly's statement was in fact part of a 'conscious effort to keep reminding him of his suspect bowling action on and off the field'. Meanwhile, Bishan Singh Bedi, who considers throwing a sin roughly in the same league as murder, declared in a column that, not just Shoaib, but the entire Pakistan bowling line-up – Shabbir, Afridi and Malik – were chuckers. Admittedly, all bowled with visibly bent arms; but that barely constituted hard evidence anymore.

I was still not convinced about the story though? Had Ganguly really questioned Shoaib's action? What had Alok da really meant? He had asked the question without a mike in the shuffling din of a large room; and it was a rather long question. As I recalled it, the words 'beamer' and 'fair' were certainly part of it. Testimonies of others also mentioned the presence of the words 'legitimate' and 'all his deliveries'.

Alok da was not around at the moment so a journalist with the proceedings on tape was sought out. The sound was muffled and distant, and we were left with the same collection of words strung together in what was certainly a many-splendoured inquiry.

Finally Alok da arrived on the scene: 'I meant if he thought Shoaib chucked or not.'

So there. But then it dawned on us group of intrepid investigators that it did not matter what Alok da had intended by the question; the only point of consequence was how Ganguly had interpreted it. There was no option now but to wait for the Indians to finish their game of team-spirit-building volleyball so that Ganguly could meet the press. He did, eventually: 'I was asked by a journalist about the beamers and whether he chucks. All I said was that you'll have seen it on TV. That's all I said.'

So there! Now we knew what Ganguly had understood by the question, but the matter was muddied further: his new answer was neither confirmation nor denial. Fresh dilemmas emerged. How to take the story forward? 'Ganguly questions Shoaib's action again'? No, that was not right. 'Ganguly denies questioning Shoaib's action'? No, no, even more false. Ignore the whole thing? Worst option. Agency reporters were in the tightest spot for they have little space for subjectivity. 'Eight-minute call to London,' said the man from Reuters, glancing down wearily at the empty credit on his phone card. 'Going with the story. Everybody knows what Ganguly meant.'

Another day in the life of the cricket reporter.

THE PESHAWAR GAME, too, had been sold out, and here too, there were mini-riots at the ticket sales. There was further skirmishing between the local journalists and the media cell of the PCB, who were accused of denying accreditations. Outside the stadium trade in black prospered. The cheapest tickets, Rs 100, were going for Rs 700-800. The passion for cricket here was the most fanatical I was to see in the country, and it took me by surprise, given the NWFP's relative obscurity for most of Pakistan's cricket history.

My first association with cricket in the region was from that old quiz question: Which Indian Test cricketer was born in Kabul? The answer is Salim Durani, the magnetic all-rounder of the 1960s; and it was tempting to think that Prince Salim, as he was referred to by fans, had some connection with the Durranis of the Durrani empire in the eighteenth century.

The most famous Pathan cricketers were those who had emerged from the traditional cricket centres: Abdul Qadir Khan, born and raised in Lahore; Sahibzaha Mohammad Shahid Khan Afridi, born in the agency of Khyber, whose main tribe were the Afridis, but brought up in Karachi. The king of them all, of course, was Imran Khan Niazi, again, born and bred in Lahore, descended from the Niazi tribe on his father's side, and the Burkis on his mother's. As Pathans are, Imran was fiercely proud of his roots, and in his book, *The Indus Journey*, took relish in describing a bare-headed encounter between his great-uncle and a leopard, the climax of which has the great-uncle shouting at the leopard, who has mounted him and is scratching out his scalp: 'If you are the son of a *sher*, then I am the son of a Niazi.' It was Imran's belief that a massive pool of cricketers in the tribal regions lay waiting to be discovered.

Homegrown NWFP cricketers were scarce over the first four decades of Pakistan's history. The only one of any note was Haseeb Ahsan, an off-spinner with a supposedly dodgy action, who played twelve Tests in the late 1950s and early 1960s, and thereafter became an active, controversial administrator. But in the last decade or so Peshawar had risen to become one of the leading teams in the country, and a glut of international cricketers had emerged from the region. Pakistan's XI for this match would contain two NWFP players, Yasir Hameed and Younis Khan; two other seamers, Umar Gul and Fazl-e-Akbar, would be added to the Test squads.

The fourth umpire for this match was Iqbal Butt, a Peshawar first-class player for sixteen years, and involved in the regional administration since. I sought him out. I wanted to ask him about cricket in the NWFP, about its growth and the reasons for its growth.

'Come, come I will tell you everything,' he said, inviting me into the umpires' chambers. He was a tall man, balding, with radiant red skin and glassy brown eyes. On this day, understandably, he was rather distracted. Just as we'd begin talking, he'd suddenly be off on a small chore, then back, rattling off the names of the NWFP local stalwarts.

'We have a rich history. This was the oldest association in All India. Before Partition, there was Karim Baksh, then there was Sher Khan. Then after Partition came Haseeb Ahsan...'

I interjected, trying to move the conversation towards the broader points I wanted him to address.

'Yes, don't worry, I'm telling you everything. Things changed really with Maazullah Khan, in 1965. He became captain of the province, a very powerful leader, and then he became the Director of the NWFP sports board...'

This had promise. But Iqbal now had to go out and inspect the crease demarcations on the pitch. He returned shortly and continued.

'So under Maazullah, the new wave started; Farrukh Zaman, he played a Test for Pakistan, there was Farooq Baig, me... then in the eighties and nineties there was a boom: Arshad Khan, Kabir Khan, Wajahatullah Wasti, Akhtar Sarfraz, Yasir Hameed, Younis Khan, Umar Gul... we have many juniors coming up, like Riaz Afridi...'

I tried prodding him again.

'Yes, yes, I'm telling you everything. Do you know ours is the oldest association in All India?'

We were not going anywhere. I stopped haranguing Iqbal. This was a day of dead ends. I should have made a day trip somewhere; I bound myself needlessly to the formality of attending preview day. Now it was too late.

I sat around. On the outfield, Ganguly was remonstrating with the groundsman to push the boundary rope 5 yards back, but to no avail.

A police officer introduced himself. He said he had prepared a definition for terrorism, so would I like to hear it? Of course, I said. He cleared his throat, widened his eyes, pointed downwards with passion and recited, 'The act of a *well-trained* person to create sensation in a *specific* community for a *specific* purpose.' He launched a brisk tirade against Israel and the Jews. Then he repeated his definition again, with more emphasis. He would like it, he said, if I could use this definition somewhere. I need not use his name; it was just that, he said, more people should know. Then he left.

I made friends with Tariq, a twenty-two-year-old, who, like me, had not much to do on this day. He was looking for a match ticket. I could not help him. Tariq had graduated in mathematics, which gave us something in common. He was excited at this discovery, and expressed his admiration for the Indian textbook for topology, by Chitale-Joshi. It was, in truth, a horrid book. But as I was to find all through this journey, the things I routinely scoffed at back home – the film award shows, the magazines, the television advertisements, the remixes, and now even the textbooks – were held here in a certain awe. It was kind of humbling.

\*

THE ARBAB NIAZ STADIUM, named after a minister in General Zia's regime in the mid-1980s who obtained the funds for it, is really a self-contained colony, a pleasant maze of gardens, residential apartments, fountains, roundabouts, when incongruously appears a set of cricket pitches and adjoining it, a sudden stadium.

As at Pindi, the stands were low and single-tiered, and its capacity, at 16,000, was about the same. Half the hemisphere was left open to the sun, the other covered by cloth shamianas; and sticking out from behind the stands like lollipops were low

115

advertising hoardings, bright red and cobalt blue, and between them one could glimpse trees. And as at Pindi, the vantage points were all taken, a towering water-tank the most popular among them. The noise, given especially the openness of the ground, was continuously spectacular.

It was a pretty morning, and the prettiest sight of all to my eyes was the grass on the pitch. I had been sceptical the previous day that it would be left that way, but there it was, glimmering specks of green awaiting a moist morning start. If Inzamam had chosen to bowl at Karachi because of the early start, this would be a no-brainer. And win the toss he did, for the third time.

The second over of the morning was the most remarkable of the series. Shabbir Ahmed's starting sequence was: wide, no-ball, dot, no-ball, dot, wide. I put myself in Inzy's shoes for a moment and felt a small pain in my chest. He had already let by a streaking chance from Sehwag in the first over. And now the extras were returning to spit in his face. Just then Shabbir produced the perfect delivery to Tendulkar, pitching off, a touch fuller to good length, moving away, and in the zigzagness that had preceded it, Tendulkar was taken by surprise, held his bat before it, and tamely nicked. Much jubilation at Arbab Niaz. Shabbir followed that with: wide, dot, wide, dot, five wides, wide and a dot. Hours after it had begun, it ended, an opera of an over: 14 balls, 12 runs, none of them off the bat, and Tendulkar gone for duck. And thereafter Shabbir settled down and stitched together a properly tormenting spell of seam bowling.

Shabbir is a mopey chap, thin and ostrich-like, with a prominent Adam's apple; a kind of longer Nehra. There is a touch of Joel Garner to his run-up, in the way he bends at the waist while running in, in the way he then stretches out to full tidal-wave length. And when he is repeatedly hitting the seam, and a length, on a surface so receptive, I suppose he can be as difficult as was Garner.

116

Sehwag fell in Shabbir's third over, caught at gully, his whip to leg defeated by a subtle straightening off the pitch. But it was Laxman that Shabbir hounded. Laxman was stuck. To get forward to a bowler of this height was unnatural, and Laxman on seaming wickets finds it harder than many. And to stay on crease was exactly what Shabbir wanted from Laxman, for it gave the ball a chance to jag this way or that and climb. For the three overs he bowled at him, Shabbir reduced the sweetest song in cricket to utter tunelessness. He whisked it away, he snaked it in, he zipped it straight through. Laxman, poked, missed, bent over, and generally responded like a man at whom knives were being hurled. Finally he edged to slip. Yasir dropped it.

Watching the contest brought to mind Simon Hughes's articulation of facing Richard Hadlee. 'Imagine being enclosed in a small, illuminated space and being fed a barrage of searching questions by an indefatigable examiner. Your responses are nervous gibberish.' A harrowed existence ultimately met its end when Laxman played yet another in-darter from the crease and was bowled through the gate. He made three off twenty. India were 37 for 3 in eight overs. Without extras, they would have been 21 for 3 in ten. And there had been two dropped catches.

Rahul Dravid had come out at no. 4 with a broad smile on his face. It was probably the result of some joke in the pavilion, but my interpretation was that he was simply pleased at the challenge ahead: juicy pitch, hot pace from one end, cold seam from the other, two-down for not-many; this was where he made his money. Joining Dravid at Laxman's departure was Ganguly, who had sensibly slid himself down to no. 5, not that it made much difference to his eventual arrival.

Both found it hard going. Dravid's first boundary was an edge; Ganguly's first two shots against Shabbir were play-and-misses. After fifteen overs India were 55 for 3; at the same stage at Karachi they had been 143 for 2, and at Pindi Pakistan 110 for 0. Cricket was making sense again.

Slowly the pair began feeling their way out of the darkness. Dravid did so by leaving more and more, and offered his body on one occasion. Seeing him negotiate these conditions was to be transported back to the Toronto tournaments between the countries in the mid-1990s. The ball would swing and seam, India's batting would struggle, and Dravid would compile a vital, hard-worked 31 off 77 deliveries, which would promptly be forgotten when centuries poured forth from all quarters on subcontinental shirtfronts.

Ganguly, of course, used to be the undisputed prince of Toronto; and fittingly, he lifted his game here, grooving himself into boundary after boundary. He was lovely as ever through the off, bat wispy like a floating cloud. Ignoring the two gullies, he touched Sami for two fours through square, and then against the slower Razzaq, drove uppishly through the covers for two more. When Razzaq pitched short, he swivelled and pulled him high over square leg for six. In a blink he reached 37 from 33 balls.

Inzamam brought back Shoaib to halt Ganguly's progress. After all the I-think-we-all-know-the-answer-don't-we stuff, this was going to be a hot contest. The crowd roared in anticipation. First up, Shoaib dug it into Ganguly's ribs; Ganguly fended awkwardly, tried to get to the other end, was sent back, and almost run out. Two balls later, Shoaib produced a 96.4 mph snorter, which Ganguly tried to evade but played down to third man. He did not push for the second. Yet, he found himself on strike to the last ball: it almost knocked the bat out of his hand. In Shoaib's next over, Dravid played a beautiful on-drive, reaching out a little, leaning over a touch, and flipping his wrists over ever so slightly at the point of impact. Past 100 now in the twenty-third over, it could be said that India had staged a recovery.

Ganguly perpetuated his string of careless dismissals by trying to dab Razzaq fine, despite the presence of a slip, in front of whom Moin dove across to hold the catch. And Dravid fell not long after, gloving Malik to Moin on the paddle. He made 33, from 86 balls, just like Toronto. Kaif departed after a four-ball one. Suddenly, Yuvraj Singh had 140 for 6 on his hands.

He'd got off to a brisk start in his hard-handed way, edging a few and playing some smoking off drives. Now he pulled Sami dismissively, with the sound of a wet handkerchief lashing skin. This riled Sami, got his blood up. His follow-through on the next ball ended inside Yuvraj's nostrils. Words were exchanged. David Shepherd, the umpire, stepped in to warn the bowler. The crowd bayed for more. So did Ganguly later, saying that such face-offs had a happy knack of involving the spectators, thus rounding off a week in which he challenged the ICC on their policies on over-rates, bent arms and player conduct.

Sami was provoked further in his next over by Powar's merry slog above cover. He responded with about the fastest bouncer there can be bowled, clocked at 98.5 mph, a measurement usually reserved for yorkers or full-tosses. Already on the day he had been twice measured at faster than 100 mph, the only man since Shoaib to be so recorded, but the broadcasters later expressed doubt over the veracity of their readings. At any rate, this bouncer was very, very fast. Long-on, Ian Chappell has said, is the best position to judge a bowler's pace, and that is where the Arbab press box, a cordoned-off section of a stand really, was located. Powar, thankfully, had not been swift enough to get fully behind the line. It would have shattered him. Bloodlust spread through the arena. 'Mooh pe maaro, mooh pe maaro' (Hit him on the face), they chanted. Powar tactfully edged the next ball for four. 'Afridi ko over do' (Give Afridi an over), they chanted.

The game hurtled on. Powar became Malik's second victim on

the sweep, this time lbw. Pathan arrived and struck Malik for a flowing straight six and then had his leg stump blasted out by a Shoaib yorker. Yuvraj expanded his innings gamely, sashaying past fifty, and then exploding into the shot of the day: a pirouette from a crouching position against Shoaib's knee-high off-stump full-toss, scudding the ball, never higher than 8 feet off the ground, into the perimeter boards at fine leg.

Balaji provided the innings a crowning glory, with 21 off 12. He on-drove Shoaib as if he were Greg Chappell; he hooked Sami as if he were Jimmy Amarnath, and then struck him, high-elbowed, for a six that was all his own. The ball landed 5 feet to the left of my laptop. Later he said he had never hit a six in domestic cricket.

India finished on 244. Forty-six runs had come from the last four overs, bowled by Shoaib and Sami. Balaji was received by a posse of grinning Indians on the balcony. In the stand next to ours, the locals sang, 'Balajee-ee, zara dheere chalo', a take on a popular Bollywood item number of the day. From the president in Pindi to the man on the street in Peshawar, Pakistan was taken by the most unlikely Indian of all.

IRFAN PATHAN MADE it to the XI only because of Nehra's injury, was given the new ball only because Zaheer had been struggling to locate the pitch, and asked to bowl the first over because Ganguly has an instinct about these things. Instantly he caught the eye. No other bowler in the series had made the ball swing. We'd seen pace, bounce, seam, but no swing.

Irfan's gift is the outswinger, the left-armer's outswinger, bending into the right-hand batsman, and it was one such that defeated Afridi's rather enthusiastic swipe to give India their first wicket. Soon he slid one across Youhana, who edged to slip, and Pakistan were 29 for 2.

But Yasir was in, well in. His had been the forgotten innings at Pindi, buried under Afridi's glitz and Tendulkar's mastery. He was working on a double-spur here. He was playing his first one-dayer on home soil. Ever since sparkling on to the scene with a pair of centuries on Test debut, albeit against Bangladesh, he'd been the darling of the locals. He was their brightest star, a true-blue Peshawari, on course to becoming their first genuine world-beater at cricket. On the streets they spoke of him proprietorially in their Pathan way: 'Bhoth achcha hamara ladka' (Our boy very good). The owner of the hardware store across the ground boasted to me that Yasir would often leave his kit-bag at the shop. His full family was in attendance.

Yasir's other spur was more headline-worthy. This tale goes back to before the Pindi one-dayer. Yasir and Rahul Dravid are in the elevator of the team hotel, in the presence of two witnesses. Rahul, ever-cordial, begins conversation with the youngster: 'You bowled very well in the nets today.' Yasir is confused. Rahul has mistaken him for a practice bowler to the Indian team. Rahul asks him whether he is related to Saqlain Mushtaq. 'I will make sure Rahul Dravid will not forget me,' Yasir vows later to journalists.

He seemed to be that kind of guy, Yasir. Later on the tour, he accosted one of India's bat-pad fielders at the swimming pool and asked him to stop yapping so much for it affected his concentration at the crease. 'But I speak only between deliveries,' responded the Indian, 'and in any case what will you do about it?' Yasir considered the question and proclaimed: 'I will *never* get out.'

Batting with Yasir now was Younis Khan, promoted in view of Inzamam's bout of acidity. He burst into three successive fours off Irfan, to such far-flung regions as midwicket, point and long-off, and took Pakistan past 50 in the eleventh over. Yasir issued a stinging straight drive against Balaji; the ball grazed his fingers, hit the stumps and found Younis outside his ground.

Shoaib Malik arrived at no. 5, and was given a working over by Zaheer, far more incisive at first-change. He nicked, Sehwag held at first slip, and the match, with Pakistan at 65 for 4, stood wide open.

Shaky moments followed for Pakistan. Yasir edged Balaji between fly slip and keeper whereupon that hole was plugged. He then edged Zaheer wide of slip but fine of third man. Heedless of these misdemeanours, he kept reeling off the strokes. Zaheer dug it in short, and he pulled him off the front foot. Thereafter, Zaheer became fodder.

Soon Pakistan were on cruise control. With Ganguly and Powar bowling in tandem, Inzamam and Yasir eased through the middle overs. Inzamam lofted Powar to the top of the pavilion for six. The 150 came up in the thirty-first over.

Tendulkar was asked to interrupt the partnership. A new tantalisation entered the game. He fooled Inzamam with the googly once; and then he did it again, this time earning an lbw, though the ball had struck Inzamam outside the line of off stump. Shortly after, a missile, a crushed wire-like object, landed near Powar at the boundary. This would be the only such incident all tour. Play continued. Ganguly brought back Irfan. Yasir played his square drive, but against a well-masked slower ball, and it looped to point. He was on 98. Arbab went quiet. 'Allah ki marzi' (It's Allah's wish), Yasir would philosophise later.

With this, suspense returned to the contest. Pakistan were suddenly six down. They needed a further 72 from fifteen overs. Razzaq and Moin were at the crease and after them only the three fast bowlers.

A delicious cat-and-mouse followed. Tendulkar bowled wrist spin to one slip and four men in the off-side ring; the three men on the leg were all posted on the fence. His scheme was to make the right-handers work against the turn. But this required extraordinary control. I marvelled at Tendulkar's confidence, and Ganguly's too.

Tendulkar kept Razzaq teetering on the brink of cutting hard, shouldering arms and tapping to point, none of which Razzaq managed to do with conviction. As over after over went by, he sort of hypnotised Razzaq, who was simply unable to find a run. On three occasions, he beat him clean. Each time Tendulkar jumped high and bounced on his toes with youthful mischief.

But runs came steadily from the other end. It was here I think that Ganguly most missed Harbhajan Singh and Anil Kumble: second innings of a day game, bounce in the pitch, series in the balance, attack and defence needed together.

In his seventh over, with Pakistan on 200 and Razzaq on 17, Tendulkar tossed one up further than any of his previous deliveries. Sensing a noose loosening around his neck, Razzaq took a stride forward and thumped it back at abdomen height. Tendulkar couldn't hold the catch. He smiled. Razzaq tried to cut the next ball and edged it. There was no slip by now. It sped away for four. The corner had been turned.

Razzaq stripped himself of all inhibition. He tonked Zaheer over the infield. He cut Tendulkar, at long last, through it. Disregarding Moin's attempts to calm him (and Miandad's from the dressing room balcony), he whipped Balaji thrillingly from outside off to square leg. From 17 he raced to 49 in 20 balls and, with just under three overs left in the game, he wound-unwound to drill Balaji resoundingly down the ground to present himself a fifty and his team victory.

So quickly it ended. With an inspired opening forty minutes and closing forty minutes Pakistan had surged into the series lead. Any chance of Ganguly's men rewriting history looked rather bleak.

Meanwhile, a canny plan had been constructed to drive through the night across the breadth of the land, from the Afghan border to the Indian border. Lahore, the finale, lay in wait.

*India 244 for 9 in 50 overs (Yuvraj 65, Shabbir 3-33) lost to Pakistan 247 for 6 in 47.2 overs (Yasir 98, Razzaq 53\*, Irfan 3-58) by four wickets*

# 5. Blue fading into green

I WAS ON the second floor this time. The dank maroon carpet was a dry moss green, matching the green panelling around the room. Across the bed, a mirror with a half-peeled Wrangler sticker, a comb tucked behind it. Across the mirror, above the bed, two dead roses cellotaped to the wall in the formation of crossed swords. I was back, unmistakably, at the Continental.

But this was the room. Outside, in the faded passageways, in the dim staircases, in the orange lobby, the Continental wore a different ambience. It was full, flowing, a melting pot, a vessel for families who had come in from India, replica-kitted, and an adda for groups of young men, such as the one headed by the local MP in the room opposite mine, a five-day hedonist hideout. As night fell, the families would dress up and leave for dinner, passing on their way out tinselled hookers in four-inch heels tinkling up the peeling corridors awash with dope. A conflux of energies was the Continental.

Aslam had not been sure how to play me. The tariff had spiralled up since I was here ten days ago. That was not unexpected, but he had been terribly vague: 'you don't worry; why are you worrying; don't-worry-be-happy.' And now he was stuck between our bond and the owner's orders. For my part, being on a per-piece arrangement with the *Guardian*, I was unable at this stage to peg down my daily budget; and I found it unfair that despite my asking he had given me no indication about the magnitude of tariff leap. Besides, the Continental was simply not worth the new rate. 'Fuck thee bloody money,' he said in his magnanimous Punjabi way, and I echoed the words, trying to match the magnanimity. But it was not clear to either whose money it was that ought to be fucked. Eventually, we settled on a rate two and a half times what I had paid the first time. We both felt we travelled more than halfway. It put a strain on our relationship, however much we tried to pretend otherwise.

But I could empathise with the Continental. The thirty months since 9/11 had been bleak for Pakistan's hotel industry. Plenty of smaller hotels had been forced to close down; many others were contemplating doing so. Financially, they needed this tour as much as the PCB. The opportunity was not to be lost. Hotels had jacked up their rates to anywhere between two and five times the usual. A standard room at that other Continental – the Pearl – was now going for Rs 25,000 per night, a figure close to the country's average annual income.

And really, there was no dearth of demand over these five days. For the Indians poured in. They came in numbers that they had never been permitted to come in before; they came by air, they came by foot, they came by road, they came by rail, using all the channels that had been opened up since Vajpayee's January visit.

Indian Airlines, which had not operated any flights to Pakistan between October 2001 and January 2004, now needed to supplement their twice-weekly service between Lahore and Delhi. On Friday, 19, and Monday, 22 March, the scheduled days, they operated with bigger aircraft, the Airbus 300 rather than the 320, to fly in 300 passengers. On 21 and 23 March they ran two special flights, bringing in 310 more. Pakistan International Airlines struck deals with Samsung, the series sponsor, and SOTC, the travel operator, and hauled in 520 passengers over two flights. A couple of hundred trickled in via the buses: the Delhi Transport Corporation and the Pakistan Tourism Development Corporation, who ran a to-and-fro service twice a week, sent an extra vehicle each for the matches. About a thousand crossed, poignantly, by foot at Wagah, as many of their parents and grandparents and possibly they themselves must have done fifty-six years ago in the other direction. But these were different times: an image for the Lahore double-header became that of a group of Sikhs, at the border, holding up a large flag of both countries stitched together, with the message, 'Friends Forever'.

The most significant movement was by train: the Samjhauta – Reconciliation – Express between Delhi and Lahore. The service, conceived at the Shimla Agreement of 1972, and hostage to existing political conditions since, had been running twice a week since January; twelve hours from Delhi to the border station of Attari by India's Northern Railways, and then by a Pakistan Railways connecting train for the forty-five minutes to the Lahore station. Now, the regular service was supplemented by two 'Cricket Specials' on 19 and 22 March, complete with branding on the carriages, cricket-themed reservation forms and ticket envelopes, and a brochure, headlined by a Punjabi quote from one of the very first drivers of the Express: 'Eh mohabbat di gaddi hai, is nu band na hon dena' (This is a train of love, don't let it stop). And so indeed, it was, for more than 2,200 passengers who made the journey. 'A non-stop party,' said one, 'even the TTE was dancing.' As they pulled into Lahore station the passengers were overwhelmed to find hundreds of Pakistanis on the platform waving the train in.

And this was the mood in Lahore over five magical days: Lahore, the best loved city of the old Punjab and the new, Lahore so sentimentalised that it sometimes seemed to curl up and rest in the air like an eternal sigh. These were days of epiphanies, of closures, of small kindnesses and large, of rediscoveries and new discoveries. Old homes were hunted down, old shops, old friends, old villages in the depths of Punjab. For younger generations, it was an emphatic tearing down of stereotypes that had been fed to them, in their textbooks, their movies, their media.

And Lahore itself, with its layers of histories and cultures, with its contrasts of sprawling gardens, crumbling monuments, broad new avenues, labyrinthine old quarters, exquisite tombs, autorickshaw hells, sandstone colonial buildings, bustling markets and ancient city gates, had so much to offer them.

They wound through the tangled mass of lanes at the Anarkali Bazaar, named so after the, possibly fictitious, courtesan supposedly walled in by Akbar when he suspected that she may have ravished his son, and where now one chaatwallah declared on a signboard that he would not take money from Indians. By night they thronged to one of the three rackety food streets, mostly the one at Gawalmandi, satiating themselves with lamb chaaps and payas and kalejis and phirnis beneath the painted *jharokas*. Or else they made for that splendid restaurant-perch, Cuckoo's Den, an ode to the prostitutes and dancers of Heera Mandi, whose bystreets extended on one side of the perch, beyond a turquoise façade, and where Lala Amarnath, manager on the first Indian tour, in 1954-55, solicited the services of two spies, a tongawallah and a paanwallah, to walk in on his players breaking curfew and enjoying a late-night mujra. And they visited, right across the other side of the perch, the colossal Mughal fort of four centuries old, and beside it, the shimmering Badshahi Masjid, its largeness, its infinite symmetry, its utter beauty, its utter power, enclosed so eloquently by four minarets that speared above the surroundings like quiet observers of history. If they had the time, they drove out east to Nankana Sahib, birthplace of Guru Nanak, one of the three gurdwaras to which Pakistan permits Indian pilgrimages and to where a direct bus service from Amritsar was now mooted; or else they drove out south-west to Harappa, to the fields of heat and mud and dust and withering dryness in which lay the ruins of the ancient civilisation. The cricketers, too, basked in the activity. They attended the Daler Mehndi concert to raise funds for Imran Khan's cancer hospital. They were hosted by the Punjab chief minister on the ramparts of the Fort at a concert by the ghazal maestro, Ghulam Ali. They swung by parties thrown by Lahore's most famous socialite, Yusuf Salahuddin, at his haveli. Ganguly even braved the midnight crowds at Gawalmandi with just the one security-man in tow. And all converged at the Gaddafi Stadium on two enthralling evenings, the cricketers at each other under lights, the fans side by side in the stands, waving their flags and the other's, holding up their posters and the other's, daubing their faces with their colours and the other's.

*

THE ELDERLY INDIAN sharing our vehicle till the Gaddafi suddenly looked confused. 'All this,' he pointed around, 'there was nothing here. It was jungle.' He wiped a tear from his eye, and continued looking out the window in silence.

Outside the stadium, the ambience was unlike anything before in this series. Suddenly there was a sea of replica jerseys, mostly blue, for travellers are usually keener players of the identity game. There were SUVs and Mercedes sedans everywhere; SUV after SUV, Mercedes after Mercedes waved through the security barriers.

There was a large mela-like crowd. A youngster approached us for help. He'd been sold a fake ticket, and his friends were already inside. There were, according to the PCB, 1,499 more like Salim, whose ticket, bought in the black market, was fake. Because of the bar-coding system used for this series, the counterfeits had been found out at the turnstiles (and at the Gaddafi there really were turnstiles).

The frauds were not restricted to the tickets. Three Indians made themselves fake media accreditations. Alas, they were caught, for they chose to enter the press box wearing replica jerseys, which, despite what you may think of some cheerleaders masquerading as journalists, was still not the most discreet tactic.

The tickets, as per usual, had sold out in a matter of hours. And, as per usual, there had been baton-charging at the sales, a situation whose grimness becomes darkly comic when newsreports start employing the word 'also', as in the sentence: 'Cricket lovers at the Egerton Road branch were also beaten up...'

The PCB, working on a commendable zero-complimentary-ticket policy for this series, now found themselves under fire for failing to invite former Test cricketers, many of whom had stands named after them at the stadium. Acknowledging the oversight, they would try to make amends by sending out tickets for the second of the one-dayers. These turned out to be Rs 500 tickets, to the raucous general stands, which incensed the former cricketers so much that four of them, Imtiaz Ahmed, Saeed Ahmed, Mohammad Ilyas and Ijaz Butt, made a vociferous boycott and called for President Musharraf to look into the matter. Genial old Fazal Mahmood was more resigned: 'After all, they are extending a courtesy. I can't take them to court for this, can I?' He watched from home.

The Gaddafi – or Gadafy, Gadafi, Gaddafy, Ghadhafi, Qadhafi, Qaddafi, even Qadhdhaafiy, depending on which translation from Arabic you prefer – was renamed so from Lahore Stadium by Zulfikar Ali Bhutto in rather excessive honour of his fellow socialist and pan-Islamist, the Libyan dictator, Colonel Muammar Gaddafi, during his visit to the city for the Islamic Summit of 1974. The stadium stood one among many in a spacious complex of stadiums and grounds and auditoriums in new Lahore. Across it on one side lay the hockey stadium, on another the open field of the Lahore City Cricket Association, and on still another the Al Hamra theatre, an identical structure almost to the Gaddafi, designed by the same renowned architect, Nayyar Ali 'Dada' Zaidi.

The Gaddafi has a certain gravitas. The curving exterior is constructed fully of brick, like much of Punjab, but its sombreness is broken by frilly fibreglass canopies over the stands, and a series of arches, beneath which, on one stretch, space has been leased to shops and restaurants. The brick ring houses the offices of the PCB, which overlook the turf beyond through broad bay windows. Up on the second floor of the ring, the media facilities are superb, two press boxes flanking a broadcasters' section. Downstairs, the area earmarked for press conferences is filled with framed portraits of Pakistan's good and great. This includes a section for Muslims who had played with distinction for the pre-Partition team, the likes of Jahangir Khan and Gul Mohammad. What is this supposed to mean? Is the implication that Pakistan has disowned the achievements of non-Muslims who played for an all-India team?

A charming tale about the Gaddafi was doing the rounds. Once the 1996 World Cup was finished, the event for which the stadium had been so wonderfully refurbished, the ground was being leased out for wedding parties and the like. After one such occasion, the groundsman here for four decades, the venerable Haji Bashir, felt such pain at the devastation of the field that he broke into tears. Fortuitously, mediamen were around to capture this. The weddings and the functions were soon stopped. For this day, Bashir predicted lots and lots of runs.

Inzamam won the toss once more; Ganguly was just bemused. There was curiosity about which way he'd swing. He liked to allow his fast bowlers a first shot, but Pakistan's success under lights at Pindi had come batting first. As at Pindi, he didn't consider the dew. He decided to bat.

At 2 p.m., under a clear sky, in a gentle warm breeze, before a crowd of 25,000, more full of banners and flags and colour than any other in the series thus far, the fourth and possibly decisive one-dayer got underway.

IRFAN SENT DOWN two wides in his first over but with his eighth legitimate ball he claimed Afridi. It was a duff stroke. A short ball, with width, and clumped heartily to the man at point. Inevitably the press box groaned: 'Should have been dropped right after Pindi. Did his job for the series.' There will never be consensus on Shahid Afridi.

At the other end, Yasir was winning against Balaji, driving him often through the off, and one time, jumping grasshopper-like up towards a bouncer and flicking it vertically over the keeper's head.

Irfan began his work on Youhana. Youhana is blessed with wonderful hands, but tends to play around his front pad, coming down on the stroke from a wide backlift. This can lead to a tangle against a left-arm over-the-wicket outswing bowler, whose natural angle slants the ball across, but the swing brings it back in. Locally, I was told, the word for this tangle is 'kaichi' – scissor – which beautifully sums up the motion of the deceived: the front foot coming out, the bat flapping across it, the upper body overbalancing towards off. Irfan hunted for the kaichi. With the second ball of his fifth over he thought he had succeeded, but he had pitched it marginally outside leg. Two balls later, he had Youhana groping once more, but now he had started too wide and struck the pad outside off. And the one after that, Irfan hit the spot: lbw. Scissored left, scissored right, scissored centre, so naked Youhana must have felt.

Irfan finished that over to figures of 5-1-14-2, and completed his spell on 7-1-22-2. By the end of fifteen overs, Pakistan had managed only 59, a credit not only to Irfan's effort, but also to Mohammad Kaif's screeching and sliding and diving and chasing all through the opening hour.

India maintained the pressure thereafter, more so on Yasir, who was beginning to twitch. His first 36 runs had taken him 38 balls, but he had since laboured over twenty-nine for just nine. All twenty-nine had been bowled by the pair of Zaheer Khan, in his best rhythm of the tour, and Murali Kartik, back in the XI after Powar's bowling had failed to rouse sufficient faith.

Kartik was operating on what, in limited-overs cricket, had become the classic left-armer's attack-by-defence line: over the wicket, pitching on or outside leg. In Yasir's case this was doubly effective for the leg was Yasir's weaker side and he did not sweep with conviction. Unable to find a way around the strangulation, Yasir finally gave Kartik the full-blooded charge, found himself to be nowhere close to the pitch of the delivery, threw himself into the swing nonetheless for the other death was far too agonising, missed the ball completely, and was stumped without making a semblance of an effort to get back.

Pakistan were 89 for 3 in twenty-one overs; and at the halfway mark they stood at 106 for 3, poised very much for a halfway total. Ganguly needed to squeeze through the fifth bowler's quota. He called upon Tendulkar, and, shortly, Yuvraj, which in retrospect could be seen as the turning point of the innings.

Inzamam at this stage was on 30. He had been electric heels! He had pushed singles and doubles and urged the partner back for more and generally been like one of Mr Bowie's tigers on Vaseline. But only two fours. Then came Yuvraj, golden-arm at Pindi, and in his second over, Inzamam smashed a straight six as he does sooner or later against spinners. He then pulled him mountainously for four. Then he pulled him for another four. Fifteen came from over number 33. Here was the adrenalin Pakistan were biding their time for.

Fours and sixes began to flow in right earnest. Energised by a drinks break, Inzamam cuffed Balaji over wide long-on for six. It was the most remarkable of strokes. He had, in truth, decided from the first that it must be a boundary. He had shaped up to hit it through the off. But the ball had pitched shorter than in his mental map, so he merely struck it later in his swing, compensating with a sharp upward jerk of the wrist to give it lift and direction. While meditating on the greatest batsmen he had seen, Len Hutton placed George Headley 'as near to Bradman as it was possible to get' – with the corollary, 'I never saw anyone play the ball as late as George.' Imran Khan's famous statement that Inzamam had more time against fast bowling than any contemporary, Tendulkar included, brought to mind Hutton's comparison. Because to watch Inzamam this series was to find oneself evoked of the pantheon. He was so extraordinarily, under-ratedly, good. Observers from another time have contemplated Gavaskar's impact upon the consciousness of the cricket world had he been an Englishman. Two decades on, I found myself asking the same question, but with a twist: how might have Inzamam been celebrated had he been Indian?

Down on the green, Inzamam bent low and swept Tendulkar for four, and later stood up tall and pasted him for six. Irfan returned to the attack, and Inzamam scampered two to bring up his century. Whereupon he leant low and tipped Irfan past the keeper, and then opened his breast and tore Balaji through the covers. In the shortest space he had gone from sprinting Inzamam to dainty Inzamam to roaring Inzamam. Gaddafi was agog. India began to come apart. Yuvraj conceded four overthrows, Irfan bowled a full-toss that Razzaq deposited over the ropes, and when Balaji tried a slower ball, Inzamam slammed a staccato six, his fourth in the last hour. Balaji pitched it fuller and Inzamam conceived a paddle of such cheek that he found himself bowled. Never mind. He chewed his gum and waddled off: 123 from 121 balls.

Razzaq was still around, still carving Irfan square of third man, and flicking Zaheer off his eyebrows fine of that same man. Two balls after Razzaq had finished his fourth mid-size devastation of the series, 32 off 24 balls, Dravid let go four byes to Tendulkar. Eighty-two runs had come in the seven overs between over numbers 42 and 49. A quick and full final over from Zaheer saw the demise of two players and a pair of unbeaten ducks from Shabbir and Sami. Pakistan's total stood at 293.

SHREDS OF LIGHTNING could have pelted the Gaddafi, aliens could have descended on the pitch and zapped laser beams, but nothing, nothing could have been so electric as the first fifteen overs of this chase; fifteen overs which saw fourteen fours, one six, four wickets, one wicket off a no-ball, one suspected wicket off a no-ball, four no-balls, eight wides, seven inside edges, four outside edges, one bottom edge, numerous play-and-misses, numerous handsome strokes, one batsman pull-out for an insect in the eye, one official break for the same, and the continuous undulating vivid gasps of a packed house under lights.

Reconstructing the sequence in detail is futile. Event blurred into event blurred into event, a green and blue whoosh in a pool of white. It began with Shoaib firing his first ball down leg, past Sehwag, past Moin, and into the boundary for five wides, then twice defeating Sehwag with 95 mphers, and then beating Tendulkar with what amounted to a leg-break at about the same pace. From there Shabbir took the baton and boomed an outswinger past Sehwag, who then proceeded to loft him over cover, flick him to midwicket and Chinese cut him to fine leg for four, four and four. Shabbir soon had Tendulkar nicking – or did he? – but anyhow he had overstepped. Shoaib finally sliced one through Tendulkar, enough to burn wood on the way through to Moin, and Tendulkar was gone for seven. Shabbir made Laxman pop one up towards gully, where Inzamam swooped like a falling star and held a catch. Another no-ball: Inzamam grimaced; Shabbir looked small; and Laxman not only eased the next ball through the covers but off Shabbir's next over, cut a four behind point, flicked another behind square, and tapped another through cover. From the other end Sehwag powered Shoaib through diving fieldsmen at point and then bunted him back through the bowler's legs. Soon Laxman was gone, bowled, blown away, a straw roof in a tempest, playing Shoaib from the crease, as he had repeatedly done since landing in Pakistan.

So when Ganguly walked in at 69 for 2 in the ninth over, the game was quaking with energy, bursting at its seams, and instantly he slid Shoaib past point for four like butter off a pan. But in the next over, Sehwag fell, caught at slip off Sami, who had replaced the disintegrating Shabbir. Ganguly on-drove Razzaq and then cut Sami for six, throwing his bat out like a cowboy on the lasso. Soon the umpires called for a spray because one of the moths which had filled the Gaddafi air had penetrated Dravid's helmet. There was a touch of the surreal to this session.

Two balls after the spray-break, Ganguly was out running Razzaq fine as in the last match. It was a feeble stroke, the waft of wafts, one hand coming off the handle. But no, still no respite. Yuvraj emerged and perpetuated the breathlessness with stiff, stylish driving. He slammed Razzaq through off, then he did so Sami, and when Shoaib returned, he did so him too, spectacularly, twice in three balls. This was a hamster-wheel of an hour.

Then Yuvraj got out. He pulled Sami, hard, fast, and rolled his wrists over more than was normal for him; even then it was not enough. Youhana dove forwards from midwicket-on-the-circle and grasped a stunning catch, so stunning that Yuvraj's wait at the wicket was more disbelief than for confirmation of whether it had been held cleanly.

And now, finally, the innings paused. Foof! Gaddafi took a deep breath. India took a deep breath. In the helter-skelter, they had found they were on the brink of extermination. One false move and finished, end of dream. Pakistan must have sensed it too.

It was not all dark for India. Though they were 162 for 5, though there was no proper batting to come, it was still only the twenty-fourth over. They were powering along at almost 7. To get home, they needed to continue at about 5. Dravid was on 29, and after some edging in the early mayhem, had been batting with keen authority. He was joined now by Kaif. Kaif's temperamental suitability to the situation was not in question, but his confidence at the moment was. He had endured a mediocre run leading up to this series, and after a fine start at Karachi, had managed eight runs in the last two matches. Coming into this game, his batting average had slipped below 30 for one of the few times in his sixty-two-match career. Were he not the best fieldsman in India, he may have lost his place for this game. There were other reasons too. As Dravid liked to say of him: 'Brings so much to the table, in terms of spirit, in terms of enthusiasm; the kind of guy you want in a team.'

And Kaif began doing what no other Indian batsman had done on the day. He started taking singles and doubles, lots and lots of them. He was past 20 before he hit his first four. This went utterly against the grain of the Indian innings. The top four had added 74 runs and 54 of them were in boundaries. Dravid and Yuvraj, even once the field had spread, had continued collecting more than half their runs in fours. Kaif's dimension was important.

Fielders earlier pushing back against the ropes now had to strain to get forward. Dravid ran superbly with Kaif, just as he had done at Karachi. More, he was still able to find the fence, piercing, especially, Afridi's dense off-side ring with cuts.

Inzamam was faced with the dilemma: should he fire his big guns or keep the second string going? Initially, he settled for mixing-and-matching, overly so, leading to a nine-over passage of play where he kept Sami on from one end, while each one of the other five bowlers – Shoaib, Shabbir, Afridi, Malik and Razzaq, in that order – sent down an over from the opposite end. It was indecisive captaincy, reactive, and at a time Pakistan needed it most, it did nothing to add a sense of purpose to their play.

Amid this hesitation, Dravid and Kaif, hot heels and cool minds, goaded India ahead. Dravid brought up his fifty from fifty-nine balls. Kaif ticked the singles. By the end of over number 34, their partnership was worth 65, and India needed a further 67.

Inzamam threw the ball to Shoaib. This was a gamble. Shoaib could win the game or he could lose it. He had left the field for a while, laying down theatrically on the turf, claiming dizziness, later explained by the team doctor as being caused due to the consumption of a high-sugar energy drink meant for another player. An off-radar Shoaib could be a costly affair.

Shoaib chugged in, very much a steam locomotive, able to generate neither full speed nor direction. He strayed on to Kaif's pads, and was glanced efficiently for four. He strained harder, and strayed further down leg, enough for five wides. This took the extras toll to 33, 19 of them wides, 14 of them Shoaib's; by the end of the evening Pakistan's series tally of no-balls and wides would stand at 98 to India's 42. Kaif rounded off the over with a deliberately frisky dabble outside off for another boundary. Thirteen from the over.

Kaif broke free now. He played the same dabble off Sami for

four and then whatever he touched turned to four. He inside-edged for four, he cover-drove for four. On one straight push off Shabbir half his bat splintered off. The ball still went for four. He replaced the implement and the first thing he did was to cut another four. He could not help himself. Dravid swapped roles with him, working the singles. India's momentum became unstoppable. Pakistani shoulders slouched into their stomachs. The fight had gone out of them.

In the dying fifteen minutes, the Indians in the crowd sang as inevitable victory grew closer. It came ultimately with a facile push from Kaif off Afridi which no fielder attacked, summing up Pakistan's deflation. As Dravid un-helmeted himself, shook hands with his opponents and ran back towards the applauding pavilion, the message on the electronic screen flashed, 'Congratulations India on your fine victory.' It was the sentiment of all Gaddafi. 'If at all there was any tension,' one Indian in the crowd told me, 'it would be resolved by waving the flags together.' 'It was strange,' said a Pakistani, 'to be feeling happy for them as they beat us.'

Back in India, Vajpayee, on the campaign trail, wooed Muslim voters in Uttar Pradesh by praising the 'splendid work done by one of your sons', Kaif. And then he rang Ganguly once more. The series was not even finished. Would this be the protocol for every victory over Pakistan?

Capitulations in Pakistan come wrapped in barbed wire. And so the question to Inzamam at the press conference. 'Inzamam, yeh kya noore kushti thi?' Noore kushti: a staged wrestling match. 'Shut up,' Inzamam roared back. Dravid was asked the same question. 'Somebody please get this guy out of the room, I mean it's ridiculous.' The association of Lahore sports journalists later demanded an apology from Inzamam. Haroon Rashid, the manager, provided one.

Rashid Latif was to voice a similar opinion on television. Proof?

141

'Even a common man could observe that the players were acting on a script because the body language of our players was not as it should have been.' The PCB threatened to sue him; the ICC told him to please furnish evidence; remarked Ganguly to *The Telegraph*: 'I think he has gone mad.' But the die had been cast.

And if Latif had not said it, someone else would have, and they did. It was said now, it would be said in the coming week, and the week after that, and the week after that, and for the rest of the tour it would hover like a shadow that nobody particularly cared for and nobody was even sure was there but everybody thought was their duty to point out to the next person. It was a strange perpetuation; I couldn't get a handle on it; it was hardly ever said with anger, more as small talk, but so widespread was the talk that it had become entrenched in the popular psyche. Perhaps it was a macho rationalising of a poor performance, in the sense that the team was too good to have been outplayed in the normal course of things. Perhaps it was a fatalistic acceptance of corruption as a way of society. Perhaps it was just an attachment to gossip. I don't know what it was. It was a phenomenon in itself. Nowhere in the world had I seen such cynicism on the street towards a cricket match. 'If nobody believes it's real,' smouldered Saad, 'why don't we just down all the stadiums and stop playing.'

Otherwise, it was an inspiring kind of night, and the image of Dravid and Kaif, wet with sweat, running back to the dressing room through the moths and the locusts and the mingling flags would linger in the mind.

*Pakistan 293 for 9 in 50 overs (Inzamam 123, Hameed 45, Zaheer 2-43, Kartik 2-48) lost to India 294 for 5 in 45 overs (Dravid 76\*, Kaif 71\*, Sami 2-50) by five wickets*

\*

## Blue fading into green

THANKFULLY, THE LIGHTS had returned by the time Aaqib arrived.

He came crisply attired: a royal blue full-sleeved shirt tucked into black pleated trousers, a leather belt, and leather shoes which made a click even on the carpet. His face had become broader; and fairer, now that he spent less time in the sun. The floppy centre-parted hair of his playing days remained, though. Strangely, he reminded me of Madhavrao Scindia, the late Indian politician and cricket board chief.

I wanted to meet Aaqib because I wanted to chat with somebody about contemporary Pakistani fast bowling. Aaqib, I had been told by Osman and Saad, was patient, talkative, analytical. Not a superstar, he would be accessible; not a genius, he would not be dismissive.

Aaqib had four fascinating traits of Pakistani cricketers.

First, he knew the tricks of reverse swing, the most spectacular contribution of any one nation to the visual drama of cricket. It was as if the single most compelling quality of every bowling art was plucked out and by magic rolled into one. It won Pakistan match after match and it changed the landscape of fast bowling.

Second, he had that aggression which bordered on the possessed. Look, he seemed to be hissing to opponents, tossing his hair back, you may have the skill and you may have your fancypants style, but boss, you just ain't ruff 'nuff for me. He was the first man to be penalised in a Test match under the ICC's code of conduct, the first one again in a one-day match, and the first to be suspended for a match in either format. I always thought one day he would just slap someone on the field.

Third, he belonged to the sizeable list of Pakistanis – see Mudassar Nazar, Zaheer Abbas, Wasim Raja, Imran Khan, Javed Miandad, Saeed Anwar – who routinely overachieved against India. If Miandad's six at Sharjah was remarked to have 'cut across the Indian ego like a knife slash', then the fallout of Aaqib's hat-trick and world record 7 for 37 in the final in 1991-92 was more tangible: India boycotted the next two tournaments there. They cited biased officialdom. The umpires were Sri Lankan.

And fourth, he had made his Test debut, if the records are to be trusted, at sixteen; and his first-class debut at twelve. Twelve!

We began with this last strand.

Aaqib's date of birth is officially recorded as 5 August 1972. First-class archives show a match played between Lahore Division and Faisalabad at Sialkot's Jinnah Stadium on 20-22 October 1984. Aaqib Javed for Lahore Division: 3-2-5-0 and 5-2-15-3, opening the bowling. Four years later, the same Aaqib Javed is playing for the Pakistan team in Australia, astonishingly, with only two further first-class matches in the intervening period.

'*First-class*?' Aaqib screwed his eyes. 'That was a *first-class* match? Are you sure? I remember playing one match when I was in school, but...

'You know, I always think that the first time I played first-class was on that Australia tour with the Pakistan team. I really hadn't played anything before that. By chance I had played the Youth World Cup. But I had hardly played any club cricket also. Even my college didn't play me! I'll tell you how it happened...'

Aaqib began his story. He seemed to enjoy it. He spoke for long and with barely a cue, mostly in Urdu the way it is spoken in Punjab, with collapsed vowels, and interspersed with English phrases and sentences. He kept fiddling with his cigarette case, lit up occasionally, and often needed to raise his voice over the revving and honking of the cars and autos which never stop plying outside the Continental.

'ONE DAY WHEN I was in college, Wasim Raja held trials at the Gaddafi Stadium for some camp. I landed up there almost as a joke. Some of my friends were pulling my leg, doing *zabardasti*.

It was the first time in my life that I had entered the Gaddafi Stadium. The system at that trial was that fast bowlers had to bowl two deliveries and *bas*, that was it. I had my turn, I bowled my two balls. I was sure that nobody was even watching. There was such a crowd, people were talking, hanging about. It was easy not to get noticed. After I finished I kept watching the trials from the sidelines. The more boys that I saw, the more I began to realise that I was actually quite good. But for some reason, I never made it to the short list.

'So I went to Wasim Raja later and told him, "I think you weren't looking when my turn came. I think I'm not bad. Why don't you give me another chance?" He was a bit surprised, but he said, "Okay, go ahead." I bowled three-four balls. They were good balls, outswingers. He selected me for the camp. The camp ran for one month. And at the end of that month, he said: "Aaqib Javed is the most talented player in this camp." I think that was a huge moment in my life. It was Wasim Raja who unearthed my hidden talent; he made me aware of my potential. That's the point when I became serious about cricket.

'Luckily for me, just two-three months down the line, the under-19 camp for the first Youth World Cup was held. This was to be in Australia. We're talking about early 1988. Wasim Raja and Khan Mohammad were in charge of the preparatory camp for the tournament, and they both liked me. I was selected in the team. I went to Australia, but it wasn't anything great. I played just two-three matches, that too the early ones. Our team reached the final and returned. But when Wasim Raja was asked to recommend the names of a few players who he thought should play Test cricket, again, to my great surprise, he took my name first. Then those of Inzamam, Mushtaq Ahmed, Basit Ali...

'But for me the crucial thing was not the Youth World Cup itself, but that preparatory camp. See, on one of the days, Imran

Khan and Mudassar Nazar had come by. The senior-team camp too was going on in the same stadium complex, and Imran was keen to have a look at some youngsters. I caught his eye. He liked my style; my run-up, my action. He asked me where I had learnt it. I started laughing. I told him I had not learnt it from anybody. I told him that where I come from, Sheikhupura, there isn't even a proper cricket pitch! That was true. Whatever little cricket I had played was on matting. I had played on turf pitches maybe two-three times. "That's impressive," Imran told me, "you are very good. If you do get selected for the under-19 tournament then that's good for you, otherwise, come and join the senior team at practice. You'll learn things there."

'And somehow my name stuck in Imran's mind. Because much later, much after the Youth World Cup, somewhere in September-October 1988, I think, there were some charity matches organised in India – Imran XI v Sunil Gavaskar XI, that kind of thing. Imran took great difficulty in tracing me out. Finally he located me. He called me and said, "You have to go to India for a tournament." I was shocked. I had been thrilled just at having been picked for under-19; after all, nobody from my area had ever reached that level. Imran organised my kit, told me I have to reach Lahore airport at such and such time. When I reached there, of course, nobody knew me. I just hung about. I saw Rameez Raja standing, so I went and said assalam aleikum and stood next to him... One year later Rameez would tell me, "Yaar, you know you came that day and gave me salaam and stood there, I thought you'd ask for an autograph, but you didn't. And I kept wondering, why is he still standing here? Why is he walking with me? What does he want? Who is this guy?"

'The first match in India was at Gwalior. We stayed at the Maharajah's palace. It was such a beautiful palace, staying there was a massive excitement for me. We reached the ground on the morning of the match. Imran was not with us. He arrived in a helicopter along with a bunch of famous actors and actresses – Rajesh Khanna, Chunkey Pandey... I met him moments before the match. "New ball *karte ho*?" he asked me. I said yes. "*Theek hai, yeh lo.*" He gave me the first over. As I went back to my mark, Imran arranged the field: a slip, a gully, square leg, mid-off, fine leg...

'Now, I'm the type of person who can't see anything being done against my nature. I feel that I should decide everything that I should do. So today if I had a new ball in my hand, then *I* would decide my field. I shouted out, "Imran bhai, you can take the square-leg fielder out and put him also in the slips. My ball only goes there." And who's batting? Gavaskar and Srikkanth! Imran laughed as if to say, 'yeh kya cheez hai!' [what a guy!]. But he gave me my fielder.

'I bowled very well. I got Srikkanth, I got Vengsarkar – and I got them in the slips. After that I played a few more matches, in Calcutta, in Madras. By the end of the tour Imran was quite convinced by my bowling. He told me: "My wish is that you come with the Pakistan team to Australia." The problem was that the team had already been announced! "But you don't worry," he said. "I'll go back and do something."

'Now, this is one thing about Imran that still amazes me: once he is convinced about something, he will never retreat. Never. So he went back to Pakistan and told the selection committee that I want this boy Aaqib Javed in the team. They said, "Who is he? We have never seen him. How can we pick him?" "But I have seen him," Imran replied. "Please change the team. If you don't, I'm not going to Australia." So the team was changed. Poor Wasim Haider was dropped. I was included. When my friends saw that in the papers, they teased me. "Yaar, tuh ne isko chhe-saat din mein kya jaadu dikhaya?" [What magic did you show him in one week?]. I said, "Maine kya karna, usne jaakar change karaya" [What do I have to do with it, he had it changed].

'And that is how I found myself in the Pakistan team at the age of sixteen. I had barely played any kind of cricket at all. It was a shock to be in the team with all these superstars – Qadir, Miandad, Malik, Imran, Mudassar. Our first match was against West Indies at Adelaide. I remember my first wicket, Richie Richardson. I bowled him a bouncer, he was caught behind. My international career had begun... We went to New Zealand, where I made by Test debut. In '91 I got a county contract with Hampshire. In '91 I also got the world record against India. In '92, the World Cup win, who can ever forget that...

'Then Imran left cricket. Looking back, I think the cricket I played between '88 and '92, I really enjoyed it. They were my best years. I think for the few years after Imran left, say till about '95, the methods he had instilled, the culture he had instilled, it lingered on. After that it kept fading. Then, Saleem Malik as captain, Wasim Akram as captain – I sort of lost interest. There were many reasons – match-fixing, politics – because of which I just did not feel happy. I did not get along well with the captains. I stopped enjoying my cricket. With great difficulty I carried on till '98.

'By 2000, I decided that I don't want to play any cricket at all. *Bas*. I was very young – twenty-eight years old. My family and friends were trying to talk me out of it. But my wife supported me greatly. She said if you don't want to play, it's your decision. So I went back home, relaxed, I only continued playing for my bank. I concentrated on my fish-farming, which was something that I had started in '97...'

So far, this was an instructive Pakistani tale of rise and decline. It encompassed several pop themes of their cricket: the uncoached talent, Imran's godfatherly touch, and the faith in youth, perhaps reflective of Islam wherein puberty and not the age of eighteen or twenty-one is considered the watershed: of the ten youngest Test cricketers at the time of interviewing, six were Pakistanis, three were Bangladeshis; Tendulkar was the only non-Muslim. And then there was the disillusionment with the system, its corruptions, its political machinations. How many Pakistani tales must there be weaving some or all of these strands?

Yet, there is an upside to our Aaqib story. He was not lost to bitterness. From uncoached youngster he returned to the system as a coach of youth, overseeing some of Pakistan's most consistent successes at the junior level. The climax had arrived barely twenty days ago, when they triumphed in the Under-19 World Cup at Dhaka. Here we must take up his narration again.

'I was basically doing my thing when General Tauqir Zia, the board chairman, called me up out of the blue. He requested me to become a selector. I tried to put up some resistance, saying I was not interested. But he convinced me within five minutes. So I got involved with cricket again in another capacity.

'Somewhere in '99, something very significant happened in Pakistan cricket. The board launched its academies. The regional academies were set up, Lahore, Karachi, Peshawar, Pindi, about five-six in all. Mudassar was the head coach of the academies. I shared a good bond with Mudassar. One day I went and told him, "Yaar, Sheikhupura has so much talent, I'm from there, I've worked hard on the making of the stadium there, they've made me selector from there, I think there should be some sort of coaching academy." Mudassar spoke to Tauqir Zia and he also agreed. So that is how I started my coaching.

'I found within one-two months that I was getting very positive results. The boys were happy. They were convinced they were learning, making progress. I realised very early that having knowledge is one thing, but a good coach is one who is able to

149

transfer it well. Australian coaches were brought in for a stint. I learnt a lot from their methods and ideas, and it really excited me. That is when I told myself: this is the job that I am looking for. Any regrets that I may have had about my playing career went away. My attitude became one of: I'm not playing but why can't I train youngsters?

'In 2000-01, I was made coach for the Under-15 Asia Cup in UAE. We won that tournament. It was the first time I think that Pakistan won any junior title. On an assignment basis now I was asked to coach a lot of teams. I became the A team coach for a few series. I was the coach of the under-19 tour to Sri Lanka, where we won. We lost the Under-19 Asia Cup in Pakistan late last year. During that tournament I had said that ours was the best side. I honestly hadn't seen more talented players than ours. Of course, I faced a lot of criticism after that. People said you claim yours was the most talented team and you didn't even go till the final. And I replied that even now I'm saying that I haven't seen so much talent at this level. Losing by small margins, it happens. And a few months later, we won the Under-19 World Cup.

'The training from academies has helped a lot. The boys are disciplined and professional from an early age. They know about physical training, diet, code of conduct. If Pakistan is now succeeding more than ever before at the junior level then this credit goes entirely to the academy system.

'At the World Cup I could see a big, big gulf in the Pakistan team and the other fifteen teams – the way we were trained. The ICC administrators, the managers of the other teams, they all came and asked us, "How have you trained these boys so well?" Sultan Rana, the manager, Sohail Saleem, the doctor, and I had a great understanding. We had given the boys everything from shaving kits to shoe-shine kits to even hair gel. We told them that when you move out of your room, you have to don everything from your shoe shine to your gel. In one month, there wasn't a single breakfast, lunch or dinner outside the team uniform, whatever our state was, whether we were tired or not. At this early age it was important to let them know that they were ambassadors, that people should look at them and feel the difference.

'The variety we had in our bowling was amazing. In my view even the Pakistan senior team doesn't have spinners who are as good. No match. Mansoor Amjad is seventeen years old but I can predict he will be another Abdul Qadir. He has a better action than Qadir. He is a six-footer. He is strong. He is so talented – I haven't seen anyone as talented in Pakistan. There is Tariq Mahmood, who actually is like Muralitharan. His outgoing ball is better than Murali's. He has learnt it from Murali, watching on TV. The fast bowlers were outstanding. Riaz Afridi is easily the most accurate bowler in Pakistan. I can say this for sure because I have done his target-practice assessment: he scores 90 per cent plus. He hardly bowls no-balls or wides. Imran Ali Pasha, he is quick. Afridi must be bowling at about 135 kmph, Imran Ali at about 145.

'In my experience over the last three years, the key to handling a bowler lies in understanding his psyche and his body – the amount of energy he spends in a match, and his recovery time after that. Some take eight hours, some take sixteen hours. We didn't make these boys practise till they recovered. Even if we made them bowl, it was two-three overs, not more. We emphasised a lot on this. At the World Cup we played nine matches including the warm-ups. But we had just five practice sessions. Everybody was mentally alert. The fast bowlers were fresh. There were no injuries. We controlled the extras. Even the umpires said they enjoyed our bowling because they did not have to call many wides and no-balls.

'You know, I am confident I can sort out the Pakistan team's extras problems within a few weeks. I have been using some techniques with the juniors. For no-balls, I make them practise their run-up like long-jumpers do, from one point to the other, then back again from the landing point, like a cycle. Each bowler is given the exact measure of his length down to the centimetre, which he marks out before the match starts. Sometimes I make them practise with their eyes closed. And for a no-ball in the nets, simple: the punishment is twenty push-ups.

'Wides also can be controlled if you remember that your line is an extension of your action. The knee of the leading foot, the elbow of the leading arm and the head should all be in one line going down towards off stump. You should concentrate only on your natural swing in the first five overs. The wrist must be locked otherwise you will just spray it around. Someone like Sami, his wrist is so loose. I have a software with which I can show him exactly where he is making a mistake. And Shoaib, his non-bowling elbow tends to come from the side. I can show him on the software exactly how...'

It was odd to hear all this from Aaqib in the same conversation in which he described his reaction to Imran's inquiry about his own cricket education as a laugh. It captured a generation shift. I wondered if the bunch Aaqib had invested so much faith in would live up to his hopes.

We changed tack, to my main reason for meeting Aaqib. How has Pakistan been able to produce the world's most feared fast bowlers for the past quarter century? The question has confounded India for years. With right earnest, systems were put in place and something of an awakening was created in the nineties – but still not a single express paceman. Whereas in Pakistan the impression was that you could reach out and, lo, in your grasp was a tearaway.

Aaqib answered with practiced scholarliness.

'Four reasons.

'One, genetic. If you compare Pakistanis with Indians or Bangladeshis – especially in Punjab and the northern areas – we have good height and build.

'Then there are the eating habits, the diet. See, you can get protein from dal and eggs but that is incomplete protein. The aggression, you get that from beef. It's not that you need to have beef only from cow. Here we use a lot of buffalo meat also. I believe that the red meat of these animals promotes aggression, and I think fast bowling is all about aggression. Your Srinath, his speed was 90 miles, but he never created terror. His body language was so soft. My speed was less than his. But the pressure I could exert, because of my body language, was much more. Agarkar can bowl up to 140-145 kmph, but there is no aggression, no body language. Pathan, he has aggression, although he is not very fast. He may be eating beef. I'm telling you it makes a difference!

'Third reason is tennis ball. Tape-ball. All our youngsters play tape-ball cricket in the streets. When you throw a light object over a distance, your joints and ligaments will get stronger, your bowling muscles will develop. When you play with the tennis ball for three-four years and then start with the cricket ball, it helps a lot I think.

'So that's three. Height, diet, tennis ball. And yes, the fourth – idols. In Pakistan we've had fast-bowling heroes. Imran was the pioneer. I loved Marshall's action but Imran was my hero. Imran's action was too difficult for me to copy! After that came Wasim, Waqar, Shoaib...'

I kind of enjoyed Aaqib's thesis. Debatable though point numbers one and two may be, it was a hearty, holistic effort. He seemed rather chuffed with it himself.

Talk turned, naturally, to reverse swing.

'It's very easy, honestly. If you go to our nets and see, even a sixteen-year-old boy, who has played cricket for six months, he will be able make it reverse swing. There is a reason for it. Our cricket grounds are so rough. At our clubs you have to make a new ball last for one month. If you bowl in such conditions from early on, you learn yourself how to look after the ball in a manner that will suit you.'

Osman had done a fine feature on reverse swing recently. He had traced its conception, from the mouth of Sarfraz Nawaz, popularly regarded as the first master of the art, to one Dr Farrukh, a 1970s club cricketer at the Lahore Gymkhana. Even so, its mechanics, why, that is, that the old ball should swerve so prodigiously, and that in the direction of the shiny side, were hard to explain. And of the maintenance of the ball there was little known. 'It's our secret, and we'd like to keep it to ourselves,' was Wasim's answer, though the secret had clearly spread through the global bowling community. Everybody agreed that high pace was an asset, as opposed, thrillingly, to conventional swing, which is more receptive to medium. There was no consensus, however, on whether reverse swing had solely to do with the state of the ball or there was a technique to delivery.

'There is no technique. The secret is how to bring the ball in that condition. It becomes more effective with speed, of course. It doesn't happen on good surfaces. If there is a lush outfield, or if there is some moisture on the pitch, it is very difficult. Very difficult. Maybe after seventy overs or something, you can get it a little bit.'

But if rough surfaces were of the essence, then how did the Pakistanis manage it in England and New Zealand?

'If you look at that tour of ours to England in 1992, they had made batting pitches, not green pitches. And in June-July the surface becomes quite dry over there, so it was not a problem.

'But the main art, I'm telling you, is to get the ball into shape. I was a bit of a specialist at that! There are many little ways. You know, bowl three-four bouncers in a row, hitting the rough side all the time. The marks will come; it will become rougher. It's a big art. It's difficult. You have to keep at it. Every one of the eleven has to be involved. Somebody catches the ball on the wrong side, and the sweat rubs on it – *bas*, the game is up. All over!'

Aaqib laughed and lit another cigarette, eyes agleam. To ask him if the laws were ever stretched would be no point: he who denies the practice altogether is a liar; he who admits it is a fool. But I asked him about how the team responded to the allegations, particularly the witch-hunt on the England tour of 1992.

'Actually, our group then – Wasim, Waqar, Mushtaq and me – all four of us were very aggressive. We enjoyed life and didn't think about much else. [The same quartet was apprehended by police on a Caribbean beach for smoking ganja.] Pressure-vresshure, these things used to just skirt us by. When you enjoy a situation, when you're giving crowds enjoyment, all that adds to your performance. If you're nervous, if you can't face people, you'll be under pressure all the time. We had won the World Cup, we had seen all the situations that cricket had to throw at us. It didn't really matter. We enjoyed and we played with aggression.'

Against India the aggression, I started to say – he did not let me finish my sentence.

'Aggression was double. I would harass Tendulkar all the time. He got fed up one day in Toronto and told me "chhod do yaar khuda ke liye tum!" [Leave me alone for God's sake!]. I felt bad. I told him then I would stop bothering him. We used to trouble them a lot: *gaaliyaan dena,* tease *karna.* We used to tease Sidhu, tell him Sardar jokes. It was a part of our tactic, it was a part of our style. We had a gang mentality, we just wanted aggression all the time. We had a psychological hold on India. India stopped coming to Sharjah at one stage because they just couldn't win.

'The Indians were polite compared to us. Who was there to abuse? There was one Jadeja. And there was one Prabhakar. Sidhu was also a little like us. He's Punjabi after all! But this Indian team is very different. They are as aggressive.'

I asked Aaqib two more questions, answers to both of which I could have guessed, but I wanted to hear anyway. First: did he think all three lbws in his hat-trick at Sharjah were out? And second: why the double aggression against India?

'Shastri *toh* looked out,' he replied to the first. 'Tendulkar *bhi* out *hee tha*. He was on the back foot. Azhar, they say there was an edge, but if you look at the replay it doesn't appear so.

'And the aggression, well, it's an emotion, a feeling. And where do these feelings come from? They come from the *mahoul*, the atmosphere. From our childhood it has been drummed into us, "don't lose to India, don't lose to India." Wherever in the world we travelled people would tell us, "don't lose to India, don't lose to India." But our relationship with the players was good. Raju, Jadeja, Ankola, Sidhu, we were close. After the match we would often sit in one room, eat and drink together. I met Sidhu this time and told him you can't go without listening to my jokes! Cricket is inside the ring.'

We finished on a philosophical note. I asked him what he'd learned from cricket.

'Willpower. I think fast bowling is for nut cases. Especially here, to run in and bowl in 50-degree heat you have to be a madman. You get hit, you don't perform, but you still have to try. I will not stop trying: that is what I have learned from cricket. I mentioned that I started fish-farming. The first two-three years were disastrous. The whole world was telling me, "Yaar, what have you got yourself into? Use your time and money well." But it is going much better now and I will make it better still. And that comes from cricket. Selectors have not selected me – *aisi ki taisi*, I'll come back. No wickets today, *aisi ki taisi*, I'll get them tomorrow. At coaching, the boys tell me they can't do something. *Aisi ki taisi*, I tell them – you *will* do it.'

Aaqib glanced at his watch and found he was running late. 'Right, ji?'

He clicked smartly out of the room.

NO, OF COURSE NOT, the evening's airy-fairy exploration of Pakistani fast bowling was not over. Point no. 3 from Aaqib's thesis was about to be tested. A friend from a TV channel had invited me to a session of tape-ball cricket organised by Shahid Anwar, a one-cap wonder for Pakistan, who, incidentally, had been part of the same under-19 World Cup team as Aaqib.

Nobody is sure as to when and how tape-ball cricket began in Pakistan. Mid-1980s some say; many go back a decade still, but no further.

My own notion of a 'tape-ball' before coming here was ridiculous. Having heard about Pakistanis employing such a contraption on American college campuses, a friend and I once tried to inject some life into our own balcony cricket with the innovation. We wrapped cello-tape around the diameter of a tennis ball to give it a 'seam'. Nothing happened. The experiment lasted twenty minutes. We went back to our old method for bowler emancipation, which was to swap the regular yellow tennis ball for the hard white MRI, so that if you hit, it at least hurt.

Our misconceptions were two. The material used was not cello-tape, but insulation tape. And it was not wound around like a seam, but across the *entire face* of the ball – except for one little

157

slit. This was to create a weight imbalance; in other words, to create swing.

Despite the assistance to bowlers, runs are made at a head-spinning pace in tape-ball cricket. The boundaries are small, and the tape imparts the ball a greater carry. And typically the games range from eight to twenty overs per side, so always there is the licence to hit.

Tonight was not a match, only a demonstration for the benefit of the cameras. The venue was Model Colony, a posh residential area in new Lahore. Streetlamps, assorted bulbs, and one car provided the light. A metal grill made up the wicket. The scene was like a tryout – a dozen enthusiastic bowlers, all shapes, all sizes, all ages, with all manner of bodacious actions, bounding in, keen to impress the camera. Some were wickedly quick, some swerved it wickedly late. Some, to broadcast their mastery, raised the ball over their heads, announced 'inswinger' or 'outswinger', adjusted the slit and their wrist positions accordingly, and then proceeded to beat the bat.

Aaqib's point about building bowling muscles by getting accustomed to hurling a lighter object held. The insulation tape barely added any weight to the ball.

Yet, this, from the outsider's vantage, did not seem to be the main point. The main point was: the fast bowler felt joy. So much happened for him – swing both ways dammit! Besides, the tape would make the ball skid off the surface, and, if dug short, rear up rather than sit up like a balloon as a tennis ball tends to do.

In India, because of the grounds, because of the weather, because of the pitches, all cricket, basically, is an excuse to bat. Pakistan should have been, and perhaps was, much the same, till somebody came up with this simple innovation which was able to change the way a boy might perceive the sport. Science tells us that the first hundred hours of exposure are key in determining a person's attitude towards a thing. This was a masterstroke.

The more I reflected on it, the more tape-ball cricket seemed to me one of the remarkable indigenous stories in cricket, particularly given the scale. Most indigenous processes tend to be personal. Bradman honing his skills by hitting a golf ball with a stump or Sonny Ramadhin spinning fruits while working the fields hadn't prompted entire nations to follow. Nor might that have met with success. But tape-ball cricket was everywhere in Pakistan: on mud, on grass, on cement, on guttered footpaths, in residential colonies, in gymkhanas, in parking lots, in private lawns, in farmland, in informal dust-ups, in organised tournaments, in cities, in towns, in villages and all else in between. Any cricket in Pakistan not with a cricket ball was with a tape-ball.

The Pakistanis couldn't see this. To them, tape-ball was tape-ball, bowling quick was bowling quick, and that's the way cricket was.

Osman, for example, couldn't understand why I kept banging on about tape-ball cricket till a week later, he suddenly turned to me: 'Wait a minute, you mean you have *no* tape-ball cricket in India?'

I nodded.

'Oh.'

*

TREND-READERS WERE not upbeat about India's chances. Of their last fourteen tournament finals, they had won one. This was not a final in that sense; it was the last and deciding match of a bilateral series. Of their last five matches in this situation, India had lost three; of the two they had won, one had been against

Zimbabwe. They had never won a series in Pakistan. A hard game was expected.

For the fifth time Inzamam called the toss correctly. And for the first time in a night game, he chose to bowl. Commentators repeated like a mantra that this was because of the evening dew but I think it had equally, if not more, to do simply with the fact that the chasers had won the last two games and almost won the first two. Ganguly said he would have batted anyway.

This was a pleasant afternoon, and at 31 C, a good two degrees cooler than two days ago. Naturally, a full and loud house was in.

Soon Shoaib barged in from the College End, across from the press box. I'm not going to dwell much on the early excitement. Must point out a few things though.

Pakistan delivered only five no-balls or wides in the first fifteen overs. Sehwag, Tendulkar and Ganguly played brisk, useful innings, one longer than the next; Tendulkar's front-foot driving into the covers, especially, cut a picture. All three were caught at the wicket, trying to play the glide to third man. Among them, Sehwag was thought out in what was probably Inzamam's only truly bright spark in the series: with the two mandatory catchers installed at short fine-leg and short midwicket, Sehwag tried to run one fine from middle-stump.

With that out of the way, we may get down to paying full tribute to V.V.S. Laxman, the most beautiful thing the world with all its wonders has known. Well.

VVS – see how it drips off the tongue – arrived at the crease in the sixth over, at the fall of the first wicket, with the total on 34. Consider the background here. His tournament to date? Benched with a stiff knee at Karachi; 4, 3 and 20 in the three innings since. His career average against Pakistan? 7.33, from six matches.

## Blue fading into green

Now VVS is a religious man – the second V, Venkata, is after Lord Venkateswara, and the S, Sai, after Sai Baba, whom he appeases with an annual visit to Shirdi – and if cricket features in his daily prayers, then surely today's imploration would have been, 'God, please give me a half-volley on leg stump first ball.' And Shoaib, thickly, obliged. And VVS, sweetly, flicked for four.

Two balls later, he jabbed Shabbir into the covers beatifically for three. A little after, he played and missed at Shoaib and berated himself for not getting out his front foot as he had been practising ever since being trapped lbw at Pindi eight days ago. Sami was called on to bowl. VVS cut him, less cut, more flashing kiss, a Japanese fan opening out. And so with three strokes and a rehearsal, VVS was on his way.

VVS is said to be a charmer. But I protest that. Anything can be charming, don't you think? Krish Srikkanth's flea-bitten twitches, Ijaz Ahmed's moustachioed nods of approval to the bowler. No, VVS does not charm so much as woo. Inevitably, we fall.

VVS is that rare player who is able to create a mood around his work. Suddenly everything becomes worth smiling at. Them-days-were-the-days greybeards are moved to nostalgia. There is nothing technical in this nostalgia. It is in fact not nostalgia. It is only mood. A curl of the arm, a flick of the wrist, a twirl of the blade, and we watch through tints of rose. There is no muscle in the art of VVS, no malice, no meanness. It is non-confrontational, innocent, lovely. Or put it this way: strip away the context, strip away the circumstances, strip away the competition and all the rest of the stuff that really make sport... strip it, strip it, strip it down to a man and a stick and nothing more and the art of VVS barely resonates any less. How many like him? Beyond this I cannot articulate the mood. But it was there at the Gaddafi.

VVS was 62, and the total 171, when Ganguly fell, for 45. VVS had, unusually, only six boundaries in this time, each one luscious. Yet he had paced himself at about a run-a-ball. By playing so, he brought to mind his childhood idol, Mohammad Azharuddin.

From 76 to 84 he moved with a painted cover drive and a late dab off Pakistan's best bowler on the night, Sami. Because of his range of ticks and flicks and swirls and glances, it is sometimes easy to forget just how accomplished he is on the off side. From 95, VVS went to 99 with a glide off Shoaib Malik. It was a full-pitched ball, and he considered the drive before allowing it to slide off the face. There was an ooh in the press box, whose glass partition had turned a distinct rose.

Then with a pat down the ground off the next ball, his ninety-eighth of the afternoon, VVS reached hundred. He took off his helmet and raised his arms, but without fuss. This was the pinnacle of a season which he spent making a nonsense of the claim that he was incapable of adjusting to the pyjama stuff. It was his fifth century in twenty-one one-dayers in the past five months. He hadn't made a single fifty in that time, reinforcing the point that when he was in, he was in. He had worked hard for it. He had improved his strike-rotation. He was getting run-out less.

Alas, it also meant that he had to sometimes go against his grain. VVS is a maker of strokes, but of ground strokes. Twice already, but only twice, in this innings had he played in the air. The first, on 52, was a pick-up off Razzaq, soundly struck, and dropped by Taufeeq on the midwicket fence. The second was an awkward hoick off Malik, dignified only marginally by a down-on-knee flourish.

With five overs to go, VVS felt it his duty to slog. These were slogs of compulsion. They were not VVS. In regular cricketers such things may suggest spunk, but with VVS they were blots, acts of corruption. But the compromise needed to be made. Better to slog than be dropped for the World Cup.

He danced down and tried to swat Malik over the top. It took the edge and went for four. He tried it again the next ball. He missed it altogether. He went for it a third time. It steepled high off the leading edge and into the hands of Sami at cover. He ambled off, loose-limbed, shadow-practising purer responses. Gaddafi to a man rose in applause.

Thirty-two runs came from three raucous overs at the death. Balaji reproduced his long-on six from Peshawar, this time off Shoaib Akhtar, and promptly broke his bat on the next stroke. 'To the next Black Bradman', John Wright would autograph it.

India finished at 293. The teams were tied 2-2, and now with identical first-innings totals in the deciding two games at the same stadium in the space of four days. Beneath everything, this fortnight had also restored faith in the power of a two-team limited-overs series.

ROARS EMANATED from inside the arena even during the break.

The flags had continued to flutter together in the stands; at one point a tri-colour kite had descended on to the field. The posters had continued to speak their message. 'Together we can beat the world'. 'We love you Lahore – Amritsar boys'. 'Pyar to hona hi tha' (Love was inevitable). There was a clever Punjabi one: 'Inzamam Tuada Haq, Samsung Cup Sada Haq' (Haq in Urdu means entitlement. So: Inzamam is your Haq, but the Samsung Cup is our right.) There was a well-meaning, but disturbing, one – 'Atal Bihari [sic] Musharaff and Pervez Vajpayee' – for the morphed image it brought to mind was not a little gruesome.

The bigwigs had continued to fly across the border. Ministers, in what were to be their last days in office, sneaking in some informal time with their counterparts; industrialists and businessmen, who took the opportunity to meet with Pakistan's finance minister; actors, models, socialites, who were bigger hits here than at home. All were overshadowed by the elegant Dina Wadia, Mohammad Ali Jinnah's daughter, and mother of the Bombay industrialist, Nusli Wadia. It was beside them that Musharraf, arriving by military helicopter and togged in military fatigues, sat for an hour.

All in all, a vibrant, gay atmosphere prevailed. There was space for everyone. This was the very apogee of the tour.

PAKISTAN HAD LEFT out Afridi. Walking out alongside Yasir under floodlights was Taufeeq Umar. His inclusion had met with general support, but given his strike rate of 56, I would have picked Imran Nazir, the man more likely to give India the shock treatment Afridi had been earmarked for. Taufeeq had composed an assured century in the warm-up game against the Indians, but Imran's humiliating 65 from 32 balls had been the stand-out performance. This was a one-off; inspiration was called for.

Rather than being hampered by dew, it appeared initially that India were benefitting from a zing off the surface. Irfan kept it on a coin between off and middle, curving it back. He started by conceding two runs: the most economical first over of the series.

At the other end, Yasir walked into a wastrel drive off Balaji's fourth legitimate delivery. It was a sharp ball, full, nipping back, and sent the off stump on a cartwheel. Pakistan's first wicket was down at 8 in the second over.

Things began to happen rather quickly now.

Yousuf Youhana entered to dancing kaichis in Irfan's eyes. He was cut up within a few minutes, for one. Pakistan 9 for 2. Taufeeq flung himself into three crashing drives in Balaji's next over, a rousing riposte, but the tide was only to turn one way. He waltzed across his stumps, smug in the knowledge that Irfan was shaping it away. I cannot say if Irfan picked the movement early but he chose that very ball to slant it in the other direction – let's just put it down to bowler's instinct. There ended Taufeeq's innings, exposed leg stump pegged back, 18 runs to go along with his two dropped catches.

Bowler's instinct was at it again, when, in his seventh over, Irfan suckered Younis Khan into slashing a very wide half-volley to point. It was a foolish stroke which looked worse than it was and accordingly left Younis open to punishment. When Saad, on a mad interviewing spree, accosted Wasim Bari, the chief selector, with a Dictaphone aboard an airplane, he was told that this shot and nothing else cost Younis a place in the Test squad.

By the time Ganguly called to a close Irfan's first spell, Pakistan were 64 for 4. Irfan was 8-1-20-3. Things had come a full circle for him at the Gaddafi. Four months ago, still playing the under-19s, he routed Bangladesh on this ground with 9 for 16, the performance that sealed his inclusion in India's touring party to Australia. Two weeks ago, against Pakistan A in the tour opener, he had been smacked for 24 runs in his first over, which led to his omission in the first two one-dayers. The thing about Irfan here was not only the three wickets. Nor even the economy of 2.5 which, in the context of the tournament, could be considered equivalent to a batting strike rate of 250. There was the joy he radiated while performing, the tousled hair, broad smile and the high leaps, surging through the team and spectators like the chorus of a rock ballad. There was the commitment with which he fielded: having sent down that pinpoint first over, he ran left and ran right at the third man fence to make two fine saves.

Meanwhile Inzamam thrived in his large ballerina way. He pulled Zaheer, he cut and drove Balaji, he looked splendid. But he didn't seem to approve of the manner in which Kartik, brought on in the seventeenth over, was pitching on leg and conceding three singles an over to a spread field. He fell back on his natural strategy: he charged down two steps, opened out his shoulders and drilled the ball down the ground with a follow-through that ended at his lumbar. From up in the press box, it looked an obvious six, the flattest of sixes, over straight long-on. But we could not, from that position, make out Tendulkar who, it emerged, had hopped sideways and backwards and plucked out the ball like a boy at an apple orchard.

And now look how life works. All around the perimeter, the boundary rope had been covered by Pepsi's sponsored toblerone, except for three or four places. The catch had been made at one of these points. Had Inzamam's bullet been a little this way or that, chances are that Tendulkar's heel would have made contact with the base of the triangle, and it would have been six runs rather than a wicket. And since it was his hundredth catch in one-dayers, it could be said to his detractors that it was indeed a Tendulkar century which had decided this quasi-final.

We may stop a detailed narration at this stage. With Inzamam gone, 200 runs adrift, the game was up. Lahoris began leaving the arena, glimpsing Razzaq perish on their way out: 96 for 6 in twenty-four overs.

Not that it stopped Malik, Moin and Sami from trying. The increasing number of full-tosses on view suggested that the dew was making its presence felt after all. But the damage had been done. Resourcefully they hoisted Pakistan till 253, at which score Balaji yorked Moin, just as he had in the previous match. A pump of the fists, a cacophony of whoops, a blue scramble for the stumps.

The series was over.

A year ago, almost to the day, Ganguly had watched Ricky Ponting's Australians tear his team apart at the Wanderers. Now, having been stretchered off in the tenth over with a sprained back, he ran out of the pavilion and hugged his mates; it had been difficult, the manager was to say, to keep him from returning to lead the team during the final overs. Fireworks went off, pink and white, like tinsel in the night sky. Below them the Indians huddled, enveloped in a thick blanket of locusts and moths.

The telly intercepted Sachin and Irfan. 'I'd like to dedicate this win to all the people of India,' beamed Sachin. 'I knew God was with me,' smiled Irfan in broken English. 'God helps.' At about the same time, *The Indian Express* was to report, Imran Khan approached Shaharyar Khan with a wounded lament: 'Intehaa ho gayi zillat ki [This is the limit of humiliation]. We must get someone like Pathan, this is too much.' Down in Vadodra, Irfan's father, Mehmood Khan Pathan, reportedly embraced the TV screen and planted a kiss upon it; 'Galli ke ladke ne hi wicket lekar dikhaya' (The boy from every street has only done the damage), was his message to Miandad; Shamim Banu, the mother, had bought sweets for she knew that Guddu would shine. In Delhi, Vajpayee offered a creaky homily. 'If eleven players working together as a team can win matches and hearts, there is no reason why hundred crore people, when they move together, can't achieve anything they want.' From Bangalore, where the Indian Open Pro-Am golf tournament had been brought forward in view of the cricket, it emerged that an estimated Rs 25 crore had been bet during the day: 'peanuts,' according to one bookie, 'compared to Delhi and Bombay'. In Kolkata, the cast and crew of the monstrous rapid-assembled film, *Silence Please...The Dressing Room*, starring cricketer-turned-soap-star, Salil Ankola, as captain of India in a cricket match played in Srinagar against the backdrop of a terrorist infiltration, celebrated its launch at a five-star nightclub before a big screen beaming the Lahore match. From Seoul to Moscow to Toronto, desis who had made arrangements to follow the matches suddenly found a vacuum in their lives. At the stadium, somebody help up a festoon, 'Thank you, Lahore.'

The series was over.

At the awards ceremony, VVS was named Man of the Match, though Irfan ought to have shared it. But it is a batsman's world. And so Inzamam was provided with the Hero Honda Award for the Highest Run Scorer: there was no Hero Honda Award for the Highest Wicket Taker; and he was provided the Hyundai Super Striker Award – a car – for the Highest Batting Average: there was no Hyundai car for the Best Bowling Average; and ultimately, deservedly, the Samsung Man of the Series award. The Indian board announced a bonus of Rs 50 lakh for the team.

'It has been a *zabardast* series,' Inzamam said at the press conference. 'The crowd has been *zabardast*, supporting for both teams. It was a lot of fun to play in front of supporters of both teams right here in Pakistan.' Ganguly requested that he be pardoned early because the pain in his back made it difficult for him to sit, but of course that was not going to happen. Asked why his team didn't do a victory lap around the stadium, he shot back with a smile: 'We thought about it, but there was nobody left in the stands.'

By the time I finished filing amid electricity fluctuations I felt overpowered by hunger and fatigue. Saad and I made for Gawalmandi and ate without shame. The paya had its moments and the mutton chaaps were colossal. Sitting there in a sea of Indians and the odd Pakistani it was well obvious that cricket had not brought the countries closer together. Food had. Such an exhausting fortnight. I felt whipped. I think I may have got a you-made-us-win-well-done call from home, I don't know. I may have felt sick after overeating, I don't know. And on the way back, asleep in the auto, I am still of the impression that Saad quoted from the Grateful Dead's 'Scarlet Begonias', which both surprised me and made me immensely happy and provided me my last thought before passing out for the night on the sagging mattress at the Continental.

*India 293 for 7 in 50 overs (Laxman 107, Ganguly 45, Sami 3-63) beat Pakistan 253 in 47.5 overs (Moin 72, Malik 65, Irfan 3-32, Balaji 3-62) by 40 runs*

# 6. A nation went potty

MY FINAL MEMORY of the Continental is a Rasputin bottle-cap tumbling on to the moss-green carpeting from the raucous room above, at one in the morning, through a duct by the window. I will miss the place.

4.45 a.m. at the bus stop. Scenes are registered in a woolly-eyed puffy-headed way. A lovely girl in black waves Allah hafiz to her family. A *buzurg* sets up his tea stall for the day. The man at the ticket booth says 'aap toh bilkul Rahul jaise hi dikhte ho' (you look just like Rahul).

The Daewoo service is clinical. The vans are nimble, clean, punctual. The tickets are priced much higher than the cheapest buses but at one-tenth the airfare. It is freezing inside. A recorded voice-over repeats the welcome two times in three languages. A hostess comes around with a bottle of chilled water and a packet of crisps. A man with a video camera records every face for fifteen seconds and then pans the camera towards a big digital clock. He does this two or three times during the journey.

The sun comes out and we see the glorious gaudy trucks rumbling on the broad highways of Punjab, glorious trucks laced with the art of the people. The drivers call them 'dulhan', bride, with love.

It is the twenty-sixth of March. We are headed south to Multan, south to the Test matches.

THE ONE-DAY SERIES had been sufficiently draining. The argument had been made that India and Pakistan were better off restricting their exchanges to Test matches, given the compressed jingoism that accompanied one-dayers, and the structural limitation, that there was no room for the middle-ground, the draw. In a sense, the great success of the series was precisely that it was able to turn these points into its strengths. The clamour of the one-day game, the hype, the incentive to be seen and to be heard, played a part in sending out as large a message as it did. It was not without superficiality. Is anything?

And it was because there is no place for the middle-ground in one-day matches that the teams were compelled to shed their inhibitions, express themselves. For the draw, in India-Pakistan history, was not the last refuge of equals. It was the wilful occupation of a joyless, castrated territory. Following an engrossing inaugural exchange – Pakistan's first ever series – in India in 1952-53, the sides played out two full series without a single result. These were the first two five-Test series in the history of the game with all matches drawn. Counting the last two games of the 1952-53 series, the run of draws in the first phase of India-Pakistan cricket, up till 1960-61, amounted to twelve. Declarations were delayed, chases were not taken up. Scoring rates hovered around 2 an over. It was a sedentary time.

A bright new age appeared to have dawned upon resumption, after the two wars. The 1978-79 series stood out not only for its two results from three Tests, but the spectacular intent required to achieve them: at Lahore the Pakistanis hunted down 128 in twenty-one overs on the final evening, and at Karachi, in similar circumstances, an astonishing 164 in twenty-five. But, as the 1980s grew longer a pall set in: fifteen draws, at one stage, in sixteen matches, many of them not even reaching a last innings.

The price of defeat, or even the failure to win, was clearly established. Of the five tours by India to Pakistan, none successful, four led to the captain's sacking: Mankad in 1954-55 (five Tests, drawn 0-0), Bedi in 1978-79 (three Tests, 0-2), Gavaskar in 1982-83 (six Tests, 0-3) and Srikkanth in 1989-90 (four Tests, 0-0). Gavaskar got through the only other one, in 1984-85 (0-0), when the tour was abandoned before the third and last Test on Indira Gandhi's assassination. At home, Kapil Dev and Mohammad Azharuddin compounded their losses in 1986-87 (five Tests, 0-1) and 1998-99 (two Tests, 1-1; a loss in the Asian Test Championship one-off that followed) with unsuccessful World Cups and were then fired. In Pakistan, Fazal Mahmood lost his job after the draws of 1960-61 (five Tests, 0-0), while Asif Iqbal announced his retirement even before returning home in 1979-80 (six Tests, 0-2).

This, then, the submission to a middle-ground of no initiative, was one of two chief characteristics of India-Pakistan Test cricket. The other was umpiring, crying about. Such copious, such passionate, such bitter tears have been shed in player autobiography after player autobiography that some must be genuine.

But there were was reason to be optimistic. For one, the Test-match draw, because of faster but shorter batting, was itself approaching extinction. For another, the officials were from a third country, and while technology was now more liable to expose their mistakes, it would presumably also see to it that two wrong decisions on the field did not translate into ten in print. Above all, the last encounter between the teams had been one for the ages. I looked forward to Test cricket; yes, very much so.

Multan arrived at eleven o'clock. Stepping out of the Daewoo was jumping out of the ice pan and into the fire. Multan is a blast from a desert.

THE SINDBAD was a government guest-house, and in high demand.

We had only managed a room because of Sonny's contact. Ours was a pleasant ground-floor room, with plants outside the meshed windows. The staff at the Sindbad were lovely, and the most efficient. They installed a shower curtain on request.

The phone in the room did not have a direct dial-out, and so could not be used to connect to the Internet. I needed to file. Getting online from the reception would mean disconnecting the Sindbad from the outside world. Attempts to connect from the PCOs outside proved unsuccessful. There seemed to be no cybercafe around. Disturbed by my plight, Arshad, one of the bearers at the Sindbad, stepped in gallantly. 'Ab toh aap Multan mein hain, kyon fikr kar rahe hain?' (You are in Multan now, why are you worrying?)

Arshad and I ventured in several directions by foot. An hour later we found Khaleel's cybercafe.

Khaleel's cybercafe was on the ground floor of a two-storey shop complex on a roundabout. In Khaleel's cybercafe it was that I felt the full the extent of the penetration of Indian pop culture in Pakistan. The master computer blared forth in extra treble, 'Luv you O Sunn-namm!', from the new Hindi movie, *Run*. On each of the other eight-odd computers sat men between twenty and thirty, some downloading Hindi songs or videos, some scouring through images of Indian actresses on websites, some, headphones on, engrossed in a Bollywood VCD borrowed from an impressive pirate shop next door. It was so seamless, so obvious – I could have been in Nagpur – so I don't know why I felt like the American who is surprised at finding Arnold Schwarzenegger t-shirts on boys in small-town India.

The filing saga continued, and by now I was in trouble. Khaleel did not have compatible software on his computers. Nor could he let me connect my laptop directly, for that, like at the Sindbad, would mean disconnecting all others. He suggested we try from his home, five minutes away. On the way I asked him what Khaleel meant. Friend, he said. He refused to charge me the next time I went to his cybercafe.

An Indian soap was on television at Khaleel's home. While Indian news channels and Indian publications were banned in Pakistan, and Indian movies were prohibited in theatres, Indian entertainment channels were allowed, and they flourished. Growing up, I remember the mother and the sister hunting down Pakistani dramas, *Dhoop Kinare* and *Tanhaiyan*, on video tapes. They were quite the rage. I think the tapes may still be with us.

Two and a half hours since setting out, I managed to send my piece through. Arshad had insisted on waiting all along. We returned to the Sindbad by auto. But Arshad warned me beforehand that I should first let him negotiate the fare.

'CHAR CHEEZE tofa-e-Multan/gard, gada, gurmee-o-goristan.' There are several English versions of this Persian doggerel. The more literal would be: Four things have been gifted to us by Multan/ Dust, beggars, heat and graveyards. For the sake of rhyme, this becomes: In four things does Multan abound/Dust, beggars, heat and burial grounds. As a variation, the beggars are replaced with shrines. And Khushwant Singh, the Indian writer, noted a fifth G during his travels – 'gadhaa', donkey. All are true.

The heat of Multan is not an ordinary heat, and the dust of Multan is not an ordinary dust. They are bedfellows, in it together, working on the skin like sandpaper. The sun beams down thorns. The dust, sand really, finds its way into the hair as after a day at the beach. It lodges itself in the creases of the neck and the bends of the elbow like crumbs of broken glass. Just as one becomes accustomed to its still silent prick, it might begin to blow, in round clouds or in straight gusts or in gentle lilts, into the eyes and nose and mouth and ears; blowing, then suddenly stopping, then pricking.

At night, up on the Fort, overlooking the crumbling town of brick. They say if someone were to dig up present-day Multan, untold clues to our civilisation would emerge. They say if Multan is not the oldest city in the subcontinent it is certainly the most conquered, repeatedly ravaged, repeatedly rebuilt. And at the Fort where we are now there remains no fort. It takes its name after a garden inside, Qasim Bagh.

Along one edge of the Fort mound is the Qasim Bagh Stadium, where Sylvester Clarke flung his brick. It was the only Test ever played here. A magnificent set of silhouetted monuments stands on the mound. The main one, the one with all the activity, is the mausoleum of Shah Rukn-i-Alam, exquisite in brick and shisham wood and tiles of turquoise, a Multani signature; and above its high sloping walls, a dome of shining marble visible from any part of Multan, but the true splendour of which can only be felt underneath it, inside.

The Fort is a carnival of pilgrims, dervishes, beggars. Stalls of lucky charms and magic potions, of candy floss, of popcorn. Large bands of travellers, some from Sindh, some from Baluchistan. Chants being sung in some corner; the waft of dope. This is not unlike the Kumbh Mela.

The thousands around the mausoleum are gathered for an Urs – the celebration of a saint's death, that is, of his union with Allah. There is an Urs on at any time in Multan, for Multan is one of the world's great centres of Sufism and other cultic, mystical branches of Islam. Their affection is for song, dance, taveez, personal *pirs*, tomb worship, all of it frowned upon by orthodox Islam.

And so there is a mystical validation for everything in Multan. The famously revatilising qualities of its clay-based soil, used in

Overwhelming as it was, the security was never really able to cast a shadow on the message of peace and love. Least of all in Karachi.

Shoaib v Sachin: the headline image of the tour. Both men gave their best performances of the one-day series at Pindi. Sachin's off-side driving in the early part of this innings was exquisite: here, frozen, the most classic of strokes.

The intoxicating contrasts of colour at Peshawar's Arbab Niaz Stadium: the garish red and blue advertisement boards, below them a sea of white and grey shalwar kameez, and down in the bowl, sky blue and deep green going at it. And pictured here is also the shot of the match, perhaps even the series: Yuvraj's flat, pirouetting six over fine-leg off Shoaib.

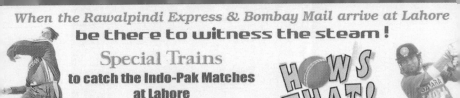

When the Rawalpindi Express & Bombay Mail arrive at Lahore
**be there to witness the steam!**

**Special Trains** to catch the Indo-Pak Matches at Lahore

The visiting passengers must have
- Valid Indian Passport • Valid VISA for Pakistan
- Valid Tickets for Lahore matches

For any enquiry regarding booking of tickets, dial 23962389 (8.00 A.M. - 8.00 P.M.)

**NORTHERN RAILWAY**
Passengers' convenience... our concern
Visit us at : www.uttarrailway.com

The headline image once more, used here by the Northern Railways. Over 2,000 Indians travelled on the 'Cricket Specials' for the two Lahore one-dayers, and were waved in by Pakistanis all the way from Wagah to the Lahore terminal. *Below*, a scene from the journey: the dust never really settles in Punjab.

Scenes from the Lahore double-header. 'Love was inevitable': one of the hundreds of peace messages carried by spectators from both countries. *Below*, outside the ground, the scenario was as familiar. At Lahore, things got nastier because 1,500 fake tickets were sold in the black market.

Lahore's batting stars. Inzamam's agility at the crease is often obscured by his bulk, but have a look here at the magnificent gateway described by his legs as he makes the cut. VVS, meanwhile, is all hands, gliding the ball virtually out of Moin's gloves to move to within a run of a sublime century.

India win their first international series in Pakistan in a field dramatically filled with insects; and above, not in the picture, the sky is filled with fireworks.

The Test series has begun. This picture stands out for a variety of reasons. For the light, not the blinding white of daytime Multan, but the invigorating yellow of early evening. For the deep placement of the man at point, which gives a far better idea of Sehwag the batsman than many action shots do. And, mostly, for how the 'K' in Pakistan is quietly resting on its side: for these weeks on tour, Kashmir almost did cease to matter.

Sehwag's demolition of Saqlain at Multan must count among the most relentlessly ruthless in the annals of Test cricket. Is it any wonder that the bowler was reduced to such mid-pitch contemplations?

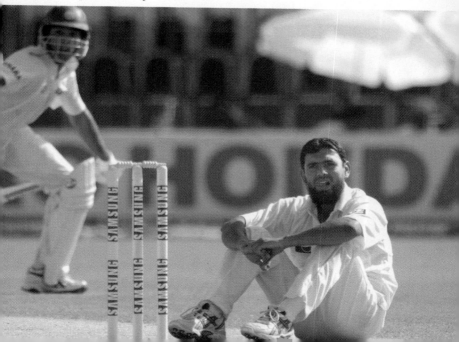

Sachin's moment of genius. The befuddled Moin Khan's position – facing midwicket, after getting bowled between his legs – is testament to the delivery itself, but much of the drama was derived from the circumstances. It was the last ball of the day, with India looking to push the follow-on, and exactly twenty-four hours after Tendulkar's comments about being declared upon on 194 had prompted many in India to brand him 'selfish'.

A bouncy pitch at Lahore, and a good time to play the pull, as the two young centurions, Imran Farhat and Yuvraj Singh, both left-handers, discovered. *Below*, all hail the baby messiah: Gul, Man of the Match at Lahore.

O Life, here I come! This tour will be remembered as the one in which Irfan Khan Pathan, all of nineteen, truly arrived.

If looks could… The Indians did not share a great relationship with umpire Steve Bucknor, not least for his unwillingness to concede lbw decisions to Kumble's flipper. At Lahore, the pot sometimes boiled over.

Two men and star at Pindi. A proper reflection of the turnout during the Tests. *Below*, Balaji, the Indian most popular with locals all tour, showed the puzzling and extremely pretty ability to move the ball one way in the air and another off the pitch at Pindi. Here he bowls Kamran Akmal with one that swung away, then sneaked back between bat and pad. Syndey Barnes would have approved.

The hero on the balcony. Inzamam, behind, can manage a laugh now, but it was not possible for long, as relations between captain and spearhead deteriorated beyond repair at Pindi. From before play on day one to the afternoon on day four, these pictures mirror the decline.

At Pindi Dravid played the longest, and among the most important, Test innings ever played by an Indian. This is a wonderful cricket picture because it establishes without fuss the core of Dravid's ethos: the care he takes over his craft. How blunted bowlers must feel.

Climax. The substitutes were on the pitch and in the huddle even before Kaneria, the last man out (poignantly, c Ganguly b Tendulkar) had managed to leave the square.

face packs, may be mystically extended to the dust: 'Yeh toh hamari Multani mitti...' (This, our Multani mitti...) And the heat, the heat is because of the saint who, when being flogged to death, called upon the sun to avenge him, so that Multan became closer to the sun than any other place on earth. And so a hardy pride, 'Yeh toh kuchh nahin, aap May mein dekhna...' (This is nothing, just wait for May...)

Multan abounds with Multani pride.

Thus, Nadeem, another bearer, an aspiring actor, at the Sindbad, on instant messenger with the nickname: 'I leave in the second oldest city of the world', flanked by red roses. Thus the gentle boast on Hamaramultan.com: 'People are polite like cotton, and sweet like mango.' And thus, Khurram, the under-19 cricketer at the stadium: 'Punjab hai woh Multan ke wajah se. Actors dekhiye aap, sab Multan ke. Politicans aap dekhiye, sab Multan ke. Cricket mein facilities kam, lekin talent mein no. 1.' (What Punjab is, it is because of Multan. You see the actors, all from Multan. You see the politicians, all from Multan. In cricket, facilities are less, but in talent we're no. 1.)

And then, with a smile: 'So, how's it passing in Multan?'

*

IN AUGUST 2001, Test cricket returned to Multan after twenty years. This is half true: the new Multan Cricket Stadium is not actually in Multan town. It is a forty-five-minute drive out by car, more than an hour by autorickshaw, off the highway south to Vehari, in the middle of farmland.

From the highway turn-off till the stadium is a stretch of road where no public buses venture. There is no public transport at all outside the stadium. By night there is no light on this stretch, and if you're stuck, as we were once, the only option is to walk out twenty minutes to the highway and hope that an auto or a bus comes by. This can take a while. I read reports that special shuttle services had been organised between the town centre and the stadium for the Test. I saw no evidence of it.

All around the stadium, flat, brown earth, criss-crossed with low mud partitions, spread out in every direction as far as the eye could see.

The stadium itself is excellent. It had been built, thoughtfully, in all brick, with occasional inserts of the Multani turquoise tile. There was a roof above every stand. Most were fitted with bucket seats or loose chairs. The media were pleased with their arrangements. There was a lustre of newness about.

The lustre extended to the cricket teams. Personnel had left, personnel had arrived. Touring parties generally find themselves boosted by this. No matter what, staleness creeps in when individuals are together for too long.

Three Indians had joined the squad: Anil Kumble, bowling Atlas; Aakash Chopra, to take first strike; and Ajit Agarkar, as standby seamer. Hemang Badani, who had played the first game at Karachi, and Amit Bhandari, the replacement for Nehra midway through the one-day series, had returned. Ganguly watched from the dressing-room balcony. The physiotherapy sessions for his back had not yielded encouraging results. He would not play. Dravid would lead.

Pakistan had made four additions and three deletions to their one-day squad. Gone were Shahid Afridi, Younis Khan and Naved-ul-Hasan; in were Danish Kaneria, our Karachi leggie, Umar Gul, a lively young seamer from NWFP, Asim Kamal, a sturdy left-hand middle-order batsman, and Misbah-ul-Haq, also a middle-order batsman (and, like Imran Khan, a Niazi from Mianwalli, where the tribe had settled in the thirteenth century), who had been with the squad for the first two one-dayers.

178

Between the practising teams, under an umbrella and a floppy hat, in a checked bush shirt, khaki shorts and bare feet, was the very large and now-familiar figure of Andy Atkinson.

I had been asked to do a little chat with Atkinson by *The Wisden Cricketer* magazine. Nothing flash, an Englishman in Pakistan type of thing.

Atkinson was a plain-speaking, middle-aged man with ruddy skin and a loud voice that complemented his frame. As a country boy, he says, he would run the tractor in his father's farm in Southend-on-Sea in Essex, a hobby which earned him the responsibility of maintaining the outfield at his local club, Rankins CC. From there he powered his way up the CCs: to Essex CCC, up to the MCC, and finally to the ICC, with whom he was now contracted as pitch consultant.

Atkinson had been roped in by Pakistan following the loss at home to England in 2000-01, a series where England stalled, stalled, stalled on lifeless surfaces, and moved in for the kill at the very end. So in typical style, the PCB handed Atkinson the grand agenda – improve every pitch in Pakistan, international, domestic, the whole lot, and equip local curators to look after the same. 'Improve' specifically meant increase the bounce.

This was Atkinson's fifth visit to Pakistan in three years. He believed his work had already yielded results, and as proof cited the previous season's series against South Africa, where one Test had a result of the last day, the other was saved on the last day, batsmen played shots, and wickets were shared equally between pacemen and spinners.

Atkinson's programme for Pakistan involved digging up playing squares at the major centres because the high content of water-retentive clay in the soil meant the pitches would always be soft. At best, an exaggerated grass cover would provide lateral movement. So a foot-deep bed of crushed stone was laid underneath, the cracks in them allowing water to trickle through. Upon the stone were piled 6, as opposed to the earlier 14, inches of topsoil. This soil was sourced uniformly from Nandipur, a few hours north of Lahore, where clay and sand merged in happy quantities. Basically, locals would be hurt to learn, the Atkinson recipe involved removing plenty of Multani mitti and replacing it with gravel and Nandipur mitti.

I asked Atkinson about grass. It served two purposes, he said. One, to bind the surface; that is, to prevent, or rather delay, its disintegration. There cannot be a pitch without any grass. And two, to siphon up moisture to the surface. It is moisture which assists seam and swing bowlers, though the dynamics of that is a separate matter. In these temperatures, though, grass dies an early death. So when they talk about the first morning being the most receptive to bowling, it is because the grass is at its most active, and because the topsoil contains its greatest reserve of moisture.

It was grass that had led Atkinson to a national bollocking after the one-day series. The fury was that, Peshawar apart, Pakistan's scalp-scorching fast bowlers were provided shirtfronts on which the Indian batsmen had prospered.

Responding to this, for the first time in an hour, Atkinson raised his, ahem, pitch.

'Mindless hysteria. I mean, people talk through their hat, grass this and grass that, and it's all rubbish. Look, first of all, this is the entertainment business. So my glib answer is simply – look at the scoreboards. One-day cricket is about entertainment, that's how the game makes money, and people don't come in to see teams making 110 and 120. It's like going to see a three-act play and they say we're going to play only one. The fact is that if Pakistan had bowled a bit better in the first fifteen overs in Karachi, they would have won the match, fact is that... I've been quite amazed by the press hysteria, really, quite amazed...'

He'd not seen nothing yet.

The pitch at the moment looked rather bald. Around it the outfield was an almost painted green, an oasis around barrenness. It was not like this, I was told, a day ago. The pitch had been shaved. Atkinson would not be drawn into a discussion. He was not allowed to. 'It will last five days...'

A casual pre-match ambience hung over the field. Javed bhai entertained a few queries from reporters. This was Pakistan's 300th Test match. Miandad had played the 100th and captained in the 200th. It's hard to imagine him ever not being there. A little boy in an oversized Pakistan jersey was taken to shake hands with Tendulkar. He was Inzamam's son. A ball came rolling my way. I stopped it with my foot. 'Typical Bengali!' Dravid called out amiably, referring to the Bengali proclivity for football.

The XIs for both teams were reasonably clear. Pakistan would open with Taufeeq and Farhat; with Yasir, Inzamam and Youhana in the middle; the all-rounder, Razzaq, and the keeper, Moin, at nos. 6 and 7; followed by the three pace Ss, Shoaib, Sami and Shabbir; and the eleventh spot to one of the two spinners, Saqlain or Kaneria.

India would open with Sehwag and Chopra; Dravid, Tendulkar, Laxman and Yuvraj would bring up the middle; Parthiv, the keeper, to follow; and then the bowlers, Irfan, Kumble, Zaheer and Balaji. The only other thought was to play a second spinner, Kartik, ahead of a seamer.

The organisers at Multan were not so sure. In the brochure prepared for the match, they had accounted for a quite different lot. Where, for example, was Narinder Sehwag? And what about Parto Patel? And that great emancipator of the southern province, Yuvraj Sindh? And where, for heaven's sake, was the ravishing Sara Gangulli?

\*

181

**Day One**
*I've been called a few things in my time – mostly by disgruntled bowlers who have taken a lashing. They have labelled me Mr. Wrong, the guy who gets away with murder.*

*Well, who cares. Perhaps I do shock the purists with a few of my unorthodox shots like the sweep and hook but the ball rattles the boundary fence more times than it rattles the stumps. And after all that's what the game is all about isn't it?*

SO BEGINS the autobiography of Rohan Kanhai. Kanhai has jumped straight into it. No preludes, no sighters. And after all that's what the thrill is with these guys, isn't it?

Urged by the prospect of this thrill, I climbed up to the grandstand above the press box, as Indian cricket's Mr Wrong smacked two boundaries from his first eleven balls.

Not a soul. Five policemen in a row of seats, rifles lamely stretched across their laps, but not a soul else. Across, above the pavilion, a few pockets of people, some of them Indians with flags. In the cheaper stands, on the square boundaries, a uniform sprinkling of spectators, sitting deep, in the shade, so that they could be sometimes heard but not quite seen. There were not more than a thousand in, a number that would swell later in the day to about 5,000. The capacity of the stadium was 28,000. The population of Multan town was 1.5 million. The population of Multan district was over 3 million. This was a Sunday.

Below, the figures in white went about their business. You could hear the calling between the batsmen, Chopra with his polite exhortations of 'nahin! rukiye, vahin rukiye!' (no! wait, please wait!); you could hear Moin Khan's big-brother admonishments, 'come on Shoaibi, oopar daal, bete' (come on Shoaibi, pitch it up, son); you could hear David Shepherd's sharp yelps of 'ouv-va'. In that sense I have never felt closer to a Test match. I have also never felt further removed from a Test match. Was this really India playing Test cricket in Pakistan after fourteen years?

In this sad desolation, there was something surreal about the sounds of Sehwag. Over after over, relentlessly, he pelted the ball, and the echoes kept clattering around the empty stands, its monotony telling the story of an innings clinical as it was violent, an innings which, when it was completed, stood alone as the most substantial body of work Indian batting has known.

It was an airless day, at 36 C well below Multan's summer peaks of 50 C, but still. If this made Sehwag's job harder, it did the bowling side's doubly so. Already Pakistan had lost the toss on a pitch that was flatter than the ambience, endowed with the truest carry, and devoid of any lateral movement. Sehwag had not looked at the pitch beforehand. He never does.

It took a while to appreciate that the Tests had begun, to adjust to the comedown. By the end of the first hour it emerged that Sehwag's callous echoing slaps and swirls had taken India to 46 for no loss. Chopra had faced 44 deliveries, for 6, with no fours. Sehwag had faced 46 deliveries, for 40, with eight fours.

He quickly added a six, a tipple over third man off Shabbir. It was the most casual of strokes, leaning back, swaying away, flicking up. This was a call to spin, as early as the twentieth over. It was also India's first little victory of the Test series. As in the one-dayers, pace had been put in its place from the start. Already Shoaib and Sami looked small, compromised.

But Saqlain Mushtaq started superbly. He bowled to three men around the bat. He mixed his speed, he varied his angle, and, on a couple of deliveries, extracted sharp turn. In his first two overs he conceded one single to Chopra and nothing else. To Sehwag he bowled five straight dots. Then Sehwag, with a whip and a cut and a loft over midwicket for six, took 14 off his third over.

In that last stroke the Pakistanis sensed opportunity. The slip was pulled out. The leg-side field was strengthened: three men banished to the deep, of whom midwicket was positioned 15 yards inside the fence.

Sehwag considered the situation, defending Saqlain's next over, even padding up a couple of times. That was ample consideration. On the first ball of Saqlain's following over, with his score on 68, Sehwag swung once more. Sami, licking his wounds at midwicket, grassed a sitter at navel height. It felt crucial. If there were people in, a hush would have fallen over the stadium. Sami would later apologise to his country.

And I think something inside Saqlain died at this moment. He played hereafter with sorrow. He himself dropped Sehwag, on 77, off Shoaib. He batted like a goose. He bowled without an ounce of conviction, hiding most of the time behind his leg-side field.

This was a pity, for Saqlain at his best is a wonderful bowler. In the last series between the teams he was ever-penetrative, prying out five-fors in four successive innings. Here he was reduced to caricature.

For only a few days ago the man who added the word 'doosra' to cricket lexicon had announced a *teesra*. And indeed, the *teesra* aroused mystery. Nobody knew how to play it. Nobody knew how to pick it. Nobody knew what to look for because nobody knew what the hell it was supposed to do. It could have been all his deliveries, or it could have been none. It could have been the one where he shuffled in from a steep angle, or it could have been the one where he hustled in from right behind the umpire. It could have been the one where he paused at the crease before delivering, or it could have been the one where he rushed right through. There was just no telling. It could have been the one he bowled with arched eyebrows. Or not. It could have been the one to which Moin responded with 'yoresalfe Seqie'. Or, who knew, possibly even not. As the afternoon wore on, the answer emerged from a corner of the press box: 'Aur yeh teesra... aur yeh chauka!' (And that's the third... and that's a four!).

It was funny then, but not by the end of it, not by the time Sehwag had bullied him to the tune of 91 runs from 80 balls, not by the time he became the only man, after Vinoo Mankad, to concede more than 200 runs in a Test innings for a second time. It was actually quite sad. The mind went to another off-spinner, the great Erapalli Prasanna, whose career ended in Pakistan twenty-six years ago at the hands of Zaheer Abbas and friends. That was Prasanna's forty-ninth Test. This was Saqlain's forty-ninth Test.

Riding his fortune, failing to fret, Sehwag brought up his century within half an hour of lunch. It was his sixth century, in his twenty-first Test. All had come in the first innings, five on the first day, five in different countries, and each against a different team. And each brilliant.

The jump from 95 to 105 was in two balls. A loose jab past gully took him to 99. He exchanged a smile with his partner as Shoaib cussed. Then he uppercut Shoaib for six. He had promised as much in some on-pitch banter during the one-day series, pointing out to Shoaib that he would have no third man in the Tests. Well, third man was in place.

I once had the privilege of speaking to Garfield Sobers about Brian Lara's batsmanship. In particular, I asked about Lara's willingness to risk shots others would not. 'But he does not take risks,' was the response. 'The great attacking batsman does not take risks. They are risks only to others' minds.'

So it is with Sehwag. For ages cricketers have been raised to the commandment 'thou shalt play in the V'. Sehwag plays in the V alright, the V between cover-point and third man. There is nothing scandalous in it. It is his percentage area. New Zealand's

Stephen Fleming once set him a field with three gullies and two deep third men. Sehwag's strategy against strategies is to pretend that there exists no such strategy.

To this end, Sehwag's technique is fascinating. His trigger movement is not back-and-across like some; neither is it the little forward-step like many others; nor is it a shuffle towards middle. Rather, he waits at the crease, his rear foot ever-ready to withdraw outside leg stump. This is his instinct to create width. If he finds the ball to be anything short of full, he retreats deeper into the crease. This is his instinct to create length. To generate momentum in his upper body, he frequently gets off the ground, sometimes with a scissoring motion of the legs. Having set himself up, he lets his marvellous hands take over, slicing, slapping, slashing, swatting above or in between the fielders in his V. Just like that, a reasonable delivery by every conventional parameter has found itself beyond the rope.

I do not know whether Sehwag found himself playing so ever since his earliest days of gully cricket, or whether it was an evolved response to slow Indian pitches, where strokemakers must cultivate creative ways to generate pace off the bat. Laxman, like Azharuddin before him, relies on extraordinary wristwork; Tendulkar on an unusually low, bottom-handed grip and an exceptionally heavy bat. Anyhow, it is ironic that Sehwag should have built his game around these bottom-handed thumps after his coach had spent hours making his ward perform hundreds of top-hand swings with a bat enclosed in a cloth case filled with mud.

By the time he got to 128, with another merciless blast off Saqlain, Sehwag had logged five sixes. Returning for a moment to our modest maestro, Kanhai: 'I've never been one for second best – that is why I never want fours, I want sixes.'

In truth, Kanhai, like Sehwag, was not allergic to fours. They would do fine. Nos. 17, 18 and 19 now arrived in one over against Shabbir. The third of those took his score to 143, from 142 balls, the first time in his innings that runs scored had overtaken balls faced.

The game, in case it was not apparent by now, was running away from Pakistan. At slip, the only slip, Inzamam stood slouched, legs apart, index finger on lips, furrow on brow. He threw the ball to Shoaib for a short burst before tea.

Sehwag responded with a straight-drive off the back foot to his second ball, a classic stroke played with a dangling, diagonal bat. Mr Wrong. Later he picked it as his favourite shot of the day.

It was also a stroke that immensely instigated Shoaib. He began to hurl bouncers and only bouncers. He went round the wicket and aimed them at Sehwag's body. He taunted him and hissed at him and gestured at him. Flat pitch, hot sun, 220 for 2: the Express needed something to stir the blood. Again and again he asked Sehwag to go after the bouncer, perhaps more than that. Word is that Sehwag at one point called out aloud, 'Yeh bowling kar raha hai ya bheekh maang raha hai?' (Is this guy bowling or begging?) Word is that giggles arose from the fieldsmen.

Two overs into the skirmish, Sehwag tapped towards square leg and sauntered an easy single. Only, he directed his path towards Shoaib and deliberately nudged him in the ribs with the bat. Shoaib was not furious. Rather, he saw it as a victory. He stood in the middle of the pitch, arms spread, smiling broadly, and generating a series of 'not on, mate' nods. He'd not drawn blood from a stone but he had made the stone react. The umpires converged on Sehwag, who argued his point, while Shoaib smiled and repeatedly nodded. Inzamam stepped in and put an arm of goodwill around Sehwag's shoulder and play resumed.

Tea came and went. Sehwag cracked fifteen runs off a Razzaq over, yawning almost as he did so. There are batsmen who endure entire careers without having taken ten or more runs off a Test-match over. Sehwag had crossed ten in an over six times already on this day. This was opening batsmanship, twenty-first century style, a force as potent as new-ball bowling.

Only in the 190s did Sehwag pause. His back had become stiff. He was mindful, too, of his experience at the Melbourne Cricket Ground three months ago, when he holed out on the verge of the double, trying to belt a six off a full-toss from a part-timer tweaker.

In all, he spent half an hour in the 190s, and faced 26 balls. On two occasions he took leave of his penance, slapping Saqlain to the square-leg fence, and later flashing and missing an uppercut off Shabbir. His tenth ball on 199 he gently clipped to long leg and ran two. It made him the third Indian double-centurion against Pakistan, after Anshuman Gaekwad, who made 201 at Jalandhar in 1983-84, and Sanjay Manjrekar, who compiled 218 at Lahore in 1989-90. In total, Manjrekar's innings was almost nine hours long. Gaekwad's was more than eleven. Sehwag, at the moment, was on a shade over five.

As Pakistan struggled in the withering vacantness, Sehwag called for his navy-blue ice collar and chilled out till stumps. 'Shot khelo,' his partner had told him all afternoon, 'lekin shot banao mat' (Play shots, but don't manufacture shots). And Tendulkar himself had crept up to a most invisible, most meticulous 60.

*India 356 for 2 (Sehwag 228\*, Tendulkar 60\*, Sami 1-54) in 90 overs*

\*

188

**Day Two**

HE GAVE OFF a hint of circumspection in the morning but no more than a hint. For the most part Sehwag flayed and slapped and swirled ever onwards, and then the iffy moments began piling up. On 267, he came close to being lbw against Shabbir. On 269, he slashed Shabbir past the man at point, who got his fingertips to the ball. On 274, he was almost run out. Also on 274, he edged Shabbir and Taufeeq Umar at slip made an effort so full of torpor that it recalled the image of the eternal crocodile resting with its mouth open. The ball raced away for four. Shabbir's knees melted under him and he buried his head in his bosom. The next ball, Sehwag, 278, timed so well that third man could not make the 10 yards to it. With this he surpassed the Indian record of 281 held by V.V.S. Laxman, who rose to applaud in the dressing room balcony, pads and earphones on. The next ball Sehwag edged again, and it touched Moin's gloves on the way to a third consecutive four. Shabbir dissipated away towards mid-off in a trail of anguish.

India took lunch at 467 for two. Sehwag was on 292.

On the stroke of 1, Sehwag became India's first triple centurion. He swaggered down two steps to the second ball he faced from Saqlain after the interval and launched into a roundhouse blast, a primal kind of blast, to the left of the man at deep midwicket, right of the man at deep long-on, and soaring over them both, over the 10 yards between the rope and the boundary boards, over the 20 yards between the boundary boards and the black metal grill, and into a thinly populated pink concrete stand beyond.

Nobody could have expected this. Everybody expected just this. Tendulkar was to smile later at the futility of his efforts. 'I talk to him. He always hears me, but I'm not sure if he ever listens to me.' It was a wise producer who remarked: 'You don't produce Ray Charles. You just get out of his way.'

189

Sehwag took 497 minutes and 364 balls for his monument. In terms of balls, it was two slower than Matthew Hayden's against Zimbabwe five months earlier. Wally Hammond's 288-minute effort against New Zealand in 1932-33 was almost certainly quicker: not recorded in *Wisden* but given in some sources as having come from 355 balls. Sehwag was the seventeenth triple-centurion in Test cricket. None of the other sixteen heralded it with a six. It is doubtful if any of them contemplated it.

India's wait for the 300 was of 374 Test matches, and 71 years and 279 days. The five countries that had produced a triple centurion had all done it quicker. Hanif Mohammad provided Pakistan one in their sixth year.

Accordingly, within six months of the feat an England-based NRI would gift him GBP 50,000; the Delhi District Cricket Association would announce the naming of a gate to their refurbished international stadium after him; Sareen Sports, a leading equipment manufacturer, would release a 'Veeru 309' range of bats; and his old university, Jamia Millia Islamia, would grant him an honorary degree, a Bachelor of Arts, I understand, in Political Science with Geography.

It is not the least bit surprising that Sehwag should have been India's barrier-breaker. 'He was not in any way inhibited,' C.L.R. James has written of W.G. Grace. 'What he lacked he would not need. All that he had he could use.' Sehwag never obstructs himself. All he has he uses. He has nothing of the image of the thinking cricketer. Secretly, everybody wishes they could think like him. His clarity I have not seen in an Indian batsman. Gavaskar, I imagine, must have had the same awesome quality.

On 309, Sehwag nicked Sami, and Taufeeq held the first of the three catches which had come his way since joining the team on the twenty-fourth of March.

# A *nation went potty*

RAHUL DRAVID DECLARED the innings when Yuvraj Singh became the fifth man out. India were on 675, their second highest score in away matches, thirty less than their highest, which had come in their previous Test, at Sydney. Tendulkar was batting 194, six short of what would have been his second double-hundred in successive Tests, and the fourth of his career. Among Indians, the first feat had been achieved only by his best friend Vinod Kambli and the second by only Dravid and Gavaskar.

Tendulkar walked back matter-of-factly to the pavilion, and did not take the field thereafter, citing a tweaked ankle.

There was a strange mood at the evening's press conference. Sehwag and Tendulkar sat side by side. The first question was not put to Sehwag about his triple but to Tendulkar about missing the double. He said: 'It's a disappointment, obviously... It's a real disappointment having got so close...'

It was a long interaction, about twenty minutes. Tendulkar was in a fairly good mood, joking and laughing and speaking glowingly of Sehwag whenever asked. The declaration question, naturally, would resurface every few minutes. I lump together here fragments of the inquisition:

Asked if he knew whether the declaration would come when it did, he replied: 'I was aware it was around the corner, but I was taken by surprise. I thought we would bowl at them for an hour or so. I thought it would come in three-four overs.' Asked if, on returning, he had asked the captain why the declaration was made, he said: 'No. If one has not been able to achieve something, there is no point talking about it. You just have to get on with the game.' Asked what the thought behind the declaration was, he answered: 'I really don't know about it. If a side is scoring at four runs an over, that is a very positive run-rate in Test cricket. When Yuvraj got out I saw Rahul calling us back, so I informed the umpires.' Asked if he had any regrets about the speed at which he had batted, he said: 'What has happened has happened. Four is a positive run-rate in Test cricket. If I haven't been able to achieve more, nothing can be done about it.'

And with that India was thrown into commotion. Countrywide, on the streets, in the newspapers, on bulletin boards on the Internet, on 'our panel tonight' on television, among fans, among non-fans, the talk was of the Multan declaration.

The press fanned the flames, some reporting Tendulkar's comments as an 'outburst', some claiming he was 'livid'. An uncle with whom I had not spoken for ages rang and inquired. Even my mother asked about it.

Stalwarts everywhere weighed in with their opinions. Allan Border agreed with the declaration. So did Mohinder Amarnath. Intikhab Alam slammed it. Vinod Kambli remarked that Tendulkar 'will not sleep tonight' and expressed his sympathy. Ricky Ponting stated he would have allowed Tendulkar the mark: 'If Sachin is feeling a bit down I can understand why.' (Twenty days later, Ponting was to slam Brian Lara's 400 as selfish: 'It's hard to imagine an Australian player doing it.') Inzamam gleefully told the press he would 'definitely have given a chance to his batsman to reach 200'.

Imran Khan threw his support behind the declaration – he had, after all, once declared with Miandad on 280, an act to which Miandad dedicated an entire whingeing chapter in his autobiography. Reminded of the event now, Imran baritoned: 'I'd do the same thing a hundred times over, a *thousand* times over...' Needless to say where Miandad's sympathies lay: 'Don't worry, Sachin, it is a part of life. Mistakes happen and your team-mates have made a mistake.'

Sanjay Manjrekar, on air at the time, called it a 'huge' moment in Indian cricket, and elaborated, grandly, in a later column: 'As I write this a fortnight later I still believe that it was indeed a very special point in India's cricket history – the start of a new vision. It was a moment when one saw the roots taking grip, the dawning of a realisation that cricket is indeed a team game... Tendulkar, understandably perhaps, felt aggrieved that he was left stranded on 194 but the surprise that he expressed at the press conference about the timing of the declaration was a little curious. You would expect someone like Tendulkar to have noticed the change in the thinking of the Indian dressing room since he first entered it in 1989.'

Ian Chappell, also commentating on the game, referred to it, equally grandly, as a 'declaration of independence' in his column. 'The fact that Tendulkar is such a superstar in Indian cricket and was on the brink of scoring a double century in successive Tests makes the act even braver and more important to Indian cricket. It will have left an indelible impression on the younger members of the team who appear to be imbued with a winning attitude and the older brigade having grown up in a different culture will now not be in any doubt about the priorities of the side.'

The worldwideweb was aflame. 'Crybaby Sachin!' one bulletin-board post was titled, the reader contending that 'Sachin like Gavaskar has always played for the record books'. Another saw the situation as something of a personal victory after years of arguing with the deluded masses around him: 'Finally Tendulkar, THE HYPED, shows his real colours'. One letter writer to a national newspaper reasoned that 'when it comes to India-Pakistan cricket, it is only natural to be superstitious', pointing out that India never won when Tendulkar made a double-century: 'Perhaps, by stopping Sachin Tendulkar from getting another double ton, Rahul Dravid wanted to be safe rather than sorry.' One shattered fan urged Tendulkar to lodge a complaint with the ICC about the deplorable behaviour of his colleagues.

Up in the press box, the initial reaction was one of bewilderment. Soon, the smell of a great story obscured all else. An occasion like this is a boon for reporters on tour. It lends itself to all kinds of space-filling – comment, speculation, reaction, source quotes, moral posturing. And what a story! It involved cricket, three superstars, and conspiracy theories. It could have been tailor-made for an Indian national discussion.

Reporters jabbed away at their targets. The Indian players, to their eternal credit, did not yield. Sooner or later, it was thought, somebody would relent. Not a peep out of anyone; not the makeshift captain, not the indisposed captain, not the extras who ran out with water and messages, not the coach, not the manager, not the media manager, not, of course, Tendulkar.

*The Telegraph* did report that a 'very senior member initially didn't believe Sachin actually spoke in the manner he did. "Is that what he said?" he asked, distinctly troubled.' An over-enthusiastic reporter for *The Pioneer* quoted Ganguly as having dissociated himself from the decision, and saying that, 'Even I would have reacted the way Sachin did.' Only, our man had not spoken to Ganguly at all. This then led to Ganguly conference-calling Dravid and the reporter on the phone to clear the air.

Best of all were the tales told during the smoke-breaks. My favourite one goes thus: Dravid, who has been watching calmly so far, suddenly jolts up from his seat at Yuvraj's dismissal and prepares to announce the declaration. The youth brigade – Sehwag, Chopra and co. – are taken aback. They try intervening with a Bollywood style slow scream: 'Raaahulll... nahhiiin'. But Rahul's mind is made up. He does the deed. There is shock in the dressing room. In the silence, VVS turns slowly towards Rahul and hushes with soft melodrama: 'Rahul?' Ganguly, meanwhile, has headed down and is already in the car by the time Tendulkar returns. And by the time Tendulkar is addressing the press conference,

Ganguly is lounging in the swimming pool of the team hotel. The sequence ends with this scene.

Finally, before returning to Kolkata briefly for back treatment, Ganguly broke the silence in an interview to ESPN-Star, with whom he was contracted:

Anyone who doesn't get a double hundred would be disappointed. If he had got out for 194 he would have been disappointed at himself. Being not out at 194 I can understand that he'd get disappointed a bit. But see, I feel we should not make it an issue. We all make mistakes. I don't want to say who's made a mistake – even if Rahul's made a mistake by declaring it at 194 or if Sachin's made a mistake making a statement... Whoever it is made a mistake it's for the team to accept it – for Rahul to accept it, for Sachin to accept it, us to accept it and go ahead... Let's finish this off as an issue because it's a side that has done well in two years – it's a side that has given hope to a lot of Indian fans and taken Indian cricket to new heights. Sachin and Rahul and myself are big contributors. Whoever has made a mistake let's just go ahead and forget it and see if we can win the series. You've seen everyone give their best on the cricket field. Among friends a lot of things happen. That's why you're friends, you forget it and your team goes ahead.

Heartfelt as it was, this, as you can see, did not particularly further the story. And anyhow, for many it did not matter what Ganguly said or did not say. He was already the culprit. One observer said to me that Ganguly's lips could be read on telly: 'double-century ke liye khel raha hai yeh' (he's playing for a double-century).

That Ganguly was in favour of the declaration was true. He

said so in almost as many words in later interviews, pointing out that he had declared at Sydney in the second innings with Dravid on 91, and that in the first innings of the same Test they had erred by batting too long – a mistake they did not want to repeat here. But to transfer the decision to declare so coolly and so fully on to Ganguly was remarkable. It did not, for one, do any justice to Dravid, who may be the self-effacing sort but certainly knows his own mind.

In any case, Ganguly was brought into the picture only by those who sought to rail against the declaration, not praise it. It was the worst kind of opportunism. Nowhere was this starker than in Bal Thackeray's newspaper, the Marathi daily, *Samna*, based in Bombay, Tendulkar's hometown. (While browsing through *Samna* archives I also stumbled upon an article headlined 'Inzamam has converted Youhana to a Muslim', a plain lie. Indeed, Youhana, a Christian, quite obviously makes the sign of the cross when he reaches a landmark while batting. And before the year was out he would captain his country in a Test match.) The newspaper carried reports and photographs of demonstrating youth burning posters of Ganguly, and chanting 'Ganguly Murdabad!' and 'Sachin se jo takrayega, Mitti me mil jayega' (Death to Ganguly! He who clashes with Sachin will be obliterated). But who, precisely, were these youngsters? Members of the Sena's own youth wing.

Two days after the declaration, *Samna* carried on its front page a most septic assault by a renowned Marathi journalist. A graphic juxtaposed the faces of a smiling Sachin and an insolent Ganguly. 'Is Ganguly jealous of Sachin?' the headline read. Just in case the rhetoric was lost, the answer was provided below, in bigger font still: 'Yes'. The writer, whose column for the series was helpfully slugged 'Maidan-e-Jung' (Battlefield), spent time building a case for Ganguly's jealousy of Tendulkar's achievements, attributing it as the reason, for instance, for his opening a restaurant

196

(Tendulkar had opened one), and his asking Tendulkar to bat down the order for a while in one-day cricket. Further, the writer argued, while Tendulkar got along brilliantly with the Mumbai cricket team, in Pakistan he had been given a golf club and a ball to play with in the hotel corridor. (In fact, this had been a late-night impromptu game to kill boredom inside the security-net at Rawalpindi, one that his team-mates joined in.) Anyway, the conclusion: 'Ganguly has used Dravid's shoulder to fire the shot.'

And this seemed to be something of a catchphrase at *Samna*. It was endorsed by a letter writer responding to the article (eight of the nine published letters were in agreement with the column). The phrase had been used, too, by Machchindra Kambli, a Marathi theatre personality, in an immediate reaction in the newspaper: 'Bengalidada has used Dravid's shoulder to fire the gun. The middle-order is so good that it is high time Ganguly takes a VRS and plays as a non-playing captain.'

Meanwhile, across the country, in Kolkata, the press largely left Ganguly out of it. Some seemed to almost go out of their way to emphasise the point. Commented, for instance, *Bartaman* (as translated in *The Indian Express*):

We are pained, angry. What kind of a decision by Rahul Dravid is this? Dravid has earned the wrath of millions of cricket lovers all over India for depriving Sachin, the legend of Indian cricket, of a certain double century.

Apparently mild spoken and not so publicity hungry, this Kannada youth used to be thought of as a cricketer of a different mentality. But Mr Dravid, extremely sorry to tell you that you have fallen sharply in one go from the high pedestal of respect you enjoyed from Indian cricket lovers.

We would like to know if Sourav had a role to play in this decision. Was it in the interest of the team or in self-interest? We all know this Test is going to be a draw, why was Sachin deprived of his feat? Is it because Dravid did not want Sachin (who has three double tons now) to touch his record of four double centuries in test cricket that he holds now with Sunil Gavaskar?

Machchindra Kambli of Maharashtra attacked the 'Bengalidada'. *Bartaman* of Bengal attacked the 'Kannada youth'. A declaration was made in a cricket match at Multan, a nation went potty, a nation stood exposed.

THAT TENDULKAR'S WORDS at the press conference were pounced on was not surprising. What was surprising was the ire that his innings provoked. Several columnists and commentators suggested it was far too pussyfooted, selfish even, and left it at that. But in less confined channels, on Internet message boards and in private conversations, a certain disgust was expressed. Shameless was the word two people used to me.

This I found extraordinary. Extraordinary not because Tendulkar's work was being husked through the same critical sieve as the next guy. That process had begun at least three years ago, and rightly. I found it extraordinary because Tendulkar's was, in fact, an incorruptibly appropriate innings. I have studied it from all angles, again and again. It is impossible to find a flaw. It did not impose itself on the consciousness. But it is not possible to find a flaw.

Let alone giving a chance, in itself rare for an innings of this length, Tendulkar barely played and missed over a day and a half. It was a minimalist innings. He tickled the first ball he faced to fine leg for four. All through he was to make a fool of that man, as well as third man. Masterpieces in minimalism, too, were the punches through cover and extra-cover, off the front and the back foot: negligible pick-up, negligible follow-through, a split-second in time seized.

I remember Tendulkar similarly occupying this high plane of minimalism on an equally flat pitch in Georgetown in 2002. Taking a cue from England a few months before, West Indies set him 7-2 fields and bowled outside off. But Tendulkar kept getting behind the line and punching it or flicking it wide of the man at mid-on. The great West Indian strokemaker, Everton Weekes, remarked that it was a privilege to be in attendance, and added, because of its subtlety, few would be able to discern the skill involved.

There had been one aerial sweep off Saqlain before, but otherwise Tendulkar's first really expansive shot at Multan came on 150, a full-fledged crack over point off Shabbir, a stroke he repeated in Shabbir's next over. Cricketers at any level will identify with the disquieting helplessness of being bled dry, the halal method. If Sehwag gave Pakistan no respite, Tendulkar gave them no hope.

Above all, Tendulkar's innings was, and this is the crucial point, a masterclass in pacing. His 194 runs came from 348 balls, that is, at 3.34 runs per over, a good if not spectacular rate by the standards of the day, and higher than his own career strike rate. But we must deconstruct further.

Breaking up the innings into fifties is tempting but would ignore the flow of the game. As it happens, it divides itself naturally into thirds; the first 60 runs – his efforts on day one; the next 70 runs – up until the point Sehwag was out; and the last 64 runs – the home stretch.

Tendulkar's 60 runs on the first afternoon took him 144 balls. This encompassed playing himself in, absorbing the loss of the two wickets which had fallen in the space of three overs, seeing through the second new ball in the final hour, and staying there with Sehwag. The pair not only remained unbeaten till stumps, but in that time added 183 runs at almost 4 an over.

Tendulkar's next 70 runs, on the second morning, came from 113 balls. Sehwag and he in this period added 153 runs in 36 overs, that is, at 4.25 runs per over. Totally, their third-wicket stand was of 336 runs at precisely 4 an over.

Tendulkar's final 64 runs came from 91 balls, and the last 40 of them in 45. India in this period added 166 runs at close to 5 an over. This included the final sprint of 110 runs with Yuvraj. Yuvraj outscored Tendulkar in their stand (59 to 40), but their *rates* were virtually identical. Tendulkar did not get his runs quite so visibly as Yuvraj, hitting only four fours to Yuvraj's eight. But I could see a logic in this. I could see it benefitting the team.

As recently as three Tests ago, at Melbourne, India had paid the price of squandering a start. They were 278 for 1 when Sehwag fell for 195. Then they collapsed to 366 all out, lost the match, and it cost them the series. Tendulkar saw to it that Sehwag's work at Multan was not undone. Test cricket is full of examples where the quest for quick runs becomes a self-defeating exercise. Tendulkar's was a deeply nuanced effort.

That left the question of motivation, the allegation that he was playing towards a (not out) 200 and nothing else. How much must we second-guess a man's motives? Or, more relevantly, who cares what he was thinking? His work spoke for itself.

My own feeling was that Tendulkar would have derived immense satisfaction from the innings. Obsessive men seek mastery not success. Garcia Marquez considers his best book not *One Hundred Years of Solitude* but *Chronicle of a Death Foretold* because, 'I did exactly what I wanted to do with it.' At the end of his career Bradman rated the 254 at Lord's in 1930 as his greatest innings not because of the strength of the bowling (Larwood absent, Gubby Allen playing his first Test), nor the conditions (1,500 runs in less than four days), nor even because of the match situation, though it was made in a series-levelling cause and while he was still twenty-one. By the usual parameters, Bradman had constructed several superior innings – the triple-hundred in a single day at Leeds; 103 not out in a total of 191 in his second innings of the Bodyline series following a golden duck in his first; 270 from 97 for 5 at the MCG in 1936-37, a point from where Australia rallied to win the series 3-2 after being down 0-2. Yet, this was his rationale behind selecting the 254: 'Practically without exception every ball went where I wanted it to.' Likewise, Dravid for a long time, even after his Kolkata 180 and several other influential knocks, regarded his 190 in a run-filled draw against New Zealand in 1998-99 as his finest innings. 'I felt in control all the way; I was in good touch throughout the innings and hardly made any mistakes.'

Tendulkar's game in the last five years had revolved around eliminating mistakes rather than defying them. At times he looked terribly careworn. At times he looked a shadow of himself. At times it was tempting to play him REM singing 'you wore our expectations like an armoured suit', in the hope that he would rip it off. But he seldom did. Every time he took the crease he primed himself for a residence in this exalted realm of blemishlessness. Now, having held his position sublimely for eight hours in this batting nirvana, circumstances had conspired to give him a *kanpat* at the very end. I felt for him.

THE TWO RUDEST declarations in Test history must be Gerry Alexander's at Bridgetown in 1959-60 with Frank Worrell on 197, and Michael Atherton's at Sydney in 1994-95 with Graeme Hick on 98.

Alan Ross, in his tour account, *Through the Caribbean*, shows little sympathy towards Worrell. At one stage, with his score past 150, Ross tells us, Worrell batted two hours for 10 runs. 'Alexander several times signalled to Worrell for some action, but Worrell, off on some pipedream of his own, chose to ignore him.' Eventually, 'Worrell remained on 197 for so long that Alexander was able to declare without evidence of malice.'

The Atherton-Hick case is more instructive. As opposed to Bridgetown, where a draw was already set in stone, this was a third-innings declaration in an Ashes series that England were trailing. Hick, by all accounts, had batted reasonably, but when he blocked three consecutive balls on 98 with the declaration imminent, Atherton pulled the plug. Looking back in his autobiography, Atherton reckoned that 'in purely cricketing terms the move was entirely justified'. But he regretted 'the disheartening effect on the team precisely at a time when we ought to have been itching to get at Australia'. He recalled going over to Hick's room that evening and finding him withdrawn. The two barely spoke for the rest of the tour.

I quite liked the Multan declaration. That it had to come round about when it did was not in question. Enough runs had been made. Enough toil had been dished out to the Pakistani bowlers. And there was a logic in declaring on one's own terms, rather than risk buoying opponents with a clatter of wickets. As ever, Tendulkar had done the sums in his head. But while anticipating an 'hour or so' of fielding in the evening, perhaps he had failed to account for the two overs of change-over time between innings: as it turned out, India took precisely sixty-one minutes to complete the sixteen overs in the evening.

It was certainly an audacious thing for Dravid to have done. Some observers referred to it as a symbolic moment. There was nothing symbolic about the moment itself. It was as direct a message as possible. And by being such a direct order, it also ran the risk of coming across as rude. Without it being intended, it had a feel of 'let's put the little man in his place'.

For, the point I think was not whether Tendulkar had been denied the double or not, but whether he had been given an indication of it or not. Later, he was to mention privately that all he wanted was a visible signal from the dressing room. Ramesh Powar did make two trips to the centre in the hour after tea. What messages did he carry? He would not tell. Tendulkar had made him promise so and he would honour it.

By expressing himself, Tendulkar momentarily betrayed a vulnerability within the team, softening the hard message the declaration was meant to have sent out. I found it difficult to hold that against him. Indeed, I found myself warming to him more than usual. His was the most human, the most natural of confessions. He was not 'livid' and it was not an 'outburst'. It was not even unfair. He played a wonderful innings and answered a question honestly and in both he revealed something of himself. Perhaps he should have slipped in a line somewhere that while he was upset, he could appreciate the team's needs. Equally, his comments could be interpreted as an indication of an evolved environment, where adults working together are able to express their points of view without necessarily undermining their common cause.

And Tendulkar and Dravid proved that by having a long chat the following morning, preventing the type of estrangement that Hick and Atherton were to suffer.

Looking back, it was quite a small thing. Looking back, the lesson from the Multan declaration was that few things gnaw at India's soul like Tendulkar.

*Pakistan 42 for 0 in 16 overs (Farhat 17\*, Taufeeq 20\*) trail India 675 for 5 decl in 161.5 overs (Sehwag 309, Tendulkar 194\*, Yuvraj 59, Sami 2-110 ) by 633 runs*

\*

203

## Day Three

THERE WAS ENOUGH weighing him down already, so when Inzamam was inquisitioned about the spectator void he sank into his shoulders and pulled his most burdened face yet. 'Abhi kya kahoon... main tikkte bhi toh nahin bech sakta...' (What to say... I can't go and sell tickets also now, can I?)

Inzamam's resignation was valid. If anybody should have been able to entice locals to the stadium it was him, but even the prospect of Inzamam, coupled with a 50 per cent discount on tickets, proved not quite irresistible to Multanis. It still ensured the best turnout of the Test.

I watched much of the second session from the Inzamam-ul-Haq Enclosure. This is bigger than it sounds. It commands a sweeping view of the field, from over the bowler's arm at the pavilion end. Inzamam's stand held, at the moment, more than a thousand, making a goodly din.

Though the Multan Division Cricket Association – which represents several districts in southern Punjab, including that of Multan – has supplied a reasonable number of national cricketers in the previous two decades, Multan town has been a barren land. A stand in the stadium is named after the Elahi brothers, Mansoor, Zahoor and Saleem, all of whom played for Pakistan; but really they are from Sahiwal district, halfway up to Lahore. As is Mushtaq Ahmed. Waqar Younis comes from Burewala, a small cotton-growing town by the Sutlej, in the district of Vehari. Shabbir Ahmed, in the current XI, and Masood Anwar, who played, and helped save, one Test in 1990-91, come from Khanewal district, adjoining Multan. Mohammad Zahid, briefly a fast-bowling sensation in the mid-1990s, is from the village of Gaggu Mandi. This leaves Inzamam, Multan town's sole cricketing jewel.

Up, towards the top of Inzamam's stand, sat one Zakir Hussain, a former Multan all-rounder, and now a coach for the Water and

Power Development Authority, one of Pakistan's first-class departmental teams. I settled beside him.

Down in the distance Inzamam was just resuming after lunch on 31. Pakistan had endured a poor morning, losing both openers in the first hour. Thereafter, Yasir and Inzamam grooved into a partnership. Inzamam was playing with loose wrists, guiding the ball this way and that and generally looking rather impenetrable.

Zakir is three years Inzamam's senior. He did not have much of a first-class career but played a lot of club cricket with Inzamam starting from their pre-teen days, and he has two favourite memories. One is from a match against Karachi; Zakir scored the only century of his first-class career in the first innings, and Inzamam, seventeen at the time, made one in the second. The other memory, this one narrated with the broader smile, is of a diving Inzy gully catch which turned a match on its head.

'He was thin, thin like a stick. And very shy, happy to be by himself. But everyone was very fond of him. He was the young one. We used to call him Affal. Some of his old friends from Multan still call him that.

'He had no vices, no addictions, nothing like that ever. Yes, he had only one addiction – sleeping. And you can add eating also, he loved eating.'

Below, Inzamam described an arty loop around Kumble's googly and dispatched it to the midwicket fence.

'The funny thing is that he started cricket as a left-arm spinner. But he was called for chucking when he was twelve years old! So then he had no choice but to concentrate on his batting. One thing that struck everyone was how much easily he would play shots. The bouncer never bothered him. No fast bowler bothered him.'

Taking a bow, Inzamam slid into a pair of exquisite boundaries off Zaheer, one stroked low on the front foot and the other punched square on the back foot.

'Yes, that is possible. He may be good against pace because of the cement wickets we played on. It is possible. There were hardly any turf wickets. Some of the cement ones were quite fast. And there was one more thing everyone could see from the start. He never felt any pressure.'

Even without Inzamam's eminence, the Haqs, a wealthy land-owning family, enjoy a certain prestige in Multan. They are believed to be Sayeds, that is, descendants of the Prophet. The father is known about town more simply as Pir Saab, and his discourses on religion are popular. Inzamam himself does talks when he can.

'When he scored in the 1992 World Cup there were parties outside his house. Of course, now he is like the Nazim of Multan. We were sad when his family moved away to Lahore last year. But we all know he is Multani. They still come back often. Their house is still here.'

Presently Inzamam went past fifty. His enclosure burst into rapturous acclaim.

INZAMAM AND YASIR had already put on 150 by the time I walked back around the stadium to the press box. It was a cool partnership, attractive, easy, and very much on the swell. The last sixteen overs had brought 85 runs. Sixty of them had been in boundaries.

Kumble was into his twenty-third wicketless over. A looping chance from Yasir plopped wide of the man at silly point. Four balls later, more bat-pad action, this time forward short leg, and this time Inzamam. It was given out. In fact, the ball had only taken the pad, but perhaps the simultaneous sound of bat striking pad had misled Simon Taufel. A slow trudge followed, even by Inzamam's standards.

Fifteen minutes later Yasir exacerbated Pakistan's situation. He'd been driving Irfan merrily for the best part of the day but, subtly, Irfan was dragging him wider and wider against a spread

7-2 offside field, till he poked at one that should have been allowed to pass untrifled. And an hour after tea, Youhana was gone, caught behind flicking down leg. The replays were inconclusive. The umpire, again, was Taufel.

This thrust nationwide notoriety upon Taufel. The Pakistan team-management went off in a huff to complain to the match-referee. Newspapers panned him pitilessly. One comment writer expressed his disapproval of Australia as a whole, having first sent Pakistan a shipment of wheat which was allegedly contaminated, and now Taufel.

'He was quite shaken,' Ranjan Madugalle, the match-referee, told me later. 'We went out to dinner and spoke for a while. Simon is very hard on himself. He's a perfectionist. He has some German genes in him, you see.'

Over the past couple of years Taufel had been unanimously considered the world's leading umpire. He represented a new, young breed of umpire, a welcome development because eyesight and reflexes do slow with age even for skilled and honest men. He worked hard at his physical fitness, and cut, for instance, a quite contrasting figure on the field to his colleague here, David Shepherd. It was common to find Taufel standing at net sessions, 'practising' his umpiring. By his own assessment he made an error every twenty-eight decisions, which, if we are to accept, would give him a strike rate of 96.4 per cent, whereas the ICC's estimate for their elite panel of umpires taken together is 92. Most players would not dispute the gulf. It was hard not to sympathise with Taufel.

They say cricket is a confidence game, and surely this must be truest for the umpire. He is always in charge of somebody else's fortune, never his own. There is no winning for him, only losing. He must learn how to conquer guilt or else he's finished.

But Youhana's dismissal had left Pakistan vulnerable. At 321 for 5, they were still more than 350 runs behind. Moin and Razzaq were their last realistic hope of averting a follow-on. The pair made a fair fist of it. By the time Tendulkar prepared to bowl the final ball of the day, to Moin, the total stood at 364.

Tendulkar pogoed in off his five steps and fizzed it out of the back of his hand. Moin wondered about it, but appeared inclined to not play at it. Then as the ball began dipping in flight he grew suspicious of Tendulkar's intentions and shuffled across the stumps. As it landed, on a good length around off stump, he had not worked out which way it would turn, for Tendulkar's wrong 'un this tour had been a thing of mystery. By and large, though, he seemed to have the angles covered. He was safe.

Next thing he found himself opened out so much that he stumbled over, stung by the googly on the inside of his left thigh. The ball ricocheted into his leg stump.

A great series of cackles erupted around him as he stood confused, bum towards slip, splayed legs facing midwicket, bat dangling in between like a tail. Cacklers from all parts of the field congregated manically at the bowler's end where Tendulkar was in the throes of the most joyfully animated celebration I have seen him in.

Perhaps one only sees what one is looking for, but Tendulkar on this day was more conspicuous than usual, always seeming to be running up to Dravid with a suggestion, or else making an outfield chase, or else bowling wrist spin. Perhaps he had regretted his words. Perhaps he wanted to prove a point. Perhaps he was just playing as he does. Whichever way, this was a moment of genius, and it signified closure to much more than the day's play.

*Pakistan 364 for 6 in 106 overs (Yasir 91, Inzamam 77, Razzaq 47\*, Irfan 2-87) trail India 675 for 5 decl by 311 runs*

\*

**Day Four**

ONE OF THE ENDURING mysteries of this Test series will be how India pried out and Pakistan conceded thirteen wickets in a single day on this Multan pitch. It really was hopelessly, hopelessly flat. And had thus caused rage.

The Taufel rage, in fact, was no more than a diversion from the pitch rage. Atkinson was the guy really copping it. The general issue of inviting foreigners was raised with passion. In time, one newspaper would query in a headline: 'Is Atkinson pro-India?' Another, underneath the headline, 'PCB spends lavishly on curator Atkinson without much gain', would reveal said amount to be USD 13,500 for the entire series. On the second evening, once India had built their Eiffel, Atkinson had been dispatched to Lahore, a move interpreted as an angry summon from the PCB chairman though actually it was to give him preparation-time ahead of the second Test. And there we will return to him.

The captain and coach took some beating too, notably from Imran Khan, who declared severally that the decision to shave off the grass was feeble and daft and played right into India's hands. The captain diverted the blame to Atkinson, saying that he wanted a hard, bouncy pitch that would suit *fast* bowlers, not seamers, and was not given it. The coach pulled the other one, saying that the pitch did indeed contain bounce and pace for how else could Sehwag hit sixes over third man. Meanwhile *The News* quoted a 'team source' pointing fingers at Youhana, whose insecurity at facing the Indian seamers on a green pitch it was that had prompted the manicure. The groundsman at the Multan Cricket Stadium blamed the entire Pakistani system. In other words, everyone blamed everyone and cricket in the subcontinent was alive and well.

For now, we must chronicle this busiest and quite unexpected of days.

Irfan set the tone. With the first ball of the morning he stunned Razzaq. Slow on his feet, least expecting a bouncer from a pitch-'er-up swingster, Razzaq fended to the keeper. Irfan bounced again next over, and Saqlain safely hooked himself out of the squad. It was a two-part effort. The first one Saqlain hooked, hideously, from outside off, and the top edge carried fine of fine leg for four. Next ball, short again, wider still, Saqlain got off the ground, reached out, and slapped high to mid-off. 'No scribe could do justice to it,' Omar Kureishi would muse, 'but a cartoonist could.' The last time Saqlain was axed from the team he phoned the coach, Miandad, and abused him, a gesture for which he just about escaped punishment from the PCB. Now he had not the right to even look the coach in the eye.

Shoaib arrived and in a trice was duped into lobbing one back to Sachin. In the first twenty balls of the morning Pakistan had lost three wickets for seven runs.

Shabbir and Sami gutsed it out for an hour and the end finally came on 407, when Kumble took his first wicket of the day. Let alone avoiding the follow-on, Pakistan had not even tired the Indians enough to make them consider not enforcing it.

KUMBLE REMOVED the pair of left-handed openers in successive overs in Pakistan's follow-on. Farhat, itching for the big drive, nicked. Taufeeq, if not wary after Farhat's dismissal, then surely by his own two edges at the start of the over, played no stroke and was lbw.

Not a run had been added after the second wicket when Yasir pushed towards wide mid-on and invited Inzamam for a tight single, as avoidable as it was gettable. Yuvraj hit. A swoop on the run, an athletic pirouette, dead-eye aim on the long diagonal to the striker's end. The hit was later agreed upon by both teams as the turning point in the match, not as in turning point, the point at which the tide turns, but the point from where the tide can no longer turn. This was the wicket not just of Pakistan's best batsman, but among the finest pressure-players of the modern era. And despite Inzamam's reams of comic highlight reels from one-day cricket, he had been run-out only twice before in Tests.

Inevitability entered the game. Yasir top-edged a sweep off Yuvraj to short fine leg. With this blow, Yuvraj's became a classic bit-performance in the annals of Ganguly's team. Usually this has been Tendulkar's domain. It was his while Harbhajan was putting the devil's touches on Waugh's Australians at Kolkata in 2001; it was his again when Agarkar was helping them to their doom at Adelaide in 2003-04. The great team performance can be judged by the strength of its walk-on parts.

Pakistan went to tea at 91 for 4, needing 177 to make India bat a second time.

In the afternoon India played inside an unstoppable aura. Every ball brought an appeal. Every appeal threatened to shatter glass. Cricket was relentless. Dravid knew Kumble would not stop and kept tossing him the ball. Kumble knew it and kept going. Pakistan knew it and must have felt unnerved. Kumble touches the spectator at a basic level because watching him more than any other spinner is to watch a physical task. Of course, this is largely visual trickery. Any bowler's success depends on repetition without error and with some wit. Kumble bamboozles as many batsmen as the next genius.

Indians could do no wrong. Razzaq middled a flick and Chopra intercepted it at short leg with one hand. Moin became sixth man out on 113, lbw to Irfan, a decision he did not think accurate for he cursed the umpire and was docked 60 per cent of his match fee. It was actually an ace verdict from Taufel, as the ball had caught pad before Moin hit it. Sami and Saqlain made tortured ducks and were leg before to Kumble's flipper and googly.

Only Youhana remained, stroking gloriously, slashing madly. In a 70-run stand for the ninth wicket, Shoaib scored only four. Of the 93 runs added after the fall of the sixth wicket, Youhana made 89. His first 50 runs took 110 balls, the next 50 took 35.

It was a desperate innings played with a swishing blade. It annoyed Pakistanis, I think, because of the association with his twenty-seven-ball fifty at Cape Town a year ago. Needing to bat two days to save the game then, Youhana set off on a kamikaze mission and holed out in the last over of the day. Unlike at Cape Town, he was down to the tail here, and what was there to be taken had to be taken. It was an innings brilliant in patches. It also suggested surrender.

With all but an over remaining in the extra half hour claimed by Dravid to try and finish the match on the fourth day itself, Kumble ended Shoaib's fifty-four-minute vigil. Tendulkar was given the final over to repeat magic. Unbelievably, Youhana stole a sharp single on the fifth ball and exposed Shabbir. Tendulkar and Parthiv, the keeper, gathered for a long chat in the manner of Warne and Healy. Tendulkar went with the fast off-spinner and Shabbir blocked it. India would have to wait.

Kumble led the way back to the pavilion. He'd been at it the whole day, walking in from fine leg, handing the umpire his weathered India cap, tugging his high-waisted trousers higher still, and propelling himself one more time into that bounding, tight-jawed run. He bowled 35.3 overs, claimed seven wickets and gave away seventy-five runs on a pitch, to use his words, with 'no cracks, no patches, nothing'.

Kumble's recent successes outside home had flushed new life into India. He knows best the reasons for his renaissance. He has said that having runs on the board has made the big difference. On this day there was another benefit that he rarely derived while playing for India: a clogger at the other end. Irfan not only began the day's slide but, in the absence of Zaheer, injured, sent down twenty-four overs of which twelve were maidens. He has been more imaginative in his variations of pace and loop, and effectively used a new grip on the googly, easy to pick, but, as he reasons, 'the batsman still has to play it'.

And as much as he likes to underplay it, one cannot help but feel that his is also the work of a competitor driven by the need to prove wrong. A few months ago one cricket reporter was surprised to find a bunch of eggs in the post. They were from Dinesh, Anil's brother. The journalist had wondered if Kumble was on tour in Australia to fry eggs. Three Tests and twenty-four wickets later, this was the answer.

And so, asked if the Multan performance had buried the theory once and for all that Anil Kumble was incapable of succeeding outside India: 'But, you know, it's still the subcontinent, isn't it? That's what people will say... that's what they'll say.' There was weariness in Atlas's smile, and satisfaction.

*Pakistan 407 in 126.3 overs (Yasir 91, Inzamam 77, Irfan 4-100) and 207 for 9 in 75 overs (Youhana 107\*, Shabbir 0\*, Kumble 6-71, Irfan 1-22) trail India 675 for 5 decl by 61 runs*

\*

### Day Five

IT WAS OVER at ten past 10, on the twelfth ball, before an assembly of mediamen and policemen and under a sudden cover of cloud. Youhana skied a pull off Irfan, Dravid held the catch and still managed to claim a stump, which he later presented to Sehwag. The Indians got entangled in their jumping huddle, their shouting resounding in the hollow bowl. Youhana felt out of place as he

213

went to congratulate them, and turned away; Irfan ran around to him later, and the others came by soon.

It was 1 April, All Fool's Day, the birthday of Ajit Wadekar, the man who led India to their first wins in West Indies and England in that golden summer of '71, and was fast asleep in the dressing room at the moment the second of those victories was achieved. In a way this did feel like All Fool's Day. Such a nothingness at the ground, such a lack of occasion.

And what an occasion, indeed, for India. Fifty years, five series, twenty-one Tests, not a single success in Pakistan till now. And at an innings and 52 runs, this was the biggest away win in their history. 'The guys can feel justifiably proud,' said Dravid, 'It's been a privilege, really, to lead them.'

Barely had the presentation ceremony concluded than the Pakistanis were ordered back out to the centre pitch itself where nets had been tied. Frankly, the strip looked good for another five days. Imran Khan made a star appearance, a total of four minutes in which he: criticised the pitch, made points to Shabbir Ahmed about the position of his leading arm and to Sami about his field placements, and even caught the interest of the Speedy One, who scowled on the periphery of the gathering. These scenes aroused photographers, and that in turn aroused security men. The lot of them quietly came to blows, as Imran's session continued a few metres away. Afterwards Inzamam was grilled over Pakistan's need for a bowling coach and a fielding coach. 'Batting, bowling, fielding, aur kya bacha...' (Batting, bowling, fielding, what else is left...) Long pause. 'Spin bowling coach *bhi la de*...'

Ganguly and Kumble left for the airport straight from the stadium, Ganguly on his way to Kolkata for treatment to his back, Kumble to Bangalore for the birth of his baby. The rest returned to the hotel, where the staff had lined up to give them a rousing reception, and from there they proceeded to the SOS

Village, an orphanage, where kids hung on to Viru and Sachin bhai's coattails. Later in the tour, both teams would participate in a polio-awareness programme and an HIV-awareness programme; at Lahore, the Indians would make a successful appeal to Indian hospitals on behalf of a ten-year-old girl whose strain of facial cancer could not be treated in Pakistan.

By evening the teams were in Lahore, a PIA flight to Karachi coolly diverted.

But for us, Keemoo's chaaps, the best darn chaaps in the subcontinent – where Shabbir had come with his friends the previous day, and the Indians had ordered in from the day before that – on a khatiya in a lane of fumes and dust, and after the chaaps, a spot of entertainment; no, not the Punjabi play *Hum Gal Nahin* starring supersiren Laila at Babur at 11 p.m., not even *Chauke Chhakke* at 10.30 p.m. at Starlight, but *Sassi Panno*, the Heer-Ranjah, the Laila-Majnu, the Romeo-Juliet, of Sindh, beneath the lavender ceiling and twisted fans at Dreamland.

So, how's it passing in Multan?

*Pakistan 216 in 77 overs (Youhana 112, Kumble 6-71, Irfan 2-26) and 407 lost to India 675 for 5 decl by an innings and 52 runs*

# 7. *Kaunsa* top-spinner?

FOR SOME REASON I didn't sleep on the way. On the highway: trucks carrying buffaloes, goats, baby camels, tree trunks, boulders, motorbikes, vans, cars, vans with cars in them. Inhabitation became thicker as we approached Lahore, and on the outskirts, alongside the margins of the road, pool tables surrounded by sharp hustlers in shalwar kameez brandishing cue sticks.

Arriving by night in Lahore felt like a homecoming. This had to do with familiarity, but also with slouching about three hours in the afternoon at Multan's Daewoo terminal waiting for a seat. And also with the fact that we came to not a hotel but a home.

'INDIAN?... WELL, Muslim at least, I hope... NO?... Then what the hell are you doing here?... Well, anyway... Where from in India?... BOMBAY!... Terrible place, terrible, and the people! Terrible, terrible people. At least Delhi the people are okay... Anyway, now that you're here...'

It was Shoaib Hashmi, actor, teacher, playwright, columnist, and a leading satirist in Pakistan. (And yes, he was taking the mickey.)

The Hashmis were acquaintances of Osman, and had lent us a roof. There was an instant liberal warmth to the Hashmi mansion, full of art and books and rugs and food and drink. Shoaib's wife, Salima, is a renowned artist, and runs a gallery in a courtyard behind the house. She is, also, the daughter of Faiz Ahmed Faiz, one of the subcontinent's best-loved poets.

Shoaib showed us to our room: 'It's small – but you must not be used to so much space coming from your Bombay. And sorry, we don't have a bed of nails like you Hindus must be used to.'

I loved the room. It was tucked away in one flank of the house, and had to be entered through a bathroom. The ceiling was high and in the walls were embedded two long bookshelves, among its contents John Arlott's *Ashes 1972* and the 1977 *Wisden*. A large window overlooked the garden. In the morning you could hear the twittering of birds and at night the hum of insects, and the light always filtered in with a refreshing tint. I felt I could have nested here forever.

But this was meant to be a temporary shelter, and I soon sorted out my accommodation for the coming week. ('Leaving? Already? Now you'll go and bloody tell everybody in India that a Pakistani threw you out of his house.') Osman too vacated a few days on; there was another lot of guests coming in. The Hashmi hospitality seemed to be a much abused courtesy.

ON THE SECOND evening Asif swung by, a bottle of Murrie beer in hand. He was dressed in a handsome black shalwar kameez, and from a pocket he pulled out a rectangle of no less handsome black. In a trice he was on the floor, legs crossed, a sheet of paper spread before him, the Murrie sitting beside it.

'Greatest shit in the world, man,' he said, as we were introduced. 'No shit like it anywhere. From the tribal areas, you know, on the Afghan border. Now, because of the army crackdowns, the poor fuckers are just sending away everything – just getting it *out* of there.'

'You know how they send it out?' He pointed to my shoes, and made a slitting motion with his left hand, the right hand holding a rizla up to the tongue. 'In the soles, luv, in the soles.'

He laughed and continued performing his task with casual mastery, overlapping two rizlas into a single one.

'Till here,' he gestured to his elbow, then went up further to his bicep – 'till about up here, that's the longest I've made. Sometime in college.'

Asif had soft, dark brown hair and small, pert features. He reminded me of Henri Leconte, the charismatic French tennis player of the 1980s. His accent was an intriguing mix, urban desi with twangs of American and north England. The colloquialisms, too, were summoned from all over, man and darling and luv and behenchod suffixed seamlessly.

Asif acts, teaches and makes ad films, one of which he had only just finished making inside some impossible deadline. He had a cool affability. We talked about India.

'Bombay stinks, man, it smells. India stinks. Bhopal stinks. But I tell you, it's a fucking free country, *azadi hai vahaan*. Let me tell you guys. In Bombay, what's that main beach *jahaan* shooting *hoti hai*? *Haan*, Juhu. There's this big bloody shooting going on. Shahrukh Khan Vharukh Khan. And I'm standing next to the sea when this drunk fucker comes next to me. The guy can barely stand. And he fucking starts pissing into the sea, behenchod. And he's pissing and pissing and the wind keeps blowing it back into his face. And he starts laughing. And the breeze keeps blowing his piss on to his face, and he keeps laughing! I tell you that fucker, he was so free man.'

He laughed and tossed his hair out of his eyes. The Murrie just waited there.

'Everybody in Pakistan smokes, man, everybody. And I really love that about this country. But the problem is that everybody is a behenchod hypocrite. I'm the only fucker who goes around toot-tooting my horn all over the place.'

We moved to a superhotbox on the other side of the verandah.

Film liners and posters on the wall and videos in the cabinets; I think there were several Kubricks in there. He flicked on the computer and played, among some impressive 1970s obscurities, three of his fifty-six versions of Gershwin's 'Summertime'. The one by Forty Two was sinuous and it worked a spell. The fan shut; the air moist with tribal.

Finally, almost an hour after he had brought it along with him, Asif fizzed the Murrie to life and swallowed it.

We drove out in his car and I cannot remember what precisely it was that played out of his stereo with the ditzy lights. He drove fast, very fast, as fast as Asad had on that first night – 'every second a different address,' to somebody on the mobile – and outside, the lights of Lahore blazed by on a blurring night of black...

... AND LIKE THAT, blurring nights of black in Lahore blazing by, one segueing into another.

One night, running with Saad on the streets, looking for nothing, and, strangely, finding it.

Another night, an early morning, beneath the falling and climbing planes by the airport, a moody room of carpets and music, the geometrical shapes of aquamarine leaping off in spectacular streams from the painted wall. 'You want anything, just ask. Anything.'

Another night, the Thursday night, the tomb of Baba Shah Jamal. Pappu Saeen and his disciple famously playing the dholak, only the dholak, one bigger than the other. A motley assembly, young and old, local and foreign, rich and poor, on the periphery, on the walls, on the branches of the trees; all urbanity in for a fix. No place to move a finger; yet filtering through no place at all, the dense laden aroma. Dervishes whirling around the dholak men; some spinning like tops; one extremely tall one with long wet hair and dressed in a black frock turning slowly about his

220

axis, hands always parallel to the floor, eyes always closed, neck always cricked at the same angle. Smoke everywhere, but no, or little and surreptitious, alcohol at this tomb of a saint. 'You could get beaten up for that.'

Another night, taking directions from strangers in a car; the car catching up a few minutes later to gift an ashtray, the offering smouldering quietly by its edge.

Lahore: hospitality, hedonism, decadence; the flavour wafting everywhere.

One night wandering through Heera Mandi with Osman. No forbidden, sequined grandeur here. Around one corner a misbehaving man, now trembling, getting beaten with a stick. Under one brothel, a creaking chariot led by a white horse pittering pattering into the silence of a winding street. And still the flavour wafting... towering from behind, from the Mughal leftovers; from faraway in the other direction, from the colonial leftovers; relics all of a decadence up and down time, the monuments not meaning anything directly anymore, but still the flavour... And Lahore, to the outsider, a mood, an aroma, thick and intoxicating, of this all.

*

BAD NEWS ARRIVED early in the morning, on running into Suhael Ahmed while checking into the Best Western Shalimar at Liberty Market. Suhael was the Cricinfo head in Pakistan, and working with the PCB on the ticket sales for the series. When I first met him, at the Karachi one-dayer, he had forlornly held up his forearms to display the bruises suffered at the ticket riots. Now, with equal resignation he talked me through the numbers: 'About twelve sales points throughout the city; tickets sold, about 1,200. Internet included, maybe about 2,500.'

This could be worse than Multan.

And upon reaching the Gaddafi, now an arm's length away, it turned out that the media crew had swelled further and was now well-placed to outnumber the spectators.

It was the usual day-before, full of idle chatter and useless excitements. Word out that Tendulkar is attacking in the nets – and upon racing around to the side of the ground, indeed, Tendulkar is attacking in the nets. Word out that one of the media liaison officers at Lahore is really an ISI agent – and upon investigation, well, evidence in that none in PCB's media cell knew where the chap had come from and why, and that his business card was different from theirs. Word out that the pitch is lush green – and upon gazing hard from afar, indeed, it looks green.

Afar was as close as curious minds got to the pitch. Our man from Southend-on-Sea was in the eye of it again.

On 3 April, two days after the Multan defeat, Inzamam had revealed this in his syndicated column: 'When I consulted the curator before the match, I was told it would be hard and the ball would carry to the 'keeper on the first 2-3 days... At the end of the first day's play, when I confronted the curator, all he could offer was a sheepish "sorry". By then, the damage had been done.'

By now Atkinson was prepared to counter rage with rage and accusation with accusation, and had unburdened the entire beast off his breast to Rediff.com:

Inzy has met me just twice in this series. Once when I congratulated him for the Karachi hundred and the second time when he asked me to shave the wicket off the grass [sic]. He can't look me in the eye. He is a coward...

He was unhappy about the Peshawar wicket also, because I gave some juice to it and it seamed around a bit. He made sure after that to have wickets with no seam movement. He just wanted hard and bouncy tracks for his fast bowlers...

I can't be blamed. After all I didn't bowl long hops and half volleys. I didn't get run out with the bat in the wrong hand.

With such hefty gales blowing, Rameez Raja had taken the supervision of the pitch upon himself, and put the square out of bounds for journalists. He was in good nick though, the CEO, narrating the following joke with pizzazz:

'Well, what's happened to your moustache, Andy?'

'Inzamam asked me to shave it off.'

Cute, but I could have sworn Atkinson didn't wear a moosh all this while.

The sharpest lashes in Inzamam's notorious column, however, had been reserved for his own fast bowlers. 'INZY'S SHOCK ATTACK' is how Bombay's *Mid Day* headlined it on their front-page. 'It is not the time to find faults and scapegoats but time to do some serious soul-searching,' the column began reasonably enough, before proceeding rapidly to find faults and scapegoats:

I have come to the conclusion that our bowlers are not really world class as the 'experts' would have us believe...

The pre-series hype about our pace bowling versus India's batting seems to have gone straight to their heads. They have forgotten how to bowl straight. Some former players have added to the hype by subscribing to this theory. When people like Imran say that our attack is world-class, everyone is bound to believe him. But right from the start of the one-day series, it is our bowlers who have let the side down.

In Multan, the hype balloon finally burst and all the hot air has escaped. Hopefully, it will bring my pacers down to earth, and they will be able to pick themselves up and perform to their potential for a change.

This was a disgruntled-fan broadside which I could not imagine coming from the captain of any other team but Pakistan. Inzy was fortunate that he had image on his side. If Shoaib had uttered these words, he would have been commanded into a corner with bent arms raised for fourteen months.

So against this background it was that the pre-match press conference got underway in the late afternoon.

'So, Inzy bhai, were you allowed to see the pitch?' he was asked first up.

Slow smile. 'Ji, they allowed me to see it.'

Over his column, he neither expressed regret, nor, bless him, blamed the ghost writer. Merely he said: 'I meant that if you see the records of Imran or Wasim or Waqar, they have around 400 wickets each. To reach that level you have to keep performing.'

Dravid was to lead India again. There was not much really to ask him. The high from Multan had receded. All necessary reactions had been gathered over the past few days. The mood in the Indian camp was relaxed. The players had visited the border at Wagah and watched movies on their laptops. The wives of some had flown in, and the parents of some. John Wright was reported by *The Telegraph* to be lounging in a lungi from Lanka in his hotel room, quoting Kipling in the land of Kipling.

This was a Sunday. Lahore appeared to be in deep siesta. At 10 a.m. on the morrow the second Test would begin. For now there was not a trace of it.

*

*Kaunsa top-spinner?*

**Day One**

THE LAHORE TEST. It has a resonance. The cricket has not always been riveting, though 1978-79 was a spicy week of bouncers, standoffs and a breathless chase. Besides that, five draws.

Still, the Lahore Test was the Lahore Test. It held a central place in India's people exchanges with Pakistan. By all accounts, the first two instances, in 1954-55, at the Bagh-e-Jinnah, and in 1978-79, at the Gaddafi, were big occasions, occasions of amity and goodwill; they were tinsel society events, a parade of the styles and fashions of the day; and an opportunity for the mingling of the common man. But we had seen this, hadn't we, at the one-day double-header?

Like Test cricket itself in Pakistan, the Lahore Test as a festival was in steady decline. The 1980s saw a progressively dwindling attendance. And now, forty-nine years since that first time, came the full rub.

At the start of play, even Suhael's projections felt an exaggeration. Outside the ground, no anticipatory hum, no developing queues, nothing; inside, on the one hand swathes of empty blue, red and white seats forming Pepsi logos; on the other, the green and white making up the star of Pakistan. Two giant vacant logos, of the corporate and the nation, this is what the Lahore Test had come to.

All manner of theories explaining public apathy were doing the rounds. That it was too hot; that the kids had exams; that the PCB had not been aggressive enough with the marketing; that the tickets were too expensive; that the security was too overbearing; that the general perception was the series were fixed (as also stated by a senior Multan government official); that the one-dayers had satiated the population; that the one-day series loss had demoralised spectators; that the scheduling was such that only two of the Test days fell on a weekend.

225

Arguably, and only arguably, there was a hint of truth in these. But really, they did not hold, not even the sum of them.

When I asked Omar Kureishi, who has covered cricket in Pakistan since the 1950s, the last time in his memory that healthy crowds had turned out at a Test match in Pakistan, he reckoned it was during India's last tour, in 1989-90. And even then *Wisden* had reported: 'The crowds at these [the one-day] matches were invariably close to capacity – whereas those at the Test matches were not encouraging enough.'

And the Tests, on that tour, were played *before* the one-dayers, as the PCB had wanted it this time around. So the effects of satiation at the one-dayers, though probably valid, cannot be exaggerated. The Multan Test had begun on a Sunday, and the turnout was negligible. So the weekend point cannot be overstated. The security was no tighter than for the one-dayers, so that did not really hold. The PCB had slashed ticket rates, making the cheapest ones Rs 25 a day, and were allowing in children for free. Even that did not work.

The only conclusion, really, was the simplest one: that a day at the Test was no longer part of the social fabric in Pakistan, the way it is in England, where Tests still draw bigger crowds than one-dayers, or in Australia and the West Indies, where they can be comparable. Admittedly Pakistan is not alone in this regard, but more starkly hit than any other country.

Kureishi did suggest reverting to the system – followed even now in Australia – where the matches would be televised in the cities they were being played at only after tea (even though Television Rating Points will surely bear out, I'm sure, as they do in India, that the viewership for Tests is a fraction of that for one-dayers, meaning that there are fewer people interested in watching the match at all). Perhaps it is worth a shot. Perhaps the marketing does need to be glitzier. Perhaps more initiatives need to be undertaken at the ground, autograph sessions and the like. Perhaps, perhaps, perhaps.

In the end, though, it is hard not to sit back and sigh. One goes to the ground for the macro, for the feel, for the realness. On moodless days at moodless grounds, needing to watch, often, from behind a glass partition that blocks sound, wind and involvement, it compels one to think that they would be better off before the television, able to absorb, instead, the micro.

It hurt all the more now because this was a wonderful, wonderful day of Test-match cricket, lit up brilliantly by youth.

From the very first it had a vigour. Shoaib's rapid opening delivery took Chopra's edge high up on the bat and squirted past third slip; the second pounded into his right thigh; the sixth ballooned up to gully off his shoulder, and Shoaib backed it up with a taunting flick of the nose in his follow-through. Chopra fell in the next over, as Sami slithered one on to his pad. It was going to be a rough morning...

And so of course Dravid's decision to bat was destined to be debated over and over again.

There was life in this surface: bounce and pace and lateral movement; it was invigorating. The grass roots, at 8 cm, went down fairly deep, so that the siphoning Atkinson had spoken about was able to work well. But the sun was out, and coupled with the low humidity, it meant that the moisture would be sucked dry in a few hours. It was a question, really, of seeing out that period.

Dravid's decision was reminiscent, in recent times, of Headingley 2002, when Ganguly had selected two spinners and chosen to bat on a seamer's paradise. That time victory had been constructed around a defensive masterpiece on the first day from Dravid himself. But if there is one thing that cricket captains know better than anybody, it is that future events not only judge the worth of a decision, but they also post-determine motivation. One moment you're brave – you've chosen to bat on a fast pitch against express pacemen, see; the next, you're chicken – look, you've lacked the conviction to stick 'em in. As they say in Guyana, 'every rope gat two end'.

History actually suggests that it matters not a whit whose way the coin falls. Upon studying the numbers it emerges that India's first seven overseas victories came when they had lost the toss. Overall, their chances of victory on winning the toss increase by less than 2 per cent. Pakistan's actually fall by 5 per cent! Either, like Steve Waugh has routinely hissed through tightly grit teeth, the toss is indeed 'there just to start the game, mate', or else there has been some continuously daft thinking on both sides of the border through the years. Reading that second option again, it seems quite agreeable actually. No, really. For look, Australia have made the toss count to the tune of 6 per cent, and West Indies more than 4. Anyway.

Pakistan had rung four changes because of injury – Shabbir's shin, Razzaq's groin, Moin's back, Saqlain's confidence – and so in came Umar Gul, Asim Kamal, Kamran Akmal and Kaneria. India brought in Ajit Agarkar for Zaheer, who had now to return home with his pulled right hamstring showing no hope of recovery.

Returning to 5 for 1.

Shoaib heaved in to four slips, one gully – and a man at backward point two-thirds of the way to the fence. Did Sehwag care? He drove, not cut, *drove*, above and fine of that man for six. Three balls later he drove again, again in the air, this time finer and less controlled, for four. At the other end, Dravid started with a serenely composed off-drive against Sami. Sehwag began stroking Sami through the off side over and over again. Shoaib went round the wicket and Sehwag bunted him gaily with the angle past cover and then bunted him straight back. And in the last over before drinks, Sami bowled five wides down leg and followed it with a no-ball.

Pakistan had lost the plot. High-octane waste. Shoaib had been ripped for 30 in five overs, Sami 36 in six. Sehwag had hit 39 in 38 balls and India were 69 in twelve overs, more than twice their score at the same stage at Multan, and now on a greentop.

Then Umar Gul bowled his second over and the match changed.

The delivery that undid Sehwag was the type Gul would bowl most regularly: pitching just outside off, on a length, on the seam, and nipping back a touch. He employed two variations to this theme: the one which nipped away off the seam, and the one which swung back in the air. In other words, he did a very good imitation indeed of Glenn McGrath, his idol – in itself an interesting point for, though his birthplace is recorded as Peshawar, Gul is believed to come from the village of Nawa-e-Khelli, from where emerged two of history's greatest squash legends, Jahangir and Jansher Khan.

Gul got on a quite unanticipated roll. Tendulkar was confronted with the ball which gives him more trouble than any other, the incoming one. This one both swung and nipped back off the seam, and caught him lbw for 2. Laxman arrived, was sliced into half with a delivery which somehow missed the top of middle, soon found himself groping at an away-seamer and was taken smartly by Taufeeq at second slip.

Accordingly, a buzz went up in the press box. Those who had contrasted Gul as the Peshawar Rickshaw to the Rawalpindi Express hung their red faces. Others bewailed India's response to seaming pitches. 'Gul is god,' beeped an SMS for Saad.

There was something terribly earnest about Gul. Earnest, and comic. So conscientiously he strained in from afar, high-kneed, long, unbending limbs jerked about as if on puppet strings. I felt he was Matchstick Man fitted with propellers at the knees and elbows. Kamran (Abbasi, the delightfully provocative London-based columnist, making a cameo appearance at the Test match) reckoned he was a flamingo.

India went to lunch at 107 for 4. Gul was on 7-2-14-3.

With his eleventh legal delivery after the interval Gul touched the pinnacle of his performance. He had the Maestro caught at slip, pushing away from his body. It took a moment to sink in. The ball had grown big on him and jagged away, yes, but Dravid simply does not do away from the body. He had so far performed expertly in the conditions. Even his edges had been regulated: if driving on the front foot, he got low and close to the pitch of the ball so that he nicked down; if on the crease, he deadened his hands at the last moment, minimising the carry. 'I pride myself on not playing that type of shot,' he was to chide himself later. But Gul, by relentlessly peppering what they call 'the business area', had drawn the error.

Saad's phone beeped again. 'Gul is Mohammad pbuh.'

Three balls later Gul removed Parthiv, padding up in a cloud of uncertainty. This gave him the five-for, and he immediately bent down and touched his forehead to the ground. 'And he kisses the ground, aww, the young man...' shrieked Dean Jones in the commentator's box, proving that you can travel all the world all your life and still remain completely oblivious to the culture of others.

Gul sent down two further overs and then left the field with cramp. He bowled no further in the innings.

There is a close parallel to Gul's performance in India-Pakistan history. Nineteen years ago on this ground, the left-armer Azeem Hafeez had taken 6 for 46, scuttling out Gavaskar's team for 156. Hafeez was twenty-one at the time and in his eleventh Test. Gul was a week short of twenty and playing his fifth. Hafeez

230

bowled swing and seam rather than pace. As did Gul. Gul's work here was done in a single spell, on either side of lunch. Hafeez struck in one 'fury spell' (in the words of a *Dawn* report at the time), on either side of tea. Gul's spell was 12-2-31-5; Hafeez's 14-5-23-6. Accounting for the inflation of scoring rates, the analyses can be considered virtually identical.

But while Gul took his wickets on a lively first-day pitch, Hafeez's damage had been done on the third day on a surface which was listless from the outset; Pakistan had made a long-drawn 428, and India got themselves together to put up a tedious 371 for 6 in their follow-on. Then again, whereas Gul was up against a line-up at the height of its powers, the lot Hafeez bowled to hadn't played Test cricket for almost a year, and anyhow their last series had been a 0-3 licking in the Caribbean.

Up in Gul's gallery were Sehwag, Tendulkar, Laxman, Dravid and Parthiv. Hafeez's catalogue boasted Gavaskar, Vengsarkar, Patil, Shastri, Kapil and Chetan Sharma. There was no doubt as to any of Gul's dismissals, whereas Kapil, after being given lbw, returned so discontented to the dressing room that he began beating his kitbag with the bat. (Patil did not dare point out that the kitbag was actually his.)

So then, which was better? You choose. But there was one other disturbing similarity. Hafeez's career ended abruptly four months after that six-for. So when a few months later, Gul was diagnosed with a serious back condition, there was reason to be concerned.

YUVRAJ SINGH had taken guard in his muscular manner in the twenty-first over at 94 for 4, a situation which was to deteriorate to 127 for 6 and 147 for 7. Crisis. He'd been there before. He'd, in fact, started there. The crisis in those days, Yuvraj's first days in international cricket, was pretty big: the match-fixing crisis.

His achievement then, as much as helping topple Australia and South Africa back-to-back in that heady Nairobi tournament in 2000, was in freshening minds which had become miserable with the mass of confessions and cover-ups and allegations and lies.

Yuvraj played an exhilarating innings at the Gaddafi. He has always had the talent which makes heads turn. After watching that innings in the cathartic Lord's one-day final of 2002, Henry Blofeld thought him to be a 'cross between Sobers and Graeme Pollock with a dash of Frank Woolley thrown in', though it remains unresolved just how much Blofeld, born 1939, would have watched Woolley, retired from first-class 1938.

He deals with pace on his own terms, a quality derived from his father's dictatorial drills against wet rubber balls on a cement pitch in the backyard. Three times on a pitch like this he stood up tall and punched boundaries straight of cover against a bowler of Sami's speed. Sami and Shoaib threw everything at him. They pitched short. He hooked and pulled. They bowled straight. He flicked fine and glanced square. They bowled wide. He cut high, cut low; cut loose.

Against Kaneria he looked to sweep all the time, a stroke over which he has yet to acquire control, as he does against spin in general. Mostly he went fine; one carried over square leg for six. Another time he jogged down and broad-batted it back dead straight over the ropes.

At the other end, Yuvraj had the most resolute support from Irfan, who played with an exemplary straight bat. The young left-handers played as one. Irfan parried, Yuvraj thrust; Yuvraj thrust, Irfan parried. Sometimes Irfan thrust. Yuvraj never parried.

Barely had Gul mopped up the top-order than Yuvraj was on the brink of a century. On 97 he snicked Sami, but Akmal failed to hold a low catch to his left. The next ball, Irfan stroked beautifully down the ground for four, and in the following over, with his score on 49, and his partner on 99, Irfan popped one back to Kaneria. In the chairman's box, his father's face fell. The pair had added 117 for the eighth wicket.

Soon Yuvraj ran a single to Youhana's misfield in the covers and completed his first Test hundred. Immediately, Balaji fell, for duck. Down to his last partner, Yuvraj scurried along, pulling Shoaib for a four that still seems to be reverberating somewhere, before one sweep too many off Kaneria fell into Farhat's hands at deep square leg: last man out, for 112, off 129 balls, fifteen fours and two sixes. You could say that Yuvraj was fortunate that Gul had been unable to bowl at him after the first third of his innings; or that Inzamam missed a trick by not confronting him with spin early on. Never mind. After applying every filter the innings comes out a classic. It will stand the test of time.

India finished on 287. Pakistan responded with solid intent, going to stumps at 61 for 1. The day had teetered constantly between attack and counter-attack, its performances bursting alive with freshness. The combined age of the three stars, a batsman, a seamer, an all-rounder in the making, was sixty, and among them they had played eight Tests.

It was to remain my favourite day from the Test series for besides this it also contained the most dramatic, the most amusing, the most engrossing, the most ruinous and ultimately the most instructive spectacle in cricket, which, of course, is the collapse. And with the home team perpetrating it, rather than enduring it as at Multan, I missed the crowd, baying and hounding the suffering towards their downfall, applauding the reprisal perhaps as they had shown the capacity to do already on this tour. But no baying, no hounding, no applauding; nothing.

The Lahore Test had died; the Lahore Test had come alive.

*Pakistan 61 for 1 in 23 overs (Farhat 25\*, Yasir 4\*, Balaji 1-21) trail India 287 in 64.1 overs (Yuvraj 112, Irfan 49, Gul 5-31) by 226 runs*

\*

## Day Two

WELL, IT HAD TO HAPPEN. The entire grain of history cannot in a stroke be reversed.

Karachi, 1955. Lala Amarnath, the Indian team manager, is seated in the room of Abdul Hafeez Kardar, the Pakistan captain. The two gents have, among other things, recently taken the unusual step of slapping each other in a hotel lobby. This is a reconciliatory tea meeting on the eve of the last Test of the series. Lala's back is to the door, and so the man who enters the room with the words, 'Any instruction for tomorrow's game, skipper?', has his guard down. The man is umpire Idris Beg.

Bombay, 1960. Pakistan's captain, Fazal Mahmood, clean bowls his counterpart, Nari Contractor, in the opening Test of the series at the Brabourne. Contractor is at an unspecified location between the square and the pavilion when the umpire, S.K. Ganguli, sticks out his arm. It is a no-ball. Why, inquires Fazal, has not the call come earlier? 'The chewing gum got stuck in my throat.'

And on the 1979-80 tour to India, Miandad begins practising without pads in the nets, so paranoid has he become that anything which hits them will be an lbw. And so on and so forth, and so on and so forth, till Imran Khan imports John Holder and John Hampshire for the 1989-90 series, who are promptly crowned Men of the Series by the almanac, *Indian Cricket*.

And here we were in the codified age of two neutral umpires, drawn from an Elite Panel no less, with a third, local, one sitting

234

on television replays, alongside a match-referee, another neutral, drawn from an Elite Panel no less...

The first session was largely peaceful. Farhat kicked off from the previous evening with a pulled four off Kumble; Yasir was out nicking a very wide delivery in Agarkar's first over; Inzamam surprisingly copped one on the helmet from Agarkar; Tendulkar bowled seam-up and coolly swung it both ways; and all the while Pakistan consolidated.

In the second session Pakistan prospered further, scoring at four an over, and Farhat reached the second Test century of his fledgling career.

But in the last session, the seams came apart. John Wright stormed into the match-referee's cabin, Kumble hurled a ball perilously close to Inzamam's noggin, Inzamam charged down the pitch shouting at Kumble in response.

What had happened? Five appeals, basically, turned down. Three for caught behind, two for lbw; one against Farhat, two against Inzamam, two against Youhana; one off Kumble, two off Balaji and two off Irfan. Of these, replays revealed that the two lbws – both off Irfan – were between very close and plumb; that Youhana had indeed nicked Kumble; but the two caught-behind appeals, both off Balaji, were almost certainly not out.

This ordinarily would not have been enough. Four things had catalysed Wright's action. First, India were struggling. The team that is winning kicks no fuss. It had been likewise at Multan. Which brought us to the second point. If Pakistan could make a complaint at Multan on the basis of a couple of dodgy calls from Taufel, why couldn't India here? Third was the fact that four of the five not-outs had come in the hour after tea. The Indian bowling at this stage was at its most urgent, having claimed the new ball as soon as it was available. The medium-pacers were getting it to swing and Kumble to hurry it on with the shine. The frustrations were compressed. And the fourth reason was the man making the decisions: all but one were made by Steve Bucknor, cricket's most capped Test umpire.

This had been coming a while. The Indians felt persecuted by Bucknor – Slow Death, as he is sometimes referred to for his delayed finger-raise. The seeds of discontent were sown, if not before, then certainly on the Australian tour at the turn of the year. Bucknor then had cut short Tendulkar's first innings of the Test series with an lbw. It was a poor decision, but not as bad as all of India pretended it was. The ensuing hullabaloo set a tone of mutual antagonism. On a later occasion on that tour, Bucknor charged down half the length of the pitch wagging his finger and shouting at Parthiv, in the middle of a jack-in-the-box appeal. Another time, absurdly, he was perceived by the Indians to be mocking Dravid by running his fingers over the side of the ball as he came out to bat – a reference to Dravid being found guilty, a fews days earlier, of tampering with the ball by applying jelly to it. Most damaging were his not-outs to a number of close, some bang-on, lbw appeals on the final day of the Sydney Test on which had hinged India's chances of winning the series.

I am inclined to give Bucknor the benefit of impartiality. If I were to make a case for it, I would say that he has famously been a not-outer all his life (why, then, the Tendulkar decision at Brisbane, Indian fans might ask). Harder to defend is the philosophy itself, one of cricket's most unquestioned traditions: to the batsman goes the benefit of doubt. Indeed, take away those last two words and you have the distilled essence of all cricket. It is a crap rule of thumb. To argue that the batsman has just the one chance is facile. Any bowler will tell you that, as often as not, one chance is all he will have to remove a batsman. Can not the footsloggers be treated as equals? Can not the benefit of doubt simply be awarded to the party whose case contains the lesser doubt?

PAKISTAN PLAYED IMPORTANT cricket on the day; gritty, unsexy. Of the four batsmen on view two, Inzamam and Farhat, crossed hundred, and Youhana fifty. Farhat's was not the most fluent effort. He got beaten a fair amount. He edged several times. He reached 50 with a top-edged hook that Agarkar at fine-leg should have caught, and on 99 he survived a raucous caught-behind appeal. He also made several crisp strokes and flashed less with time. He put runs on the table. Later he called it a better hundred than his first, against South Africa the previous season, because the opposition was India. His family, he said, had always wanted him to succeed against India.

That family included Humayun, his wicketkeeper elder brother who had made his international debut in the same series as Imran, and Mohammad Ilyas, his father-in-law, who had also opened the batting for Pakistan and who now declared in the press box that this was a prouder moment for him than his own Test century. Among Ilyas's cousins you could count Mudassar Nazar who, like his father Nazar Mohammad, had carried his bat opening for Pakistan. That made it four Test-opener centurions in an admittedly extended family. Even the magnificent Mohammads had managed just three – Hanif, his younger brother, Sadiq, and Hanif's son, Shoaib – but then we haven't scoured through their *mamus* and *sussars* and the rest.

Farhat's century went to demonstrate that when Inzamam prospers, so do his colleagues. Over the past three years, it has been calculated, Inzamam scoring more than 30 leads to a 40 per cent increase in the productivity of the rest of the top-order; of Inzamam's eighteen previous hundreds, thus, thirteen have resulted in wins, and only two in losses.

Inzamam did hard graft. The Indians came at him full pelt. He cut the frills and played the ball under his chin. In the face of appeal after appeal, he kept his calm. Late in the afternoon, moments after bringing up his century, and about the same time that Wright must have been huffing out of the match-referee's cabin, he was stirred into confrontation. Inzamam is not readily provoked but when he is provoked, as a chump of a heckler in Toronto has found out, he is provoked. For size, outward peace, inner rage, I link him in my mind always to the Pacific Ocean.

Kumble, at the end of an over, had flung the ball back to the keeper. Only, it would have taken out Inzamam had he not ducked. Inzamam bristled down towards Kumble, yelling and gesturing. A demonstrative exchange followed. Laxman dragged Kumble away. Dravid got involved and the battle waged on. The umpires made a quick dash to the scene of mischief. Soon Kumble was back in the frame. Tendulkar pulled him away now. The captains continued to trash it out, the umpires and Youhana lending their ears. It was an image for the day, a good old-fashioned hothead day of fighting like cats with Pakistan coming out tops.

It had been a hard session for Kumble. He'd got Youhana caught behind but it had counted for nothing. The delivery immediately after that reprieve had been allowed to run away down leg by Parthiv, and though it appeared to have grazed Youhana's person, it was declared byes – which meant that the runs were ticked off against Kumble's name. Shortly after the Inzamam pow-wow, an exceedingly eager throw from Yuvraj had raced away for four overthrows – which, again, went against Kumble's figures. Two balls on, Youhana edged inches wide of slip, for four.

At last the day ended. Kumble and Inzy returned to the pavilion together, Kumble's arm around Inzy's shoulder, Inzy's arm around

238

Kumble's waist, a smile upon both their faces. Later, at the hotel, Parthiv was summoned by Madugalle and slapped with a 60 per cent fine for overappealling, overdissenting and overcelebrating. This is not as bad as it sounds: the sponsor contributes two-thirds to the Indian cricketer's match-fee, indemnified against fines and such.

Did I mention there was a mild earthquake at 2.30 this morning? Anyway, I slept through it.

*Pakistan 355 for 3 in 113 overs (Inzamam 118\*, Youhana 62\*, Farhat 101, Balaji 2-63) lead India 287 by 68 runs*

\*

THE MIND STILL throbbing with appeals and verdicts and the like, *Mid Day's* Ehtesham and I set out for the home of Ansar Mehmood Bajwa. We found him waiting for us on the main road. He led us into an unlit lane, which had the feel of industrial wasteland, strewn with debris and patches of dried cement. In the darkness of the lane, Bajwa, in his pristine white shalwar kameez, was a beacon.

We entered his house through a tall steel gate that opened with a loud groan, and settled in a plain living room with chalky walls, mosaic tiles, a single tube light, wicker chairs and a formica table on which rested a bunch of synthetic flowers. Somebody, I think it was his brother, came out with two glasses of Roohafza.

We began going through the list, one by one, the appeals and the verdicts.

- Fayaz Ahmed versus Wasim Akram. For appearing in the Royal Stag advertisement. Status: Rs 24,000 in damages awarded to the plaintiff.

- Najmal Abbas versus Wasim Akram. For applying for the post of Indian bowling coach. Status: case withdrawn after it was established this was untrue.
- Najmal Abbas versus Tauqir Zia, chairman of the PCB. For the early exit from the 2003 World Cup. Status: case withdrawn after the team's success in the next tournament at Sharjah.
- Syed Muzzamal Hussain versus Shoaib Akhtar, Ramiz Raja and Aamir Sohail. For attending a fashion show on the holy night of Shab-e-Barat, and that with a key one-day match slated for the following day. Status: case withdrawn towards the start of this series, to prevent distraction.
- Najmal Abbas versus Shoaib Akhtar. For demeaning Pakistani cricket greats in an interview to the *Guardian*. Status: case withdrawn towards the start of this series, to prevent distraction.
- Najmal Abbas versus Wasim Akram. For statements from Irfan Pathan and Zaheer Khan that his coaching had helped them. Status: case dismissed by a Lahore court.

In the space of fifteen-odd months, Bajwa, a lawyer for seven years, had colluded with citizens to file six Public Interest Litigations against Pakistan cricketers and administrators. Cricket PILs were not unheard of in India but they were yet to become a one-man cottage industry.

Routinely, the most libellous statements are made in Pakistan cricket and not a thing comes of it. And, side by side, the Bajwa litigations. It is all accepted with the same fatalism. Newspapers report it all in the same unblinking vein. PCB chairman involved in cricket gambling, says Sarfraz. Miandad blocking my son's career, says Majid. And with that: Akram sued for helping Indian bowlers. Or: Shoaib receives legal notice for attending fashion show. I suppose it was all of a piece with Pakistan cricket: the bizarre bazaar, the flavours of Saqlain's mystery balls blending naturally with the Bajwa litigations.

I asked Bajwa why he did it.

'It's my duty. Being a lawyer, I can represent the public opinion, I can spread the voice of the common man. People approach me themselves to represent them.'

But was this not a dangerous precedent? Could not it become a racket?

'I think journalists are good judges.' His voice contained no obvious irony. 'They will not support us if our motives are wrong. That is how we know we are on the right track. Journalists have supported me. The public knows what is wrong and what is right. After all, public opinion must count.

'It was in late 2002 that I handled the first case, the Royal Stag case. Fayaz Ahmed was the plaintiff. He's a twenty-four-year-old youngster. He was my client for some other case. That's how I knew him.

'Now, everybody knows Royal Stag is alcohol. I have myself seen the advertisement on ESPN. "Royal Stag *hai mere taakat ka raaz.*" Fayaz Ahmed told me that what Wasim Akram is doing is not correct. We should do something about it. And I agreed with him. Wasim Akram is no. 1 cricketer. But he is misleading the youngsters. Alcohol. Match-fixing *ka chakkar*. Jeep *ka chakkar* [alluding to another case, where Akram was accused of filching a friend's jeep].

'He can do what he likes in private. I don't mind. But he is a role-model for so many youngsters. He is giving Pakistan and Islam a bad name. His brother, he is like a gangster, the way he approached us when all this was going on.'

Keema samosas were served.

Bajwa had won only one of his six cases, the Royal Stag one.

It did not matter to him. Won, withdrawn or dismissed, Bajwa was of the belief that 'our purpose was achieved'. It was admirable how this always worked out.

In the bowling-coach case, for instance, Akram put to the court in writing that he had not applied for such a job and Jagmohan Dalmiya, the Indian board chief, said to newspapers that no job application had been received. So no chance Akram would become bowling coach of India. In the Tauqir Zia case, the errant players at the World Cup had been dropped and a brand new team under Rashid Latif won the very next tournament, at Sharjah. Purpose, thus, achieved. In the two Shoaib Akhtar cases, the public were made aware of Shoaib's sins so that wherever he went he would be faced with their wrath, thereby driving home the message. Only in the last Wasim Akram case, the passing-on of tips to Irfan and Zaheer, was the purpose not achieved. Reason? 'Wasim Akram is a powerful man in Pakistan. What can I say – now, you be careful about how you write this – but the judges were changed and all that.'

Of the lot, the *Guardian* interview case was my favourite, not because of the premise per se, but just look at these paragraphs from the Speedy One (see, in particular, the Wasim 1996 bit):

I deliver the ball to the edge of the bat, it gets nicked but one of the fielders has to catch it. I can't run round to the slips and take it. So I try to make a lot of my dismissals bowled or lbw. But sometimes you have to rely on your team-mates.

Imagine if I was playing for Australia... With [Glenn] McGrath and [Jason] Gillespie softening them up, then I come on, I'd have got more wickets than anyone ever, mate. Because when I play for Pakistan, with Wasim [Akram] and

Waqar [Younis] they are in decline. They were great but they're not match-winning bowlers any more. Wasim has not won a match since 1996. So I have to make it all happen on my own. There is so much expectation on my shoulders. But, if I come on after those two [Australians], when the ball's a bit older and swinging. Imagine, it would be 'see you, mate, talk to you later' every time.

'What will the youngsters reading this think?' Bajwa asked.

We challenged Bajwa on the last case, Akram passing tips to the Indian seamers. Was that not a healthy thing? Has it not been remarked that 'cricket, like art, is international'?

'But why before the tour? Wasim Akram has the most swing bowling secrets in the world. He knew the Indian tour was coming up. It was not right for him to reveal these things. It was against national interest. Nobody would have minded after the tour.'

Would he have objected if, for instance, Sunil Gavaskar shared his nous with Pakistan's young opening batsmen?

'No, I would not have minded. It would be in national interest, after all. You have to do what is in national interest.'

But, he added, he would not react the same way now.

'Ab toh dosti ki hawa chal rahi hai [Now the wind of friendship is blowing]. It has never been like this. This tour has been totally different.

'And besides, I'm getting feelers from the courts that they may no longer entertain my cases.'

*

**Day Three**
SPECTATORS WHO NEVER came didn't even have time to not take their seats when the captain fell, on his first ball of the morning,

243

lbw to Irfan on the kaichi. Youhana made two velvet drives off Balaji and then got bested by his subtle away-seamer. Akmal and Sami came and left like passing thoughts. In the first forty minutes Pakistan lost four wickets for 31 runs. And after toiling without success for thirty-one overs, Irfan now had three wickets from six overs, two of them leg-befores. Only yesterday he could be heard singing, like Blondie before him, 'In Babylon, on the boulevard of broken dreams, my willpower at the lowest ebb, oh what can I do?/Oh bucca-nor! Can ya help me put my truck in gear?'

Foolish me. That is not buccanor but buccaneer. And anyhow the man upholding Irfan's appeals this morning was Taufel. Foolish me.

Sweet languor descended after the Irfan strikes. Over after over ticked by, no wickets, no runs... lolling in cricket's silly lap, it was vastly comforting, watching Shoaib Akhtar, the speediest thing the world has known, do rigid defence and more rigid defence, drifting, up, up and away, cricket performing its time-honoured function, drifting on a soft white cloud... until the Express improperly awoke all with an explosion, which, it turned out, was a slap of pure lust over mid-off.

Soon it was time to lunch.

Asim Kamal resumed with a four first thing after the meal, and India reached out for an old trick. The field was spread, Kamal was allowed singles. This trick, of course, has not been known to work. Kamal manipulated the Indians. He accepted the singles and also found the boundaries. When least expected he hit sixes. The first of three came from the supplest of on-drives off Irfan. Kumble he swept a lot. To reach fifty, he tapped a two off Tendulkar when the whole idea was to never allow him two in the first half of an over.

Kamal was unusual in Pakistan's scheme of things in that he

had worked the domestic circuit for six years and been given a Test cap at the age of twenty-seven. That was last year, against the South Africans. He made 99. And then, after one further Test, he had been dropped until now. Journeyman left-hander coming to the rescue with the tail – the Indian fans had seen it before. Two Tests ago, in fact, with Simon Katich during a crucial phase at Sydney. Then, Katich had added 105 runs with Jason Gillespie for the eighth wicket. Here, Kamal added 84 with nos. 9 and 10.

There was something to be said for the efforts of nos. 9 and 10. Shoaib Akhtar successfully batted like Shoaib Mohammad. And what strokes Earnest Gul played! He leant into a square drive; he stood up, high-elbowed, into an extra-cover punch; he sashayed across the stumps and pinged it to square leg as Vivian Richards in his pomp would and Yashpal Sharma once did in a fit of inspiration at the 1983 World Cup. He made an extremely well-meaning pull off Tendulkar which scampered away to the fence but found, alas, that his keen footwork had disturbed a bail.

Kamal was the last man out, on 73, gloving a reverse sweep. Pakistan finished 202 runs ahead.

THE LAST TIME INDIA had faced a deficit this large was at the MCG a few months earlier. The weight had told, and, though not without a fight, they had succumbed to their lowest total of the series. Among Test cricket's fascinations is detecting dread in the movements of perfectly good batsmen in these situations.

Like in the first innings, Chopra collected a boundary off the edge and then fell leg-before to one which skid on. He opened his eyes wide and stared at Bucknor. Then he examined the face and the edge of his bat and nodded his head, a routine he maintained till the time he walked off the field, at which point it was widely expected that he would march up to the commentator's box to make an announcement of it. To be sure, it had hit the bat; but not, replays revealed, before it hit pad. This was a superb decision: Bucknor had correctly laid the benefit of doubt where it belonged. Not that it would console Indians.

Chopra's dismissal having come on the last ball of the over, Dravid took the pitch at the non-striker's end. Sehwag pushed to cover and called Dravid for the single. Imran Farhat pounced on the ball and made a muscular direct hit: 15 for 2, India's captain and best batsman gone, without facing a ball. The symmetry with Inzamam's run-out at Multan was compelling.

Tendulkar took guard after tea and observers watched with interest. Sami was bowling fast and straight to a circle of fielders swooping and diving with new life. Presently he got one to scurry on to Tendulkar's pads. Tendulkar went down on his haunches and instantly looked at his bat, the two acts suggesting that the ball had kept low and that there had been an inside edge. That he had misread the length and missed it entirely was probably closer to what happened.

Tendulkar's squat was not an unfamiliar sight. He did it from time to time in the course of an innings, surprising for a short man. The one image it recalled at this moment, and with Tendulkar there is always a reference point, was the time he was bowled by Pedro Collins after a glittering 86 at Jamaica in the deciding Test of 2002. With that squat had evaporated hopes of a heroic 400-plus chase of the type Gavaskar, Viswanath and Amarnath had orchestrated in the Caribbean twenty-seven summers previously; and with that, another dream of an overseas series win. The team had reacted spinelessly to that squat, not least the tailenders who tossed away their wickets the following morning minutes before a great rain came down, a rain of eleven days, flooding the rivers of Jamaica, clogging its roads, bringing all life to a standstill.

Truth was that Tendulkar had bailed India out of an almost identical situation against West Indies at the Eden Gardens sixteen months ago. Truth was also that contenders everywhere were performing more valorous deeds more regularly. 'The responsibility of being a champion,' Jack Fingleton has written of Bradman, a touch sympathetically, a touch unsympathetically, 'is that the champion is never expected to be anything else – come weather, come age and all the ills and little upsets that champions must suffer.'

Pakistan were hot. Laxman stroked two fours before Gul spectacularly did him in with one which arrowed into middle and took top of off. Yuvraj replicated Laxman – two fours, and gone, open-facing Sami to the keeper. 105 for 5, and the Test match sealed.

Sehwag was still in, still paying heed to the voice of Rafi in his head, 'Barbadiyon ka sog manana fizul tha/Barbadiyon ka jashn manata chala gaya' (Futile it was to mourn my ruin/So I kept on celebrating my ruin), and accordingly raised fifty in fifty-five balls with ten fours, none badly hit. It was the first second-innings fifty of his career. He finished the day on 86, a performance comfortably eclipsed by Pakistan's rousing all-part effort of early resistance and late hustle.

As the players returned to the pavilion a heartfelt round of applause went up in the media box. An announcement had just come through. There was to be no press conference.

*India 149 for 5 in 40 overs (Sehwag 86\*, Patel 13\*, Sami 2-61) and 287 trail Pakistan 489 (Inzamam 118, Farhat 101, Kamal 73, Youhana 72, Balaji 3-81, Irfan 3-107) by 53 runs*

*

247

## Day Four

WAS SEHWAG ASKED not to be himself this morning or was it of his own conception? It was not before the seventh over of the morning that he went for the ball like he goes for the ball. His senses had been dulled by then. He nicked it.

Whereupon Irfan came to the centre, for the first time in this series as far as fast bowlers go, to a catcher both at short leg and silly point. The first delivery would have burnt a hole in his right armpit had he not managed to flail a glove in its path. The ball fell to the right of silly point. The second honed in on his ribs, and this time the splice came to the rescue. The ball drooped down before short leg. The third delivery hissed past his nose. The fourth was a repeat of the third, but closer to the body. It looped up off the bat-handle to Taufeeq at second slip. Five balls, four bouncers, two wickets, game up. Come on down, Mr Express.

It was good to see the smile back on Shoaib's face. Dressed down after his Multan performance, he had melodramatically offered to sit out this Test. Sulking, he had skipped two practice sessions leading up to it. Then he bowled like a duffer on the opening morning. Now, after his success, he was to make the most poignant confession of all: 'I'm no angel'; and to prove the point, he went and embroiled himself in a row with Muhammad Ali, Assistant Superintendent of Police, by dragging his sexy red Ducati 600cc bike till the dressing room, thus violating numerous security regulations at the ground.

Parthiv and Agarkar stroked fast runs. An hour more of the stuff and it would have begun to count. Kaneria wrapped the tail around his finger and finished on a hat-trick. As soon as Balaji became the last man out, with India 39 ahead, Earnest Gul raced towards the stumps, yanked one out of the ground and began motoring towards the pavilion. Soon he registered the bewilderment on the faces of his team-mates and umpires, and it dawned on him that Pakistan were to bat again. 'Excite ho gaya main zaada' (I got a little overexcited), he said later, earnestly receiving his Man of the Match award from Fazal Mahmood, invited to do the honours after the ignominies during the one-dayers.

Inzamam played wounded winner to perfection. Craftily ignoring his own column, he laid into critics of the Pakistani team, not least the former players, making it well clear that he was doing so on the back of victory so as to not make it sound like an excuse, and that he would have no qualms, like Miandad, in resigning should such criticism continue.

As at Multan, it was generally an easy last day. The gaze had shifted to Rawalpindi since the previous afternoon. For the moment there was nothing severe to contemplate. No tension. Pressmen whistled and mopped up, grateful for a fourth-day finish. I filed quickly and hopped across the ground to keep my four o'clock date.

*Pakistan 40 for 1 in 7 overs (Yasir 16\*, Balaji 1-15) and 489 beat India 241 in 62.4 overs (Sehwag 90, Parthiv 62\*, Kaneria 3-14, Shoaib 3-62) and 287 by nine wickets*

\*

MY FIRST CONTACT for him came through a business card passed on by a colleague. ABDUL QADIR, King of Spin, it said. It was the colour of heather, with a white oval patch at the side, in which he was pictured bowling. The salient features were enumerated:

* Millenium 2000 No. 3 Sportsman From All Sports (The Sunday Times England News Survey)
* Pride of Performance (Pakistan)
* Life Membership From M.C.C. (England)
* Ryder Medal From (Australia)
* Life Achievement Gold Medal Award From (P.C.B.)

* Founder of Cricket Academy in Pakistan
* Abdul Qadir Cricket Academy for Boys and Girls

I had dialled the number on the card towards the end of the Multan Test, to request an interview. My assignment was to juice every drop of leg-spin wisdom from the man.

'*Janaab*,' he had said, 'you come, you are my guest from India, I will give you a cup of tea. But *janaab*, neither do I have any interest in having my photographs published, nor in seeing my name in any headlines. Unless, of course, it is done professionally. You see, this won't pay my electricity bills or feed my children. But you have my phone number and you can get in touch with me if you can make the arrangements.'

I left it at that. The amount I could have offered would have been insulting; besides, it was against company policy. I was disappointed, but I appreciated his point of view.

Later, I mentioned this to Kamran. He pulled out his mobile at once. After some twinkle-eyed bonding, he concluded the conversation thus: 'Yeh mera dost, Rahul, usne aapko phone kiya tha? Ji aap please usey interview deejiye. Bada shareef ladka hai. Bilkul jalebi ki tarah shareef' (My friend, Rahul, he had called you? Please give him an interview. He is a very decent boy. Decent like a jalebi).

And so like a jalebi I had again called Qadir bhai.

Qadir's business card was no match for the hoarding outside his academy. It was a large green work of tin. ABDUL QADIR INTERNATIONAL CRICKET ACADEMY, it declared, GRASS ROOT IS OUR ORIGINAL FUTURE. Qadir was painted in the centre like in the movie posters. He has just released the ball and his tongue is sticking out in follow-through. In red wispy handwriting running diagonally across his abdomen and left thigh were the words: 'Millenium 2000 No. 3 Player All Sports in Sunday Times England'. And below the painted Qadir: MESSAGE:-

LEAVE COMPUTER T.V. CABLE JUST FOR FEWHOURS. COME TO GROUNDMAKE YOUR NAME IN SPORTS ALSO MAKE YOUR BODY STRONG. On either side of him, two further exhortations: SAVE YOUR KIDS FROM EVIL SOCIETY, and, GREAT FUTURE CAN BE FOR SCHOOL BOYS.

When I found him, Qadir was on his haunches, a hose in hand, peering loftily at the compact mud through the spray of water. He was wearing a bright yellow and dark blue polo-style t-shirt, tucked into brown denim. He looked much younger than his forty-nine. There was no hint of vulnerability in his mane of black hair, and the skin on his face was smooth and radiant; you could see the pores on them.

'*Aao, janaab,*' he welcomed me. I got on my haunches beside him. He continued doing his work, and began speaking in such a mellifluous stream of Urdu that I was convinced he was reciting poetry from the masters until he came to an abrupt halt with the words, 'No Bullshit'.

'No bullshit,' he reiterated, 'I believe in no bullshit.' He grumbled briefly. Then he began speaking once more in Urdu, and now I could follow, about the beauty of life, the beauty of nature, the beauty of manual labour. He dropped the hose and patted the earth in front of him. 'I want turf pitches here. We will make it ourselves.' He bellowed out to a boy to hurry up with a basket of mud. Poor chap stumbled. 'These are the beautiful things in life,' he said, gazing through the spray, nose sharp in profile. 'No bullshit.'

Qadir's academy was tucked away in a corner of the Lahore City Cricket Association grounds, adjacent to the Gaddafi, and had been open for about a year now. I asked him how it was getting along.

'I'm not running on any financial help, from PCB or the government or anybody else. I have taken this plot on lease. Promises were made. But I know I have to coach the children of this country, both boys and girls. The girls' wing will start soon. After all, *I'm* because of Pakistan, *Pakistan* is not because of me.'

He began grumbling again. Something was clearly bothering Qadir. It was the fallout from his comments on national television a few days ago.

He was an expert on the daily cricket show on PTV. Asked why Pakistan's pacemen had been unable to extract reverse swing in this series, he had stated: 'We all know the ball has always been made up by Pakistani fast bowlers, but with so much scrutiny on this series, this has not been possible. Even against Bangladesh in the Peshawar Test last year, the fast bowlers were unsuccessful, till after a break wickets fell in a heap.'

For this PTV had summarily dismissed him. Qadir was threatening to go to court over it. Presently, an Indian news channel arrived to obtain Qadir's reaction.

A surge of vigour overcame him. He bounced up to the camera, insisting on speaking in English. Gesticulating immensely, he attacked the nature of PTV's contract with him. He called the producer of the show an illiterate so-and-so who thought the national channel was his father's property. He defended his comments, on the one hand maintaining that at no stage did he mention 'tamper', and by 'made up' he simply meant looking after the condition of the ball by legal methods; and on the other claiming that 'the problem is nobody wants to hear the truth'.

On the completion of an extended and rather entertaining rant, he was asked about Sachin Tendulkar. Against a veteran Qadir at an exhibition match in Peshawar it had been, in 1989-90, that a sixteen-year-old Tendulkar had smashed 27 runs off a single over.

Qadir broke into a glow of affection. 'Darling boy, *bilkul*. Real darling. I treated him like my little brother, I took him everywhere. I took him shopping, I encouraged him to hit my bowling. He is still a darling. *Badhiya insaan, badhiya* batsman. Double-wicket tournament at Sharjah, you remember? I threw him a challenge that time...'

He did not stop for breath for fifteen minutes. The reporter tried interjecting but to no avail. It was like trying to swim up a waterfall.

The topic turned to his young son, Usman, and upon the very mention of the name, Qadir purred like a lioness. He called out to a boy with rosy cheeks and coy eyes, maybe about twelve. He yanked him towards himself and planted a kiss on his cheeks. 'Look at him, so beautiful, so fair!' He raced to the practice pitches and returned with a set of stumps. He hammered two stumps into the ground, at about thrice the normal width, and balanced the third stump between them like a bail. He summoned Usman to demonstrate his wares before the camera. '*Yeh* leg-break,' he exclaimed gleefully from the sidelines. '*Yeh* googly. Aur *yeh* yorker...'

One of Usman's elder brothers, Salman, had just batted and bowled off-breaks for Pakistan's under-19 team at the Youth World Cup, but Usman was clearly the apple of his father's eye. 'He is Test player. *Haan, haan, pakki baat*, inshallah. I think he can become better than me. He has everything. Look, he wakes up at seven and goes to school and studies till four in the evening. Then he comes here and jogs around the ground – look at the size of this ground. Then he starts practising, he bowls, he bats. I start to worry sometimes, but he just does it! Everything he does on his own. He only needs a little guidance. Jab machine chaalu nahin hoti, tab junction dabbe mein tel-shel lagaate hain. Bas waise' (When a machine doesn't start, you put oil in the junction box. Just like that).

He planted another kiss on Usman as he finished. 'So beautiful, so fair, just like his mother. Not like his father!'

253

And after ninety minutes of standing by and absorbing the moods and energies of this most fascinating of men, I managed to sit Abdul Qadir down for our chat on leg-spin bowling.

RECALLING HIS THOUGHTS while facing Qadir for the first time, the England spinner Vic Marks wrote: 'Good Lord, he's bowled me a high full toss. Where shall I smash it? Hang on it's a low full toss. Not to worry. Maybe it's a half volley. Oh no, it's a length ball and I'm groping hopelessly.'

Watching him as a young boy, the subtleties of Qadir's flight and dip were lost on me. But I do remember his action. I more than remember it. It is my single most vivid cricketing image from the 1980s. I, and I was not alone, practised it endlessly. I internalised it. It was the greatest joy.

Starting from a forty-five-degree angle to the stumps, hands – the ball in the left – curling up alternately to the tongue, the body rocking forwards on to the stretched and slightly bent right foot, then back again, then another forward rock, and back again, and then a stutter!, and another!, and some momentum now, arms swinging like vines in a storm, a jerking parabola to the wicket, and on the seventh stride the body collecting itself into a twisted jump with, at one point, both arms pointing straight up and both feet off the ground, and then the snap-wristed release, the hair flowing behind and tongue protruding ahead, what contortion, what climax!

Being what it was, the Qadir action has been ensured perpetuation. Mushtaq Ahmed took the baton, and then passed it on to Kaneria, each action, like Chinese Whispers, getting more mangled, or in this case, less mangled, as it moved along.

I wanted to start by asking Qadir about his action. But that led me to backtrack to the more basic question: why leg-spin at all? It was an unusual choice for the time. Pace and swing ruled the planet in those days. The best spinners were finger spinners: Bedi, Prasanna and Venkat; Lance Gibbs, Derek Underwood. B.S. Chandrasekhar was slotted as a leg-spinner but was really in a genre entirely of his own. Johnny Gleeson briefly mystified West Indians but his novelty soon wore off. Mushtaq Mohammad and Intikhab Alam, accomplished all-rounders, both bowled leggies with great success on the county circuit but in a combined thirty-seven years of Test cricket mustered just about 200 wickets between them. Subhash Gupte played his last Test in 1961, Richie Benaud in 1964. Not a single leg-spinner of consistently world-beating calibre purveyed his craft in the 1970s, the time when a young Qadir would have sought idols.

I asked Qadir this first. Why leg-spin?

'I wanted to do something in cricket, you see. I used to sleep with the cricket ball. I was twelve-fourteen years and I used to go to sleep with the ball in my hand! It has to be *your* enthusiasm, *your* determination, *your* concentration...'

No, no, but *why* leg-spin? Or why *leg*-spin? I tried to discuss the background. It wasn't much use. This was too pedantic a line of thinking for him. It was the domain of a theorist not a performer. He became impatient with the question.

'I mean, my wish was I should be a leg-spinner, not anything else. I wanted to bowl leg-spin, that's all... I mean, if you want to eat rice, it's entirely up to you. If you want to eat banana...'

And so on to the action.

'That was all artificial.'

Artificial!

'Yes, it was not natural. My action was beautiful, you see. When I bowled with a natural action I was a better bowler, a better finisher.'

So then?

'As soon as I started playing Test cricket I started picking up things. I started studying the psychology of batsmen. I added up all the things I learnt to create some impression in the minds of batsmen. It was an artificial body language. But very successful.'

Would that be the same sort of impression that had led Imran Khan to recommend him the French beard, with the additional incentive that 'it works with the women too'?

Qadir laughed.

'Yes, Imran told me, "You look like real magician with the French-cut beard." The combination of my beard and my bowling, he really liked that. I think it matters a lot, what sort of personality you have, what sort of image you have, how you face up to being hit, what sort of enthusiasm you have. Leg-break bowling one should bowl with a big heart.

'I'll tell you what is special about leg-spin. Where nothing else can succeed, leg-spin bowling can be successful. That is the beauty of leg-spin. Where the ball is not breaking, the leg-spinner can make it break. Where there are only runs in the pitch, the leg-spinner can bowl variations. If he has control over line and length, he can bowl defensively as well. He can buy wickets, if he is of high calibre, he can stop the runs. Where nothing else can succeed, leg-spin can succeed.'

Qadir stretched incessantly while we spoke, suddenly extending his leg out and touching his head to his knee, or rotating his head, or spreading his legs out and holding his hands out before him like a martial artist. He tended to finish his sentences, in English, with 'you see' and in Urdu with '*samajh gaye*?'.

I had the opportunity, recently, to watch on video the first of the two Karachi Tests in the 1982-83 series, where Imran's legendary spell – it *is* legendarily stunning – of high-speed late swing and cut with the cross-breeze (the stands at the National Stadium were low and open in those days) had flattened the Indians in the second innings. Yet, does anybody remember that it was Qadir who had pried out four wickets on a first-day pitch, hastening the Indians towards 169 all out? The last of those four was Maninder Singh, Test average, admittedly, 3.80. As the ball descended on a length fuller than good, Maninder froze in his stride, holding his bat near his pad, not too close, for what if it turned and took the edge, and not too far, for what if it snuck through the gate? It did neither of the two, but zooted back, low and fast, into his pad. Greater, much greater, batsmen have been had by the Qadir googly.

I asked Qadir about his variations.

'Leg-break is original, googly is original, flipper is original, *samajh gaye*? Leg-break, googly, flipper. From these, it is up to you what you can go on removing.

'I could bowl the same ball in ten different ways. Ten leg-breaks, ten googlies, ten flippers. I couldn't bowl from one place. That's not my style in life. I've seen people bowling in one style, and that's it. But not me. I wanted to do miracles, you see.'

Who taught him?

'Koi coach nahin. Halaatein thi meri coach [No coach. Circumstances were my coach].

'My new book is really exclusive. I have made three frames of shoulder, three frames of wrist, three frames of crease position. These different combinations you keep using for your variations. Leg-break, googly, flipper are three originals, and you use these positions to keep removing more.'

Three originals and nothing else? What about all the deliveries Mr Warne has told us about? What about the top-spinner?

Qadir became agitated.

'Bakwaas [Nonsense]. Koi top-spinner nahin. Kaunsa top-spinner? What is definition of top-spin? *Janaab*, if top-spin means that the ball will jump up high by your command, then I think eleven top-spinners would be enough for any batting line-up.

257

There is no top-spinner ball, *samajh gaye?* Only those who are less educated in cricket, when they have to keep speaking while giving commentary, only they say things like "that was a great top-spinner".

'Spin bowling hai variation ko kheechna [Spin bowling is getting the most out of your variations]. This is what I had told Anil Kumble, you see, which he is still using very well. This I'm telling you on the record. When Sachin Tendulkar brought Anil Kumble to me in 1997, he asked me how he could make the ball break more. I told him, "You want me to tell you how my ball will break more, but I want to tell you that your ball will never break more in your whole life. But you keep bowling variations. In the first three days of a Test this will come in handy for you." What I thought suited his bowling, I told him. And he is still using that very well.

'Spin bowling is four things. One, line and length. Two, variation. Three, using the crease. Four, using fielders. That is spin bowling.'

Now suddenly he stopped stretching and tapped me.

'And you know who is leg-spinner? If a person is bowling from dawn to dusk, when he goes back home he should still have something left in the bag. *He* is leg-spinner. If there is nothing left, he is not leg-spinner.'

He seemed pleased. To Qadir's mind, with prayer-time approaching and the BBC still waiting its turn, my interview was finished with this quote, a splendid one, I have to say. But I greedily persisted for more, trying to challenge his claim that spinners today have it easier, suggesting that superior bats, shorter boundaries and batting pitches had perhaps made it harder. Once more he summoned an analogy, this one to represent the weak Test teams to have joined the international fray.

'Aap dus bande ke saath kushti kar rahe ho, do hi taaqatwale nazar aa rahe hain, aath aur ko to aap giraa dete ho na? [If you are in a wrestling ring with ten men, and two are formidable, you will defeat the other eight, won't you?] *Samajh gaye?*'

He was growing very restless now. I had not quite extracted my treatise, but it was time to let go. He had shared a fair amount, and it was good of him, particularly given the circumstances.

'So, my friend Chris,' he turned to the BBC man, an old acquaintance.

I rested my head back on the grass, beneath the softening evening light, content listening to the sounds of bat on ball on one side and the words of Abdul Qadir on the other. 'See Chris, I realised that *I'm* because of Pakistan, *Pakistan* is not because of me...'

Chris completed his interview. We strolled towards the nets to take pictures. Qadir majestically put his leg up on a slab and gave us a profile. A large concrete rectangle next to him held the 'COMPLETE THOUGHT OF LIFE BY ABDUL QADIR'. The words DISCPLINE, TRUTH, UNITY and FAITH were arranged in four rows, each word repeating itself three times. Towards the bottom were four more rows with the headings, DISCIPLINE, HARD WORK, HABITS, AVOID. Each had a four-point programme. Point no. 4 under AVOID, for instance, was 'Lies.'

We finished taking photographs. Qadir came across, momentarily mislaying his nervous energy. '*Janaab* Rahul,' he said, stretching out slowly. 'I can give some *zabardast* programs. Hot programs, *bikne waali* programs. You know anybody who will be interested? TV, radio, whoever, let me know. Match-fixing *ho ya* ball-tampering *ho*.'

'Match-fixing?' I pressed him gently on the subject. 'Ab bhi?' (Even now?)

'Pehle, ab, sab' (Then, now, all). He rattled off a string of player names. 'I'll call one-two bookies. They will put their hand on the Qu'ran and say everything. Of course, they will want a price for it.'

What price were we talking about here?

'One England tabloid, they were giving one bookie 15,000 pounds. But that was too little for him.'

All of a sudden it occurred to Qadir that he had delayed his prayers beyond all levels of decency. He pardoned himself, turned around, broke into a sprint, pulled out his prayer mat and spread it out on the plot of earth he had been tending to when I first found him.

# 8. Champagne

THE DAYS BEFORE Pindi were well utilised. I had my visa extended, with the help of a kindly retired colonel who took me to a batchmate of his son in the civil services. I felt kind of important when, seated in a small room in an old building in Lahore's secretariat area, Saleem, the visa officer, pointed out a man in sunglasses through a slot in the ply partition of his cabin. 'See that guy? He is ISI. Every move I make he watches. I must pretend I don't know.'

For reasons not known to anyone, least of all him and me, Saleem felt I'd be able to provide a friend of his tips on launching a fashion magazine in Pakistan. He took me to meet said friend at his high-walled bungalow-office the following day. It swiftly emerged that I had inadequate expertise at hand, and also that Saleem was rather more keen on his friend starting the fashion magazine than the friend was. Nevertheless, contact details were exchanged with the air of parties signing a crucial treaty.

During the meeting, Saleem advised me against travelling outside the zones specified in the visa – the match venues – and to build his case, supplied horror stories of unfortunates who had been found straying. This provided extra incentive for venturing out to Harappa.

On the way to Harappa I was temporarily adopted by a village. The village did not have a name. It went by a number, 135 A/9-L, and it lay beside a highway petrol station, the closest

Daewoo stop for visitors to the site. In one direction from the petrol station was Sahiwal, well-known in cricket as the venue where Bishan Bedi conceded a one-day international out of disgust on the 1978-79 tour, when, as the Indians were poised to home in on a tricky target, Sarfraz Nawaz began bowling unreachable bouncer after unreachable bouncer with the blessings of the umpire. Far off somewhere in the other direction from the petrol station lay the excavations. Leave alone a shuttle service, there was not even a signboard about.

It was a parched hot summer day and the landscape was bare. I began drifting and presently encountered a man sitting on a khatiya, gazing passively into the scorched fields across the road. I asked him for directions. Instead he invited me to take a seat and have some tea. Soon, the entire village was at the khatiya, led by the patriarch, tall, bony Mr Rana, the grandfather of hundreds, a voice like bottled thunder. From the khatiya we gravitated into the terrace-room of Mr Rana's home, 135 A/9-L excited by the prospect of an Indian, the Indian overwhelmed by the attention and affection accorded him by 135 A/9-L. Mr Rana came from Ludhiana, and showed me portraits of his father who'd served in the police there, Mrs Rana encouraged me to bathe and nap and eat since I must be tired and hungry, and the girls and boys asked questions about Indian movies and colleges. Thereafter, rambling through the burning remains of an ancient civilisation was an anti-climax.

I returned to Lahore that night by a ruffian big bus with vomit floating in the aisle, rushed to purchase a new suitcase to replace the one which, bought expressly for this tour, had dissembled some way ahead of the shopkeeper's assurance of 'minimum five years', slept for three or four minutes, and departed for Islamabad. It was my third 4.30 a.m. start of the tour. Was this the journey where I imagined myself fielding at silly point and the batsmen kept shouting, 'don ghe, don ghe' (take two, take two, Marathi), after repeatedly tapping the ball to my feet?

THOSE WHO JOKE that Pakistan's capital is not in fact in Pakistan aren't far off the mark. Islamabad is a haven constructed for bureaucrats, diplomats, military chiefs, the retired and those who fancy a second home in Pakistan. For in Islamabad the weather is always lovely, and the air is never polluted, and there is no visible poverty, and there are pleasant weekends to be spent in the hill-stations in every direction. With its grids and sectors, its designated blue areas and white areas, Islamabad retains the feel of a place which never left the architect's table, which it only did less than half a century ago. And so the garden is green and the dinky parked next to it is shiny and the Lego-man with a briefcase is walking to a building with clean lines. Like Chandigarh, it can instigate lunacy. And to some, the notion of Islamabad, in a country where over a third are poor and over half illiterate, is revolting.

I could see the point, but I cannot pretend to have been revolted. And lunacy wasn't much of a threat. Islamabad proved soothing, a relief. This had been such a breakneck journey, into its sixth week now; and the days at the Pindi Cricket Stadium, half an hour away, were to be more challenging than elsewhere. We stayed at the Western Lodge, one of many bungalows in the residential sectors converted into a guest-house. The rooms were large. The surroundings were unobtrusive. Walking around in the cool of the night, in the shadow of the mountains, beside the rustle of the leaves and the calls of crickets, one could feel at peace.

The days before Pindi also provided a final occasion for social activity. Miandad hosted his old friend Dilip Vengsarkar, and his wife, at his Lahore home, as also Tendulkar, who took along a couple of younger team-mates with him. Nehra joined Shoaib for an outing to a friend's farm. Dravid, Parthiv, Balaji, Irfan and Rameez Raja addressed a gathering at the Lahore University of Management Studies, where the students chanted for Balaji. The Indian and Pakistani cricket fan clubs organised a get-together. Later Imran Khan would throw a party for players, officials and friends, but would controversially omit Miandad.

The great Waqar Younis formally announced his retirement during these days – though, with the ways of Pakistan cricket, nobody entirely ruled out the possibility of him making a comeback, as captain, in the last Test. It had been a year since Waqar last played for Pakistan, leading them to the worst World Cup showing in their history, following which he was sacked from the squad altogether. His announcement was made at a press conference at the Marriot – convened by the PCB, attended by the chairman and the CEO; later that evening there was a dinner party in his honour, again organised by the PCB, attended by the media and the players of both sides. The send-off went beyond indicating a reconciliation between Waqar and the establishment; it held the promise that Pakistan cricketers, notorious for leaving or having to be dragged off the stage kicking and shouting, would be given farewells that did justice to their talents.

But Waqar's shimmering poolside dinner was overshadowed by another contemporary giant. A world away Brian Lara was approaching a quadruple-century in a Test innings. Accordingly, all were in thrall. Some guests arrived late, some guests left early, some guests whisked away to the giant screen in the coffee shop.

Rahul Dravid watched the moment on the TV in the gymnasium area. With him was the Marathi journalist and editor, Sunandan Lele. Dravid marvelled at Lara's technique, which allowed him the option of a defensive stroke or an attacking one to every ball till the very last moment. Above all he marvelled at Lara's appetite. Lele had just interviewed Dravid. He had asked him about his dry run in this Test series. 'Vees,' Dravid had held up two fingers and replied, 'vees houn dya' (Twenty, just let me get past twenty).

\*

THERE WAS MUSIC at the nets. It was Urdu rock, Junoon, I suspect. Whether it was the disturbance picked by the speaker-wires or the acoustics in the stadium I could not work out, but every time bat hit ball, the sound of an electric whip striking a metal plate stung the air. The Pakistani bowlers worked the air-guitar at the top of their run-ups and laughed and chatted. '*Batein nahin, batein nahin,*' Miandad remonstrated in the tone of the elder who was secretly enjoying the fooling about.

But beneath the free spirit, Pakistan were so besieged by injury and insecurity that they had picked a hundred-man squad for the last Test, eighty-one of them fast bowlers. Or, closer to the truth, a seventeen-man squad, six of them fast bowlers. India, for home Tests, pick fourteen. Australia pick twelve.

The big blow was that Gul, down with a back injury, was not among the six quicks. Sami was, but he was said to be struggling with back spasms and a bout of food poisoning. There were four relative rookies in – Naved-ul-Hasan, Ifthikar Anjum, Abdur Rauf and Fazl-e-Akbar. Naved hadn't played a game since the first one-dayer at Karachi and had never played a Test; Rauf and Ifthikar were uncapped seamers from the Punjab hinterland making themselves a name in domestic cricket; Fazl, a Test player briefly, was, at 23, already a grand-daddy on the domestic circuit, hauling in bucketfuls of wickets with his old-England-style gentle swing and seam. That left Shoaib Akhtar. Which is never a straightforward matter.

Shoaib's relationship with Inzamam was in visible decline all tour. He had been too profligate in the one-dayers for Inzamam's liking, and his dismissal in the final game, run-out, shirking from the crease, afraid of being hit by the throw, could scarcely have placated his captain. Then came the Tests. So disappointed was Inzamam with Shoaib's wicketless showing at Multan that, claimed those in the know, he reprimanded Shoaib while the team went through their stretching routine on the final morning, telling him, basically, that he had lost Pakistan the match. On the heels of that came the hype-balloon-has-burst-and-the-hot-air-has-escaped column. Thus Shoaib's offer to pull out of the Lahore Test. On the third evening of that Test a little incident occurred on the field, innocuous in itself, but I suppose these things add up. With India under the cosh, three down for not many in the second innings, Shoaib made an outfield chase of supreme lethargy, ambling alongside the ball, criss-crossing it luxuriously, looking back, looking down but not bothering to bend down and pick it up, converting a two into an easy three. Inzamam normally reacts to such misdemeanours with passive disgruntlement but on this occasion he yelled at Shoaib from afar, charging briskly in his direction, clapping his hands over his head. It had been almost half an hour since Shoaib had finished his spell so there really was no excuse.

The latest strain between the two concerned the sudden and bitter departure of Taufeeq Razzak, one of the two doctor-cum-physio-cum-trainers attached to the team. When Razzak was asked by the board to provide reasons for the spate of injuries in the Pakistani camp, particularly among the fast bowlers, he blamed it on Inzamam ordering excessive net-bowling. This angered Inzamam, who, to quote Razzak from his later press conference, 'confronted me in front of the entire team accusing me and degrading my abilities and professional knowledge. I had a heated argument with Inzamam. And the captain kept on saying baseless things that were a shock to me. Thus I decided to part ways with the team.'

Now Shoaib and Razzak were close friends. Pakistani journalists cynically referred to Razzak as 'Shoaib's personal trainer'. Indian scribes identified him as the bloke who jogged with Shoaib in the evenings. And during the previous year's World Cup, reported *The News*, Razzak had been sent back home after players had complained about his preferential treatment of Shoaib.

Razzak certainly took great pride in the association. When he first examined Shoaib four years ago, he said in an interview, not putting too fine a point on it, Shoaib's 'shoulder was gone, he had a ligament injury, his rotator cuff was damaged, his 12th rib used to hit his pelvis while bowling – he had a stress fracture over there – his back was gone, both his knees were badly injured, especially the left one. Then his ankle had a ligament strain, so he had problems in bowling and running.' He added: 'Shoaib Akhtar is part of me now... Every time Shoaib takes a wicket, I believe I have done something for Pakistan.'

Whether or not Inzamam's spat with Razzak was directly linked to Shoaib, it certainly did nothing to bridge the gap between the captain and his ace bowler. Nor did the walkout of a staff member ahead of a crunch match do much for team spirit. As ever, Pakistan's challenge was to rise above chaos.

But it was hard to escape the feeling that they, a young bunch, did not have anyone to look to. No captain has it all – some of the best have been called blocks, stones, worse than senseless things – but in one way or another his leadership must count. If Inzamam was proving to be a weak inspirer, as well as a weak tactician, as well as a weak manager of personalities, then there wasn't much point. Inzamam made no bones of the fact that he'd never sought the job; that it came to him by default. And – despite his honest intentions – it showed.

THE INDIANS WERE CAUGHT up in a dilemma of their own. In many ways it was a routine selection dilemma, but discussion over this one grew larger and larger, and gained such a proportion that one writer described it as a 'clash of civilisations'. The question was who to drop now that Ganguly was fit.

One option was to make the straight swap, Ganguly for Yuvraj. The other was to drop Chopra, in which case a cunning arrangement would have to be worked out for the opening position.

Ganguly, plus a few, preferred the second option. The rest preferred the first. Ganguly plus a few liked to view this team as a mace: a small central core with protruding lethal spikes, never mind that the spikes could puncture one's own self; the rest envisaged it as a log of oak, suitable for both attack and defence, never mind that the implement could be cumbersome.

Speculation had reached a fevered pitch over the past five days. 'All I can reveal,' remarked Wright wryly, 'is that the opener will be a left-hander or a right-hander.' Ganguly laid it out more clearly: 'It will either be Yuvraj or me.' Me? 'If I have to do the job, I have to do it.' So, for the moment, that brought an end to the chatter that Parthiv Patel would be thrust into the customary keeper-on-tour role. Commiserations poured in for Chopra, the favoured incumbent both in the team and the media.

Several sympathy bouquets had already been delivered to Chopra at Lahore. Before he took guard in the second innings, Ganguly, in Kolkata at the time, had been quoted as saying that Yuvraj could not be dropped for the last Test after making a century. Perhaps it was not the most tactful comment, but it was simply absurd to blame that, as many were doing, for Chopra's second-innings failure. In an interval during the classic Lord's Test match of 1963, the West Indian batsman, Basil Butcher, opened a letter which told him of his wife's miscarriage back home in Guyana. Butcher went back out and resumed what became one of cricket's great match-saving, almost match-winning, centuries. Later, he didn't think he had been heroic.

I suppose allowance must be made for the unique pain caused to the Indian fan by the opening failure. Ever since Gavaskar departed there had been a hole at the top of the order, a hole whose shape alternated between a question mark and a teardrop. It was filled with modest success and lavish failure by an assortment of all-rounders, wicketkeepers, middle-order converts, lifelong openers, plumbers, bureaucrats, oncologists, butterfly-collectors, carpenters' wives and none of the above. Between Gavaskar's retirement in 1987 and now, twenty-six players and *forty-one* opening combinations had been tried out; that is, a different pair every third Test.

But the Gavaskar fixation had become a burden. Gavaskar had defined too much too strongly for too many Indians. So when an S. Ramesh or a V. Sehwag came along and succeeded with his loose ways, the general response was grudging acknowledgement, till one or two failures, at which point the knives would come out. By contrast, when an S.S. Das or an A. Chopra arrived – short, compact, obdurate, right-handed – a reassurance bordering on self-delusion spread across the land; great meanings would be derived out of decent performances, and rank failures would be explained away. It was like the English detecting Ian Botham in any chap who could bat and bowl; only, I think, they were more aware they were doing it.

India's Gavaskar fixation had blurred into another fixation, a specialist-opener fixation, specialist being one who has always opened. I'm not sure if that has ever been a necessary criterion in Test cricket, and it certainly was not one in today's game. Scanning team rosters at the time of discussion, the world's premier openers would be: the Australian pair of Hayden and Langer, the South Africans Gibbs and Smith, England's Vaughan and

Trescothick, the Sri Lankans Jayasuriya and Atapattu, New Zealand's Richardson, the West Indian Gayle, and Sehwag.

*Six* of these eleven – Gibbs, Jayasuriya, Atapattu, Richardson, Gayle and Sehwag – did not begin their first-class careers as openers. Indeed, most were extreme cases. The first time, for instance, that Jayasuriya and Sehwag ever opened in first-class was in the match immediately preceding the first time they opened in a Test; Richardson (like Ravi Shastri: in all conditions India's best opener between Gavaskar and Sehwag), started life as a left-arm spinner who batted at no. 9 or 10, and crawled up the order over the years.

Certainly Chopra had been of value in India's campaign in Australia. He had been assigned a specific and important function, to see out the new ball, and he largely fulfilled his brief, particularly in the first innings of the matches. Moreover, he and Sehwag ran well between the wickets and had the happy knack of putting up stands. One point, though, was not being given sufficient attention. Chopra was one of twelve specialist batsmen on either side. The series averages of the other eleven were: for Australia, in batting order, 46, 64, 101, 42, 45 and 70, and for India, 58, 124, 77, 82 and 47. Chopra averaged 23.

It should be fairly clear by now where I stood in the clash of civilisations. More than anything, I had been stirred by Yuvraj's Lahore century. I wanted to watch him play again, and felt no guilt at this yearning. Besides, I also considered him the superior batsman, in better form, and so more likely to produce something decisive.

And I had a few stats to fall back on. Largely unremarked, Yuvraj's first century in first-class cricket had come while opening. His second had come at no. 3 – but he was at the crease fourth ball of the innings. And, when prodded by Ganguly he opened this domestic season, he began with a hundred and an eighty.

And the clincher: Yuvraj's first-class debut, too, was made as an opener. Would it weaken my case terribly if it were to be revealed that he made duck?

Otherwise Ganguly's men stood on the cusp of a big thing. They had been on the cusp before. In Zimbabwe, in 2001, they won the first Test but lost the second. In Sri Lanka, a few months on, they drew level in the second Test but lost the third. In West Indies, in 2002, they took the lead in the second Test but lost two of the following three. In England later that summer they hit back to equalise the series in the third Test but could not win the final. In Australia, most recently, they surged into the lead in the second Test, lost the next, and drew the last. So, apart from a one-off in Bangladesh, they had never won an away series. And apart from that and a 1-0 defeat of the Sri Lankans in 1993-94, India had not won an away series in seventeen years. Of course, India had never won a series in Pakistan before.

*

**Day One**

THE PLAYERS WERE presented gold medals by Hanif Mohammad before start of play: this was a golden jubilee Test, the fiftieth Test between India and Pakistan. And about time. India and England had already played ninety-one times. Australia and England, admittedly over twice the period, were on 306.

Shamianas had considerably been erected above the stands, above all but one stand. Shamianas, Golden Jubilee, series decider, none of it mattered. As at Multan, as at Lahore, a hundred here, a hundred there, a dozen here, a dozen there.

The pitch was almost identical to the one at Lahore. India retained three seamers, with Ashish Nehra coming in for the insufferably loose Agarkar. Sami emerged fit for Pakistan, and Fazl-e-Akbar won the race for the third spot. All other personnel on either side were the same as at Lahore.

Ganguly won India's third toss of the series, a fitting response to Pakistan claiming all five in the one-dayers. Learning from Lahore, he decided to field. Besides, it was in keeping with him.

In the past thirty months Ganguly had inserted (in reverse chronological order): the world's, perhaps history's, most formidable opening partnership in the form of Hayden and Langer at the Gabba; the West Indians at Jamaica with the series at stake; England at Mohali with a novice attack at his disposal; South Africa at Port Elizabeth and Sri Lanka at Kandy with the series in the balance both times. By opting to field now for the sixth time out of the sixteen occasions on which he had won the toss, Ganguly's ratio of insertion, pardon the expression, was quite unrecognisable from that of India's early leaders.

In the 1950s Hazare won tosses eight times and never fielded, and Umrigar made one insertion in six opportunities. At the turn of the decade Contractor enjoyed the option seven times and batted every time. In the 1970s, Wadekar stuck 'em in once in seven chances, Bedi once in thirteen, and Viswanath and Venkataraghavan never did in the four opportunities between them. Gavaskar made four insertions in twenty-two chances. The only departure had come in the 1960s under Tiger Pataudi who, despite his spinners, made six fielding decisions out of twenty, most of them to protect the batting, four of which led to losses and none to victory.

But this could not be seen as a captain's fetish alone. The broader pattern that emerges concerns the evolution of the Indian bowling attack. For, from the mid-1980s onwards, Kapil Dev, Krish Srikkanth, Dilip Vengsarkar, Mohammad Azharuddin and Sachin Tendulkar together made twenty-one insertions from the sixty-six available chances – a proportion not quite as high as Ganguly's but not far behind.

The reason is that there were new-ball bowlers in the house. India's inadequacies in this regard are legend. My favourite story is that of Budhi Kunderan, who, on a miserable tour of England in 1967, opened both the batting and the bowling in a Test match: Kunderan was a wicketkeeper. In this particular match, though, due to a spate of injuries, India were compelled to play both Kunderan and Farokh Engineer. 'What do you bowl?' Pataudi had inquired of Kunderan. 'Don't know,' Kunderan muttered back. Upon which he was thrown the ball.

India are yet to produce an express bowler, but thanks to the emergence of Kapil, and the institution of Chennai's MRF Pace Foundation in the late 1980s (and thereafter such clinics as the one run by Frank Tyson in Bombay for a while in the early 1990s), there was at least an awakening to the power of seam. One of the reasons that Ganguly was given to playing three seamers in his XIs in away Tests was that he had the option of doing so.

But this decision still remained a risk, judging by Ganguly's own experience in the matches listed above. At Brisbane, the Australians had rattled up 262 for 2 from the sixty-two overs possible on day one. At Jamaica, on the grassiest pitch Michael Holding, a local, said he had ever seen at the venue, the West Indian openers sailed to 88 for no loss by lunch and the innings finished on 422. At Mohali against England, it was Harbhajan who had done the damage after tea. At Port Elizabeth, South Africa had made 362 despite Srinath's six-wicket toil. Only on that first occasion, at Kandy, had the move truly worked, when Sri Lanka were bowled out for 274 on the opening day and every wicket, except a run-out, fell to seam.

Not much in the early exchanges at Pindi suggested a departure from the trend. Irfan and Parthiv conceded four byes down leg in the first over. Balaji's second ball was hoisted by Taufeeq into the square-leg fence. Then he bowled a Test-match wide. He continued straying and was replaced by Nehra after three overs. Brought back later from Irfan's end, Balaji bowled another wide. Pakistan were off to their most assured start of the series.

A point of interest was the man Ganguly positioned, briefly, at short leg – himself. He had chosen to omit the team's best bat-pad catcher. This was his way of showing his men and the world that he would not shirk from the dirty work; or perhaps, returning from injury, he wasn't in the best condition to field in the circle.

Balaji bent the fifth ball of his second spell into Taufeeq, at a yorker length almost, surprising him and trapping him lbw. From the other end, Nehra nipped one into Imran Farhat's pads off the pitch. Another leg before. 34 for 2.

Inzamam and Yasir flowered amid the seam, driving avidly and repeatedly through the covers, Yasir a touch too avidly, for he was dragged into a wide nick off Irfan. Just as he had been at Multan. And, by Agarkar, at Lahore. Fool me once, shame on you; fool me thrice... Once more Nehra provided the follow-up, with an immaculate deception. He had just swung one into Inzamam's pads and ought to have won an lbw appeal; the next ball, same line, same length, but angling away; Inzamam, pushed and snicked.

And just like that, Pakistan at lunch, much like the Indians at Lahore, were 96 for 4. Nehra had bowled ten on the trot and on resumption straightaway bowled four more.

Pakistanis dropped off like dead petals after the interval. Youhana played on carelessly to a so-so ball from Irfan. But Irfan's stonking previous over had certainly played its part. It was the fifth time in the seven meetings on the tour that he'd removed Youhana. The batsman, an accomplished one, was in his seventh year of international cricket, the bowler in his fifth month.

Balaji re-entered the game and fashioned it with the most prodigious display of old-ball swing bowling by an Indian in recent memory. It was marvellous to watch, and hard to explain. A gentle breeze blew across the ground, gentle but no more. Repeatedly, Balaji curled it away like a wisp of smoke. One such trapped the left-handed Asim Kamal lbw; another duped Kamran Akmal into nicking to second slip, where Laxman held a swooping catch. On occasion, Balaji managed the inswinging leg-cutter, a delivery not known to prosper outside the hands of such wet-wicket demons of yore as Sydney Barnes.

Shoaib's dismissal deserved the thousand super slo-mo replays it got. Balaji started from wide of the crease. He gripped it straight up the seam, which did not point to fine-leg, as the textbook says it must for the inswinger. Nor did he pull his fingers down the outside on release, as is meant to be done for the leg-cutter. And yet the ball did swing in, and yet the ball did cut away from leg. It was off on its way with a quick back-snap of the wrist, the stitches staring straight down, hypnotically, into the batsman's eyes, the ball drifting further and further in, not merely with the angle, but over and above the angle, making soft contact with the earth and then shooting away in the opposite direction and into the off stump.

Singled out for special mention Balaji may have been by the president of the nation, serenaded he may have been by crowds across the country, all the rage he may have been at a college function, impudent sixes he may have driven over long-on, and bowled he may have with an honest heart, but really, to stake his claim on this tour, Balaji needed a performance which could be recalled. Here it was.

At 137 for 8, the wheels had fallen off Pakistan. Sami played the best innings of the day, defending surely, but still managing to smack seven fours. Fazl-e-Akbar offered comic resistance, for he belonged to that classic breed of tailenders who opted to bat without bending their elbows. In the main he defended, but every so often he stepped away to leg and swatted with his rigid levers. India drifted briefly.

After tea Kumble nipped off Fazl, padding up to a googly, to end a 70-run partnership. Sami was soon run-out, agonisingly, on 49, even as his mates gathered on the balcony to applaud what would have been his first Test fifty. The man making the direct hit was Irfan, who himself had been out on 49 at Lahore.

Pakistan finished on 224. Eight wickets had fallen to seamers. India had mopped up Pakistan for fewer in the first innings of a match on five previous occasions. Only on two of those instances had seamers been comparably dominant. In 1954-55, on the matting at Karachi, G.S. Ramchand's medium-pace had pried out six wickets on what used to be his home ground, and Dattu Phadkar had chipped in with one. At Kolkata in 1998-99, Srinath's morning burst had reduced Pakistan to 26 for 6, and to his five wickets could be added Venkatesh Prasad's two. At Karachi, Pakistan had clawed back to draw. At Kolkata, they had won.

SO MUCH FOR my pontification. Yuvraj did not open the innings. Neither did Sourav for that matter. Parthiv did. He had opened once before in Tests, on the most difficult pitch there was to have done so, at Hamilton in 2002-03. He lasted four balls. That experiment had gone pretty much the way the one with wicketkeeper Sameer Dighe the previous year, similarly thrust into the role in the last innings of the series in seaming conditions, at Harare. He made 4. And that experiment had gone the same way as the one with wicketkeeper M.S.K. Prasad two years previously at Sydney. He made 5 and 3.

I could not work out this decision and I was disappointed by it. Ganguly said later that it was during the tea break, with

Pakistan at 169 for 8, that he had taken the call, reasoning that if the new ball was negotiated the middle-order could cash in conclusively. But when Parthiv himself was asked, he said he had been readied for the task two days in advance; that is, even before Ganguly announced to the press that either Yuvraj or he would open. It had been another appalling day for Parthiv behind the wickets, conceding fourteen byes in a small total, repeatedly fumbling simple takes, and dropping a sitter of sitters from Sami when he was on 34. I wondered how he'd respond to this challenge.

Sehwag took strike to Shoaib. He was out first ball, whipping to leg but caught at gully, on the third attempt, by Yasir.

Observers pounced on Ganguly: had Chopra been playing, he would have taken first strike and such a tragedy would not have come to pass. The fact that Sehwag had recently lost his wicket for 0 and 1 in consecutive Tests batting at no. 2, with Chopra as partner, was quite easily overlooked. This annoyed me so much that, on reflection, I think it was now when I threw my weight behind Parthiv and Ganguly, willing them to prove everyone wrong. That's the thing about Ganguly; with the merest step, by simply being who he is, he is able to create us-versus-them situations. For the most part, it has served India superbly.

India watchfully played out the fifteen overs till close. Later in the evening, Dravid excused himself early from the dinner table. He wanted to sleep well, he said to his companions, because he had to bat all day tomorrow.

*India 23 for 1 in 15 overs (Parthiv 13\*, Dravid 10\*, Shoaib 1-4) trail Pakistan 224 in 72.5 overs (Sami 49, Balaji 4-63, Irfan 2-49, Nehra 2-60) by 201 runs*

\*

279

## Day Two

PRESUMING AN OPENING stand longer than one ball, the Maestro was a touch late to the crease the previous evening, still attiring himself as he reached. But now, after a good night's rest he fell clean out of his groove. The good 'uns still make it count; and maestros, of course.

He was just not feeling it. Sami had a close lbw shout against him on the fourth ball of the morning. Soon he edged Shoaib out of the reach of third slip. On 21, he was a goner, surely, struck again by Sami on the pads. Not given.

This was not an easy morning for India, nor was it expected to be, for the grass still had not fully browned and there was movement about. Parthiv was briefly troubled by Shoaib's bouncers. Ill-advisedly, Shoaib bowled only bouncers, all for a macho smirk at watching a little guy leap about. The one time he had pitched it up, Dravid had edged. Why was he not doing it more? Parthiv grew in stature. He does have a terrific ball sense (while batting). A lot of his strokes are executed with a dangling bat; dangling square drives and dangling glides and dangling cuts, all timed sweetly. He was well at home against the medium pace of Fazl and frequently clattered him for boundaries.

Shoaib returned after a while in the manner of The Slickers' Johnny Too Bad, a ratchet on his waist and a pistol on his waist, robbin' and a stabbin' and a lootin' and a shootin'. He shouldered Parthiv away at the non-striker's and swigged his queue. He bounced it over the keeper for four byes and fired a round in the air. He bounced and bounced and bounced. What was rude boy thinking? Why was not the captain speaking to him? Was this the plan? Was it, really?

By lunch, Parthiv reached 65, already his highest Test score – higher, too, than Chopra's highest Test score from fifteen innings. As the pair returned to the pavilion, Ganguly led the applause from the balcony. This was his tactical victory.

Parthiv fell soon after the interval, pushing Fazl away from his body. Buoyed, Fazl served up a jaffa to beat Tendulkar's outside edge first thing. Next ball he did locate the edge, but the ball squirted past gully.

Shoaib was produced at the other end. First ball, back of a length, steaming hot, climbing, shoulder height, off stump, wicked, evasion from Tendulkar, jubilation from the keeper, appeal from Shoaib, no response from umpire, Tendulkar walks, 130 for 3.

In the snap of a finger the game had opened up. Pakistan needed to break the door down. Some magic, some madness, some inimitable Pakistani inspiration; this was the moment, now was the time.

Nervous moments followed for India. VVS, the new man, made a wristy edge off Shoaib. Dravid top-edged Fazl over the keeper.

But Shoaib was taken off after two further overs, the second of which cost him ten runs, four leg-byes followed by repeated revolving-door ticks from VVS.

Fazl and Sami strayed on to the pads of these Indian gents, an irredeemable error, and accordingly were creamed for boundaries. Dravid began treating Sami's bowling with increasing disrespect, taking two more off-side boundaries, but on 71, with the total on 177, he allowed himself a flailing up-and-under cut, the type he rarely indulges himself with. Yasir plonked it at point. It was, as they say, a lollipop. Sami's Multan blunder had come back to haunt him. It is hard to express Pakistan's agony of the moment. Perhaps Yasir did it best when he said a few days later: 'I haven't spoken to Inzy bhai even once after that... I can't show him my face.' He added, endearingly: 'Sometimes you get so engrossed in watching batsmen like Rahul Dravid and Sachin Tendulkar that you lose focus on your job.'

Dravid continued to buffet rough seas. On 77, there was a prolonged inquiry into a caught-behind off Kaneria. It was, even on the slowest replay, a not fully discernible flurry of bat, boot, earth and ball. My own impression from the freeze-frames was that it had gone from bat to boot to the keeper, which should be out. Misery was piled on misery as Dravid edged a cut wide of slip in Kaneria's next over. From the other end Shoaib bowled another bumper, which jarred Dravid's finger, and the physio was summoned out. This was a wretched innings. But look at the score.

Tea was taken, and after it VVS opened his wings and soared away. There was nothing to do but blush. On three occasions he took a pair of boundaries off Fazl. He flick-pulled him into midwicket, and punched him into the covers; he punched him into the covers and flicked-pulled him to square-leg; he punched him into the covers and touched him straight down. Pakistan's fieldsmen may as well have retired to their tents for VVS was not about to hit to them. To his five boundaries in the ninety minutes before tea, he added seven more in just thirty minutes after. Dravid picked his own pace, hooking Fazl unconvincingly and straight-driving him utterly convincingly. Pakistan were not stuck between a rock and a hard place, more like between an advancing wall and a dancing swordsman. Whatever is the chemistry that these two share, can it please be bottled up and stored for all time?

With a turn to leg off Kaneria, Dravid reached his seventeenth Test hundred. He now had a century in and against every country barring Bangladesh, an anomaly he would rectify before the year was out. On only one of these seventeen occasions had India lost.

Inzamam claimed the new ball as it became available. Shoaib drew an edge from Dravid, it flew, down, wide of second slip, and two slips were all there were. It was impossible to remember a Dravid innings as coarse as this.

Out of nowhere, on a day he had spent peppering his own toe, Shoaib screeched an outswinging full-toss past a half-flick and into the middle stump halfway up, leaving VVS blinking at a blur. It was the fourth time out of eight dismissals on tour that he had been bowled. Later he would say that he lost the ball in the air, and Shoaib at this point was the fastest bowling he had faced in his life. But, 71 off 99: a gorgeous innings, and which had stroked India into the lead.

Ganguly was greeted by a leg gully, a forward short leg, many slips and crimson flames blowing out of Shoaib's nose. On the first delivery to the Indian captain, Shoaib tumbled and fell in his follow-through, leading to a long break wherein his left hand was bandaged. He completed that over, but two balls into the next he left the field. Some forty-five minutes later he re-entered, was told by the umpires that he could not bowl for a while as per the laws, upon which he left again. He did not return.

Pakistan's attack, lacklustre, luckless, sank into submission. Planes flew over Pindi, the sun fell away, and Ganguly prospered, cutting away, cutting every bowler, cutting till the final ball of the day, from Kaneria, to bring up an effortless fifty. Dravid, too, approached his inevitable best in this last hour. Chatting with the press at the end of the day, he remarked: 'When things go your way, you have to make it count, you have to hang in there.' Asked if he was eyeing Lara's 400, he broke into a grin: '400? For me to score 400 the Test match would have to go into a sixth day.'

*India 342 for 4 in 105 overs (Dravid 134\*, Ganguly 53\*, Laxman 71, Parthiv 69, Shoaib 3-47) lead Pakistan 224 by 118 runs*

\*

## Day Three

WHEN GANGULY WAS run-out, for 77, forty-five minutes into the morning, it was history in its seventh repetition as farce. Of Dravid's seven run-outs in Tests, four had been in collaboration with his captain, and out of Ganguly's three, all had been in duet with his deputy. They were magnets configured to always face each other the wrong way, jolting madly towards one another when they needed to stay far away, repelling madly when they needed to move towards one another with alacrity.

The previous evening Ganguly had been all but run-out after a mix-up, and there had been a close call already this morning. When it did happen, it was not out of a misunderstanding, but no less embarrassing for that. Ganguly pushed Kaneria into the covers off the back foot and set off for a single. Imran Nazir, the best fielder in the land, on as substitute, pounced on the ball and made a powerful throw. As the ball was released, Ganguly's eyes were fixed on the fielder, so that he was looking sideways and backward – not the best technique while surging forwards – and his path to the non-striker's was a diagonal. The intention, I suppose, was to position himself between the fielder and the stumps to deter the throw, but once Nazir released the ball, there was no longer scope for bluffing; Ganguly ducked and shirked, the ball hit the top of the stumps, and though Ganguly's bat was well behind the crease, it was not grounded at the moment of impact.

Otherwise Ganguly played a handsome innings, and had not his indolence intervened, looked set for a century. His wagon-wheel was an indictment, too, of Pakistan's own mental torpor. Fifty-three of his seventy-seven runs, and ten of his twelve fours, had been collected in his favoured region, on either side of point. Apart from an occasional second gully, Pakistan had done little to plug this gap, and even less to bowl straighter to him.

Of course, Inzamam missed his best bowlers. First Gul. And now Shoaib, who didn't make an appearance at all on this day.

There was no clarity as to what had gone wrong with Shoaib. From first being informed of an injury to the left wrist, the media were sometimes told that Shoaib was suffering from a side strain, sometimes it was that he had torn a muscle in the back and sometimes broken a rib. Safe to say Inzamam bought none of this. Up in the press box they called him Shoaib Actor.

Shoaib has never made a pretence of being a good boy and that did not help matters now. Indeed, he'd been going around to the Indian dressing room, asking the team manager to help with visa arrangements for a commercial-shoot in Bombay. And he rang up Rashid Latif, or so Latif claimed on national television, to complain about Inzamam not giving him the field placements he wanted. While this stuff always seems funny to the outsider, I was beginning to empathise with the Pakistani supporter.

Sami burned his soul through a thirteen-over spell in the morning, but he could gain neither Gul's deviation off the wicket nor Shoaib's bounce. And reverse swing continued to be elusive. Whether this was, as Ganguly believed, because the hosts had erred by choosing not to prepare dusty tracks and sparse outfields to catalyse the scuffing of the ball, or that the bowlers were unable to perpetrate whatever the mysteries there were to this art, the end result was that their raw pace on these pitches was a bit like shark's teeth without the shark.

Besides, there was Dravid to contend with. He had spent most of the previous day smoothing rough edges, and now his bat did not have any. He consolidated diligently with Yuvraj, committed to 'bat once, bat big', as per plan.

An hour after lunch Dravid reached 200, just as he had reached 100, ticking Kaneria to leg. Inzamam came over for a handshake. Cynics suggested this was only because of the criticism he'd faced for having not done so when Sehwag reached 300 at Multan. I'd like to believe it was a spontaneous acknowledgement from one modern master to another.

When Yuvraj fell lbw to Sami, the pair had added 98 runs for the fifth wicket. Dravid had put on 129 runs with Parthiv, 131 with Laxman, and another 131 with Ganguly. Two runs more with Yuvraj and he would have become the second man in the history of the game to have shared four century-stands in an innings. The only person to have done so was the PCB's Special Guest for this Test, Hanif Mohammad, during the mother of all epics, the sixteen-hour rearguard against West Indies at Barbados in 1957-58.

Only after tea, once they had flattened Pakistan out as a rolling pin does dough, did the Indians begin taking risks. Irfan lofted Farhat for four; Dravid pulled Kaneria and was dropped by Imran Nazir at midwicket; Irfan lofted Kaneria and was caught at long-on; Kumble batted twenty-three balls for two runs and then lofted Farhat for six; Dravid raced on, with sweeps and magnificent inside-out drives, one of which soared for a six.

With the total on 593, and his own score on 270, of which 136 had come from 181 balls on this day, as compared to 134 from 314 before, Dravid pulled out the reverse sweep from outside leg stump to Farhat's part-time spin, testament both to the adventure he had added to his game and his refusal to play for a milestone ahead of the team cause. He was bowled. Thus it was at quarter to four on the day recognised by the Islamic calendar as the twenty-fourth in the month of Safar that Indian cricket's longest batting journey came to end.

Of all Dravid's tours de force this was the most physical. Twelve hours and twenty minutes says plenty, but not everything: apart from the intervals, Dravid had spent all but *one ball* of virtually three full days on the field. This was especially challenging because he is prone to losing fluids much quicker than the next sportsman. Dravid always takes measures. In Perth a few months ago he had visited a specialist, who prescribed him a fluid mix which would aid his rehydration process. And he was, according to John Wright, 'in the top 10 per cent when it comes to physical training', which meant, essentially, that in a squad of sixteen he was number one or two.

As things stood, India had now made four centuries in the series to Pakistan's three. Not much in it. Except that the sum of the Indian four worked out to 885 runs to Pakistan's 331 from three.

This was not Indian overperformance. It was a natural progression. Five of the six highest scores in their history had come in the last three years. Four of them had arrived in the last five months, each of them outside India. Since Sehwag joined the ranks, in late 2001, the quintet of Sehwag, Dravid, Tendulkar, Laxman and Ganguly had among them piled on thirty-one centuries and forty-four fifties in thirty Tests (this one included). Their combined average in this time was 55.85. *Nineteen* of these previous twenty-nine were away Tests – and not a dud among them; tours to Australia, South Africa, England, New Zealand, West Indies and Pakistan and nowhere else. India emerged from these nineteen (current Test excluded) with four wins and six losses. For prolificacy, for seizing moments, for always having a man, or two, for every occasion, the quintet could not match the buccaneering band of contemporary Australians, but what they had achieved was turn India, despite their limited bowling attack, into contenders in any part of the world. Finally.

If Ganguly's and Wright's appointments as captain and coach were significant steps in this regard, Dravid's ascension to batting leader was equally so. Indeed, it is not possible to dissociate the events. (And it is one of the poetic beauties of Indian cricket that

Ganguly and Dravid should have made their debuts together, with a century and a ninety.)

Ganguly's first Test as captain was against Bangladesh in November 2000 (Wright assumed his position one match later), a time where Indian cricket had hit something close to rock bottom. Dravid himself was in a slump in the period leading up to it. In the space of seven Tests his average had plummeted from 55 to a 'mere' 47, and he did not manage a single fifty in those fourteen innings. In the forty-one Tests and forty-one months between then and now, Dravid averaged 70, eight points clear of even Tendulkar in the same phase. He strung together sixteen fifties, three of which were nineties and another three eighties. He constructed eleven centuries, *five* of them doubles, each bigger than the previous, more than any Indian had ever done in an entire career let alone in three and a half years. Not one series passed without bearing the mark of the Maestro and rare was the Test win, home or away, which remained untouched by his work. He was there at Kolkata with VVS, scripting among the most dramatic turnarounds the game has known. He was there with Ganguly five months later at Kandy making a long fourth-innings chase against Murali and cohorts, the longest successful one there has been by a visiting team in that country. He was there at Port Elizabeth three months later saving a Test a day after Mike Denness had infamously hauled the lot over the coals. He was there at Georgetown four months down the line averting a follow-on while popping painkillers to soothe a jaw that had swollen to one side as though with a gulab jamun. He was there one Test later at Port of Spain etching out more than a hundred forgotten runs over two innings in a famous victory. He was there, four months on, entrenched at Trent Bridge for the final four sessions, saving still another Test. He was there at Headingley in the next Test taking blow after blow to the body on a bowler's pitch under glowering skies, sculpting one of the great defensive innings in one of the great Indian wins. He was there, unforgettably, at Adelaide, batting, batting, batting in a trance to victory. He had been India's batsman of the 2000s as they had unfolded so far, and his had been as significant an extended run as there had been by any batsman anywhere since the second war.

Watching Dravid is an inspiration because at a most visible level Dravid's lessons are the lessons of life. After a point all achievement is appetite. In 1997-98 he scored fifties in six successive Test innings. Five years later, he scored hundreds in four successive Test innings. How much can you keep biting off? How much can you keep chewing?

Balaji hit one last parting six, a flying kiss to the crowds, then lost his wicket. India were all out for an even 600.

BY A NEAT SYMMETRY, Pakistan had fifteen overs to play till close, the same as India did on day one. Their first wicket fell on 30, when Farhat made a poke at a ball from Balaji which ought to, particularly in the circumstances, have been left alone on both line and length. Four runs later, Taufeeq followed, lbw to Irfan.

This was Pakistan's great batting failure of the series. The young lefty openers took turns in pursuing each other into the pavilion. At Multan in the first innings, Taufeeq went in the twenty-fourth over with the total on 58 and Farhat at 73 in the twenty-ninth; in the second innings Farhat at 33 in the eighteenth over and Taufeeq at 44 in the twentieth. In the first innings here Taufeeq went at 34 in the eleventh over and Farhat in the twelfth on the same score. And now, Farhat at 30 in the tenth over and Taufeeq at 34 in the eleventh. Only at Lahore had one of them gone on to make a big score and it was the only time they did not expose two new batsmen simultaneously. The results followed.

Inzamam sent out the young wicketkeeper, Kamran Akmal,

who lasted till stumps. Irfan finished the evening on 7-5-7-1, with one four having come off the edge. In the second innings at Multan he had bowled spells of 8-6-3-0 and 9-5-11-1. At Lahore 8-5-4-0 and 7-3-11-3 (one edged four). Of these five, only the first of the Multan spells had been broken by an interval. Already, he had sent down more overs, and many more maidens, than anyone on either side in the series, Kumble included. India seemed to have unearthed the real thing. Pakistan were on the precipice.

Later, after midnight, on a ramble with Saad: me moaning about the lack of texture in the three Test matches, each never wavering from the path it set out on, Saad moaning about his evening in the company of ranting bitter alcoholic former cricket greats who, unlike the chaps of today, always scored a 150 or at least took nine wickets in an innings. We ran into a group of young men about to begin a game of tape-ball under streetlights in an empty parking lot. They refused to let me join in. 'Rahul? Rahul aapka naam? Nahin, hum aapke saath nahin khelenge. Aap ne hamare khilaaf aaj 270 kiya.' (Rahul? Rahul is your name? No, we will not play with you. You made 270 against us today.) We played joyously, raucously, for an hour, maybe more.

*Pakistan 49 for 2 in 15 overs (Akmal 10\*, Yasir 8\*, Irfan 1-7, Balaji 1-30) and 224 trail India 600 (Dravid 270, Ganguly 77, Laxman 71, Parthiv 69, Shoaib 3-47) in 177.2 overs by 327 runs*

\*

**Day Four (and after)**

SUCH AN OPENING HOUR nobody expected. Under a canopy of cloud, Balaji and friends moved it as if on a string, Pakistani batsmen grabbed the string and constructed nooses around their necks, and Indian fielders gently untied the knot. It was a strange, mocking time, every man trying to pull a fast one over the other.

Akmal tried not to play at a ball from Balaji but ended up playing it to Laxman at second slip and Laxman waved it away for four. Akmal popped a dolly off Irfan to Yuvraj at short leg and Yuvraj gargled it between his hands, forearms and chest before letting it fall. Then Akmal was bowled by Balaji, who expanded his Syd Barnesesque repertoire to include the outswinging off-cutter.

Yasir square-drove Balaji. Tendulkar grassed it at point. Inzamam was opened out and laid bare by Balaji. Dravid plopped it at first slip. Yasir slashed at Irfan. Kumble failed to hold at gully. Battling all odds, Yasir succeeded in losing his wicket, to a superb catch by, of all people, Parthiv, down leg. Since a pair of centuries on Test debut, Yasir's scores were 23, 18*, 39, 18, 16, 20*, 21, 17, 80, 3, 59, 91, 23, 19, 16*, 26 and, now, 20. He was a very good player striving for anonymity.

Youhana arrived and guided Balaji to point. Yuvraj spilled it. The next ball, a smirking away-goer, caught Inzamam's outside edge and Parthiv held.

And so in the first forty-five minutes there were three wickets (two of them to Balaji), six dropped catches (four of them off Balaji), six fours (five of them off Balaji), several misfields and several edges (most of them off Balaji). Of course he had to be the tour favourite.

At 94 for 5, Pakistan needed 282 runs to make India bat again. Youhana could be relied on for nothing-to-lose boundaries if not much else. With Youhana was Asim Kamal, who had been put out of commission the previous evening, when, fielding at short leg, a stinging pull from Ganguly had crashed into the elbow of his right arm, his leading arm, that is, while batting. Often he would stroke the ball and wince with pain. One time the doctor came out to administer him an injection.

In seventeen overs the pair added 81 runs and would have gone to lunch unseparated had not the interval been put back by half an hour to accommodate Friday prayers. Kumble deceived Youhana with both flight and turn to pouch a caught-and-bowled, proof of the delicacies he had added to his craft. With the first ball of his next over, he had Sami caught at slip, leaving him on a hat-trick with what were to be the last five balls before lunch.

Who emerged out of the squat Pindi pavilion? Not Fazl, not Kaneria, but the multiply indisposed Express.

Six crouching fielders gathered around the bat: four in a ring on the off, one at forward short leg, another tucked behind, at leg gully; from afar they resembled a noose. First up, rather oblivious to impairments in the wrist, back, side or ribs, Shoaib wound up, got on his knees, and made a tempestuous slog sweep which took the edge and trickled over the rope at third man. Next, a no less tempestuous swing down the ground, third bounce into the fence. Next, dot ball. Then more wholesome swinging, this time over extra-cover off the outer half of the bat. The cameras panned to the dressing room, where Inzamam rose from his seat and paced about, disgust on his face. Fifth ball, the most violent swipe of all, depositing the ball on to the green cloth shamiana behind midwicket. And on that note, lunch. It would be an interesting interval in the dressing room.

Shoaib returned to smite another four and a six before holing out to end a 14-ball innings of 28, all runs in boundaries, none designed to make even a pretence of saving a match, and none suggesting a man in pain.

Two wickets stood between India and their historic quest. Kamal brought up a brave half-century, but only two Pakistani players, the youngsters Akmal and Farhat, came out to the balcony to applaud him. At least he was given a rousing ovation by the crowds. The ambience on this concluding day was the closest the

Test series came to a carnival. My guess was that it was the biggest crowd of the Tests. Certainly it was the most frolicsome; the noisiest of the lot was the women's enclosure, clapping and hooting at the flood of activity.

With little thought for Kamal's efforts, Fazl made repeated kamikaze heave-hos, and eventually was caught on the skier to become Kumble's fourth victim on the day. Two flighted balls from Tendulkar were sufficient for Kaneria to throw himself into a hopeless hoick. Ganguly got underneath it, the captain who had to wrenchingly sit out the victory moment in the one-dayers. By the time the ball landed in Ganguly's hands, Tendulkar had ripped a stump out of the earth. Soon there was none left standing. Soon the substitutes were on the field. Soon there was the great hurrahing huddle. Soon the secretary of the board was on the pitch, and the manager, and the media officer, and the Pakistani masseur attached with the Indian team. John Wright, ever the background man, remained on the balcony, with the physio, the fitness trainer and the computer analyst. In any case the bedlam would move to the dressing room. Soon the champagne was uncorked, soon the music was flipped on, soon bhangras were done. Soon the board announced a second bonus of Rs 50 lakh. Soon the Indians stood atop the balcony; atop, really, the world.

*Pakistan 245 in 54 overs (Kamal 60\*, Youhana 48, Kumble 4-47, Balaji 3-108) and 224 lost to India 600 by an innings and 131 runs*

\*

INSIDE THE LONG DUNGEON in the Pindi pavilion building, they tore like piranhas into Inzamam and Miandad. Some of it, both the questions and the manner, was the vilest I have seen at a press conference. At any rate, Inzamam did not hide his contempt for

Shoaib, saying that he was 'as surprised as you'll were' to see him bat so freely after having refused to bowl; and that, not to worry, if the phone call to Rashid Latif was true then 'action would be taken'. About the estranged Dr Razzak's contention that the fast bowlers were being overworked at the nets: 'You'll were the people complaining about the no-balls and wides in the one-dayers. If they don't sort it out in the nets, then where? In their rooms while sleeping?' Even in anger Inzy retained his touch.

I left to catch the mood outside as Shaharyar entered. Later Osman told me that only then did the real shouting begin.

The shouting never stopped. The following day the English press were scathing. It was nothing, I was told, compared to the Urdu press. Unintended comedy arrived via the slug accompanying the front-page report in *The Nation*: 'Historic Defeat'. Less amusing was a headline on their sports pages: 'Revisiting Kargil in Cricket'.

Words of tragedy and rage poured out from the keyboards of two of the most eloquent commentators on Pakistan cricket. Thus began Omar Kureishi's column in *Dawn*, under the headline 'Pakistan Cricket's Blackest Day'.

I am not certain whether the poet is Byron but these lines come to mind: "If Greece must perish we thy Will obey/But let us perish in the face of day." Not for Pakistan the face of day, not even a tame surrender, just the silence of the lambs. I was hoping that I would be lost for words and would, therefore, be spared the agony of writing about a day, the blackest in Pakistan's cricket history, that has caused so much pain to its supporters.

Kamran Abbasi was far angrier looking back later in *Wisden Asia Cricket*. He called for Inzamam's head, 'a captain without solutions, a captain without spirit', and contended that:

> One of the mysteries of this decade will remain Pakistan's performance in this historic series. Rarely in the annals of cricket can so many talented young men have played so gutlessly for so long... There is no shame in defeat, provided it is defeat with dignity. There is no shame in losing to a better team – which this Indian side clearly is. But there is shame in losing with a whimper. There is shame in failing to compete in the biggest contest of your life.

Shoaib became the obvious scapegoat. Offered the CEO, Rameez, in his column:

> I was really disappointed at the way Shoaib Akhtar conducted himself right through the Test. These green-top pitches were made for him after we decided to bow to public demand. After we provided favourable conditions, I was surprised to see that he was not really committed to beating India. For a Pakistani player, if you can't fight against India, then you won't fight against anybody... Besides his on-field performance, the way he conducted himself as a senior bowler in the side, with the youngsters, his captain and his coach, was really not a reassuring sight for Pakistan cricket.

Shaharyar did a balancing act, standing up for Shoaib at times, laying into him at times. But Shaharyar's actions spoke louder than words. Rapidly he instituted a four-man medical commission, at once a shameless witch-hunt and a useless bureaucratic distraction tactic. The primary motivation behind convening the commission, to quote from the first paragraph of its report, was 'to examine & substantiate the authenticity of injury sustained by Pakistan's Fast Bowler Shoaib Akhtar during the third test match between Pakistan and India.' For this insult, Imran Khan urged Shoaib to sue the PCB. As for the other stated purpose – to assess the injuries of the five Pakistani players during the series – the competence of the commission could be judged by the fact that they failed to detect any trace of the three stress fractures in poor Gul's spine, diagnosed in South Africa a few months later. Shabbir Ahmed did not even depose, as he was required to.

And Shoaib deposed a week late, for he had taken off straight after the series to Bombay, where he was photographed at nightspot after nightspot, and where, in a glitzy colour-supplement, he would lend his byline to a column containing sentences such as: 'Fast bucks, fast cars, buzzing lounges, dope, smoke and sex – I see a smoky realm growing grittier by the day, as it accumulates into varied psychological and physiological stress', and, 'We live in aggressively market-driven times and the unpalatable truth is that "fame" has become society's narcotic and the youth's doorway to this ephemeral fame is partying.'

Eventually, surprise, surprise, the medical commission was unable to ascertain whether Shoaib had bluffed or not – but for good measure the chairman of the commission still made it clear that there was a strong chance that Shoaib had in fact faked it. Thus was achieved both eyewash and witch-hunt.

Everyone began going after everyone. Our old friend, Mr Bajwa, the Public Interest Litigator, was back with a bang and slapped a lawsuit on Shoaib (Rs 100 million only) for letting down the nation. Shoaib retaliated by slapping a lawsuit on two of Bajwa's former clients for malicious prosecution (Rs 70 million) and mental agony (Rs 30 million). Rameez was subjected by the media to so many allegations of malpractice, including that of selling thousands of tickets in black, that the PCB released a complete statement of his entitlements, showing how he had, for example, forsaken the privilege of a cook. The treasurer of the PCB resigned with a dynamite letter wherein he accused Shaharyar and Rameez of splurging unwarranted millions on consultants and lawyers and chairs and mobile ticketing booths, and accused Allied Bank, with whom Rameez was a marketing executive, of withholding payments to the PCB knowing that with Rameez on their side the PCB could easily be dictated to. Meanwhile, *The News* reported that the treasurer's allegations were, in fact, rooted in the ignominy of having been denied 400 match-tickets for friends and family. A Standing Committee of senators in the upper house of the national parliament began a sustained and vociferous probe into all matters of the PCB, from its constitutionality to its appointments to its selection procedures to, of course, reasons for the shameful loss to India. Shaharyar routinely appeared before the senators with various documents and routinely he was grilled to charcoal. Seizing on the vulnerability of the moment, the state associations formed an 'action group' and made a list of demands, starting with the restoration of democracy to the board. Under pressure from all quarters, the PCB were driven to a feeble branding initiative, replacing the catchphrase of the team, 'Proud to be a Pakistani', with 'Team Pakistan', in order to 'emphasise more on the team aspect'.

Inevitably, heads rolled; by force or by will, one after the other, every fortnight someone fell. The treasurer had announced his explosive departure three weeks after the series ended. Soon Miandad lost his job (and by the year-end would serve a legal notice to Shaharyar) to the highly-regarded Bob Woolmer, brought on board at many times Miandad's salary, while Barry Richards and Greg Chappell were hired as batting consultants. The two team doctors were sacked for a South African pair of a physiotherapist and a fitness trainer. The head of the media cell quit his post. Ultimately came the resignation of Rameez, unable to sustain his triple life of commentator-columnist, board CEO, and marketing executive of a bank which did business with the board. In three months, therefore, we were talking six middle- and top-level exits from the team management and the PCB management, and a parliamentary inquiry which is probably still continuing at whichever time you read this.

There may have been no public demonstrations, there may have been no burning of effigies, and there may have been giggling and laughter in the stands as the last rites at Pindi were performed. But this was India versus Pakistan. This always ends in tears.

It had been fascinating, surreal even, watching Pakistan close-up in action over the last month and a half. How do they do it? How do they do it despite themselves? This is a commonplace lament in the cricketing world. Really, the rest of the world does not have a case. No, not strictly for level of chaos, which several others, not least India, can muster, though not so relentlessly. We mean here chaos offset against results.

It is simply astonishing that Pakistan are history's second most successful team, behind, in terms of win-loss ratio, only Australia; ahead of England, who had a head start over every other country by virtue of having invented the game; ahead, by a whisker, even of West Indies, who for two decades roamed the earth with an invincible swagger; and ahead, by *twice*, of their big neighbours, India. They burst on to the scene in the fifties, young upstarts, and by the time their first captain, Abdul Hafeez Kardar, had called it a day, he had led Pakistan to the extraordinary feat of a Test win against every country, and a Test win in every country they visited. I cannot know how it was watching Kardar's lionhearts, but while growing up, no team spoke so directly to me as the Pakistanis, no team quite stirred the blood so. The big hair, the cuss on the breath, the red-hot pace, the late swing, the googlies, the yorkers, the reverse sweeps, the inside-outs, the keeper shouting down the bowler, the bowler shouting down the fielder, the captain shouting down everyone, the victories snatched from nowhere, the defeats snatched from nowhere, the, what's the word, *junoon*... it was, minus the late swing and the red-hot pace and arguably the googlies, cricket as I knew it in the empty plots of Secunderabad or in the L-shaped building compounds of Bombay. The Pakistanis were always around to provide reassurance that cricket was well worth losing your head and manners and inhibitions over; that cricket, really, was the fight for survival. But where was that Pakistan now, where was that irrepressible Pakistan? Chaos still surrounded them but where was the junoon? What happened?

So while luxuriating in the glow of India's achievement, I could not help but feel more than a tinge of emptiness at Pakistan's surrender. Yes, I did feel vacant.

# 9. *Safar*

I SUPPOSE the greater part of it was end-of-tour vacantness. Suddenly no requesting the 7.30 morning milky tea. Suddenly no encouraging the room-mate into first use of the toilet (no chance with Saad) to steal an extra twenty minutes of sleep. Suddenly the lovely Shakeel bhai, former Pakistan cricketer who now worked in the media cell, has presented a goodbye t-shirt. Suddenly every other sentence is 'achchha, khyaal rakhna' (all right, take care), if not 'yaad rakhna' (remember us).

The weeks after a tour require infinitely more energy than the weeks on it. A life ends with a tour, for every tour is a life. Over weeks a world is built, every character, every event, contributing in ways nobody can predict to a conclusion which nobody knows, and then that world with its intricacies, patterns, ironies, irrelevancies, beauties and stupidities is not so much dismantled as razed to the ground. The mind must let go, unlearn; a purpose is lost. It is disconcerting. Days pass and months do and years do and then there is only a reminiscence of a world, a state of mind, a state of life, once inhabited with such gusto, such fervour, such an over-rated world, such a delightful world.

It was in this condition of slight disorientation that I went to meet Ganguly at the team hotel the morning after. I could not find him anywhere. I waited, as journalists must, shrewdly parking myself on the piano-stool in the lobby from where every angle could be monitored.

Fans, both Indians and Pakistanis, were out in force in the lobby. Irfan's parents were by the concierge, the mother in hijab, the father, a muezzin, in Jinnah topi. They had travelled out of India and by airplane for the first time. The son was not around, so they were besieged for their own autographs.

I had unwittingly drawn a moment of defensiveness from Irfan when I asked him if he had any family in Pakistan. 'Nahin, Hindustan ka hi hoon' (No, I'm from India), he replied emphatically. He had probably been warned against this type of question; it could trap him. But my question was not at all 'how does it feel to be a Muslim playing against Pakistan'. I'd only wanted to know if there was a side-story worth following up for the magazine. However, it was in Irfan's fate, the son of a muezzin, in post-riot Gujarat, to represent the ideal of a plural India in its days of darkness. I wondered how he would reconcile, if he had not already, to the full weight of his symbolism.

A man with large eyes greeted me. I could not place him but he said we had spoken briefly at the Pearl Continental at Lahore, the day the Indians first landed in town. Gosh, how long ago was that! He could not have been mistaken because he remembered me desperately trying to retrieve my mobile phone from the cushion-crack in the sofa. Tanveer claimed to be great friends with Tendulkar and the poet-director Gulzar and later emailed me his photograph taken alongside each of them. He had a manic way about him. He spoke in rapid torrents and everchanging modulations. All of a sudden he leant into my ear and whispered, 'I hate border'. I couldn't quite get him. 'I hate border,' he repeated, 'I hate fucking border.' I can still see the humongous white expanses of his eyes as he whispered the words.

I did the Ganguly interview in the coffee shop. Rawalpindi had been a big moment for Ganguly from a personal point of view. It was his fifteenth win as Test captain. With that he had overtaken Azharuddin as the most winning captain in Indian history. Azhar's fourteen had come from forty-seven Tests. Ganguly's fifteen had taken thirty-eight. Azhar's team won once outside India (in Sri Lanka). Rawalpindi was India's seventh away win under Ganguly, and in the seventh country. And at an innings and 131 runs, Rawalpindi had surpassed Multan as the largest Indian away victory. As Test matches go, the only comparison in Indian cricket history to the back-to-back 1-1 in Australia and the 2-1 here was the twin series wins of 1971, in West Indies and England. Attempting to rate the historic significance of the two events, or even their worth as cricketing achievements is silly, and when Wadekar, present here as a PCB invitee, himself declared this one to be the better team, to me what it really meant was that at long, long last, about a quarter-century too late really, somebody had taken things forward.

'You've got to do that,' Ganguly said, leaning forward in his chair, playing with the Dictaphone, eyes bright behind spectacles. 'At least people will say this team has taken Indian cricket forward. You cannot push back Indian cricket by being negative or just looking at personal goals.'

We spoke only for fifteen minutes, maybe twenty, and though his answers were mostly short, a news piece could have been woven around virtually every one of them. 'People will remember you only if you win, says Ganguly.' 'Playing football made me competitive: Ganguly.' 'Parthiv's batting the biggest plus from the series, says Ganguly.' 'Yuvraj future opener for India, says Ganguly.' 'Ganguly surprised by Pakistani softness under pressure.' 'First I pick 'em, then I persist with 'em: Ganguly's mantra for nurturing youngsters.' 'India second only to Australia, declares Ganguly.'

This was Ganguly, wearing his ambitions, his pride, his achievements, on his sleeve. Many of his plans and ambitions would come unstuck in the following months, he and his team unable to summon the strength to keep from getting sucked into the whirlpool of distorted realities that success brings, especially for an Indian cricketer; and bogged down further by a disgraceful, rotting cricket board. But regardless of where Ganguly would go from here, he had played his part, a huge part it was, a part few expected him to play. He had taken Indian cricket forward.

I asked him, finally, his favourite memories from the tour. 'I know there were a lot of things attached to this tour,' he maintained, as he had done all along, 'but for the twenty of us in this team it was cricket. And winning the series, both the series, is the biggest memory we will take back with us.'

A few hours on, the Indians departed by a chartered flight aboard which they cracked open more bubbly. On arrival in Delhi they were led out secretly as they had been at the arrival in Lahore. Reports spoke of hundreds of fans having gathered at the airport. Most photographs I saw showed hordes of BJP workers carrying the party flag, or dancing men wearing t-shirts with the branding of Sahara, the team sponsor, and Samsung, the series sponsor. The tour had begun with appropriation and so it would end. In between it was beautiful.

I proceeded to Karachi where five days passed in a haze of deadlines and jadedness. Soon I found myself poking at a toast-omelette in a cold and desolate restaurant at the departure terminal, waiting for an early-morning flight home. It was too early and too cold to think much. But I thought of 135 A/9-L, and I thought that for six weeks I had been made to feel special and that would now go away.

For now I must wind the clock back a month.

*

304

*Safar*

A WARM LULLABY wind blew the afternoon Saad and I travelled out in Shaukat's taxi. This was the twenty-third of March, the second gap-day between the last two one-day internationals. It happened to be also, Pakistan Day, the anniversary, the sixty-third now, of the Lahore Resolution, wherein Jinnah's Muslim League first made their demand for a separate Islamic Republic culled from British India.

We drove along the canal, which then stayed by our side for most of the way. Past the conurbation of Lahore, families picnicked by its grassy banks, youngsters pushed one another in. The canal-network was a legacy of the Raj, and scholars are still debating whether it built the economy of Punjab more or ruined its ecology. The canals were a symbol, also, of one of the few things at which the two governments had managed reasonable and sustained co-operation, the sharing of waters.

Every now and then we passed small settlements, canal colonies, fronted on the highway by a dhaba. Behind, the fields yawned away into a shining golden horizon, the flatness broken only by occasional brick kilns.

I asked Shaukat what fields these were. He replied: 'Pakistan ke hain, India ke nahin' (They are Pakistan's, not India's). Immediately he looked embarrassed. He had misunderstood my question. I told him I meant what was being grown on them. He said wheat, though it could well have been mustard. His face fell.

Soon we passed Batapur, a factory village. The logo – red, italicised, running-hand font – was incorporated into the village name and splashed on signboards everywhere. Pakistanis, I had found, like Indians, assumed Bata was theirs. In fact it is Czech.

Thirty minutes into our drive, the milestones for Wagah, spelt on this side as Wagha, began to appear ever more frequently till there was one every kilometre.

THE LONG HORIZONTAL banner above the gate was sponsored by Dawn Bread. Welcome to JCP Wagha, it said. There was a dhaba outside the Joint Check Post too, and a number of cigarette and cold drink stalls. I looked for a visible sign of a border on the fields. I could not make out any. I was told there was a fence; a low, non-electric fence, as I found later in a photograph of Tendulkar, who was granted permission to stand with a leg on either side.

There was an awful lot of dusty activity at the JCP. And a montage of sounds: the impatient buzz of the waiting, growing beyond a buzz now; the high-pitched electronic crackles of the Walls ice-cream cycle boys; the afternoon, asr, call to prayer from the mosque across the dhaba.

A set of Rangers guarded the gate. This gate, I came to understand, was a valve; the arena of the ceremony, as it were, was more than half a kilometre beyond, and already packed with people. The area leading up to the gate was patrolled by a pair of Rangers, whips in hand, atop chestnut-brown horses.

Slowly, but discernibly, a certain bedlam was beginning to set in. Nobody knew the criteria for getting through the valve. Besides, the wait for many, it was clear to see, had been for hours. The crowd was much bigger than usual, I was told, because this was a national day.

Every now and then, a wave of people would attack the gate. The foot Rangers would brandish their lathis. A few would squirt through. The men on horses would swing into action, backing the rear of the animal into the wave, making everyone run backwards, resulting, sometimes, in a domino-fall. It was a wonder there wasn't a full-scale stampede.

The crowd kept swelling. There was a large number of families, many of them with children. There were several bedraggled groups who had the feel of refugees, as at the visa counters at Delhi.

There was a collection of sightseers: a few Indians, an orange-haired Japanese twenty-something with a videocam. The Ten Sports crew had arrived to shoot a sight-and-sounds clip, but, for the moment, was not being let through. Khalid Ansari, the founder-chairman of the *Mid Day* group, came with a couple of Pakistani friends, who were meant to have been granted easy access. They were not.

Meanwhile, the waves got stronger and more frequent. If both horses were pressed into action on the left, there would be a compensatory attack from the right. Children would begin crying, and women shrieking, half out of fear, half out of fun, whenever the horse's bum approached. Suddenly the horse might turn, revealing large glistening eyes, cavernous nostrils, and a sliver of frothy spit. I got a tail in my eyes.

And so the game continued. The masses swayed to and fro, going to the gate one minute, running away from the grunting horses the next. Except for those in government vehicles, the number of people squeezing through the valve kept reducing. The dust, kicked up by the wave-game, flew into the eyes, it blurred the vision; hundreds of people coughed together.

People began to get hurt; an elbow in a face here, a hoof on a foot there. One of Mr Ansari's companions turned out to be a friend of Saad's father. In one horse-induced retreat, he was thrown backwards, and might have been badly injured and trampled upon had Saad not, quite heroically I must say, caught him in his arms a few inches before he hit the ground. It was all getting rather ugly. We could have turned back at this point, taken a stand against the indignity. But we were desperate. I could not fully comprehend my desperation. But I was desperate.

Wagah is the only point along India's 2,900-odd km boundary with Pakistan where crossing is permitted. I was not sure of it back then, on the twenty-third of March, but the cross-border movement of Indians during the cricket tour was the greatest there had been since the early years after Partition. Indians came on cricket visas, tightly configured visas, valid for no longer than two or three days after the match ended, and valid, in name at least, only for the venues of the matches applied for. Crucially, they bore the stamp 'Exempted from Police Reporting', meaning there was to be no presenting oneself to the cops first thing on arrival as is required of casual visitors to each other's countries.

How many crossed? We must hope that one day the Pakistan High Commission in Delhi, from where all visas were issued, makes the information public. Till then we are down to guesswork. What we can be certain of is that the figure was more than the 8,000, as was initially declared by Pakistan's Interior Ministry, and less than the 20,000, which Shaharyar, a former foreign secretary, repeatedly claimed after the tour. Ringing, writing, and generally haranguing the High Commission for months on end brought either evasion, or throwaway, often contradictory, numbers. On request, a journalist better connected than your author was told that 11,000 was probably an accurate number, with approximately 5,000 for the Lahore one-dayers. After piecing together fragments of information obtained from the Northern Railways, the Border Security Force, Indian Airlines, Pakistan International Airlines, Delhi Transport Corporation and the attendances at the matches, that is also the estimate I'm inclined to accept.

There seems to be agreement that the other great movements would have also been on occasions of cricket, and those from east to west. Ten thousand, according to *A Corner of a Foreign Field*, attended the Lahore Test of 1954-55, but those were times when the border was still fairly porous. Reports in *The Times of India* during the other significant series, in 1978-79, suggest that not more than a couple of thousand crossed.

So this was it, then, the single biggest window there had been in almost fifty years, the single biggest window for a people to talk to another. We talked pretty well I think. And in the name of a contest.

A LAST-GASP BOUT of violent opportunism saw us through the valve, not without a volley of lathi hits, five minutes before the ceremony was to begin.

A fanatical cheering became audible as we approached an imposing brick archway. The archway was flanked by white minarets, from which curved out a semi-circular amphitheatre. One half was reserved for ladies and children. We tried to get up into the other section, but it was occupied almost twice over. The guards sent us back down. We tried to make our way through the archway, and to the side of the road up which the soldiers were to march, but there too people had lined up, seven and eight deep. The guards wouldn't let us through. Every place we tried to squeeze into, a guard with a rifle was there to stop us. Finally, I played the India card. 'Achchha, India ke hai? Pehle hi bol dete...' (From India? You should have told me earlier...) He let us pass, with a smile. Saad grimaced.

We found a spot on the sidelines. Chants rented the air. Pakistan Zindabad. Allah-u-Akbar. A cheerleader who had almost knocked over Saad with his flag at the stadium was running up and down, waving his crescented cloth, urging the masses on like the coach at tug-of-war. The flag had been designed by Jinnah so that – I quote from a Pakistan government website – 'the white and dark green field represents Minorities & Muslim majority, respectively. The crescent on the Flag represents progress. The five-rayed star represents light and knowledge.' It was a striking creation, and a powerful symbol.

Barely had we taken our spot than the crowds erupted into a

delirious roar: a guard had begun marching towards a gate, some 50 metres past the brick archway. Marching is a euphemism. He stomped so hard as if to create holes in the earth, a severely built man in immaculate uniform, a magnificent turban, boots of gleaming black, and wearing hate on his face as he had been told to. Even amid the chanting and hooting and clapping, the clamping down of the hobnailed boots could be made out. And since I sat cross-legged on the road up which he marched, I could feel the vibrations through my body.

The guard powered on till the gate, where he spread his hands like a performer, maintaining the hate on his face, and shaking his head vigorously in the manner one does after downing a Patiala Peg; high on induced hate. The hands were lowered to the sides in a series of theatrical gestures. Another guard followed, and another. Sometimes they went in twos and threes. As they reached the gate, one after the other, and played out their hate, the crowd was stirred to a frenzy. A depravity hung in the air.

The Pakistani gate was an intricate iron work of green, with a large white crescent and star. Ten metres or so beyond that was a cream Indian gate. A thick white line – *the* line – ran between these gates, an arrow from each gate pointing to the line.

Beyond the cream gate, in Bharat, a similar process seemed to be underway. I could not be sure. I read somewhere that the Indians had decided to tone down the posturing from their end. I read somewhere else that the commanders of both forces were to meet and agree on softening the gestures. What I do know is that the last time I contacted the Border Security Force, six months after the tour, I was told the ceremony was just the way it was, without any softening.

Amid a blast of bugles there ensued a rigorous confrontation between a pair of Indians and Pakistanis on the thick white line. High-stepping, goosestepping, they criss-crossed each other fiercely, the Pakistanis in olive-black, the Indians in khaki, to a crescendoing noise.

A chronicle by a visiting westerner likened the ceremony to a European football game. This was ironic, instructive. Where Orwell had likened sport to war minus the shooting, here was wilfully calibrated war minus the shooting – shadow-boxing, in uniform, at the border – being likened to sport.

At last a pair of guards from either side shook hands, and the flags were gently lowered. This signified the closing of the border for the day. Both gates were slammed shut together, with immense force. There was a sudden, shocked silence, and in the silence of the moment, the metal rang in the ears. The silence continued for several seconds. The silence was a lot of things: a brief mourning, the acknowledgement of an attachment, of a shameful history; it was a symbolic reconciliation; I think it was, in large part, embarrassment at the preceding depravity.

I have read that at this point people from both sides are allowed to run up till the gates and look across for a couple of minutes, into one another's eyes, into one another's countries; that some broken families fix this as a meeting point. There was such a great spilling out of crowd, from the sidelines, from the amphitheatre, thousands, perhaps three, perhaps five, perhaps more, but thousands pouring out on to the road up which the soldiers marched, that I could not tell for sure.

Suddenly music blared out from the speakers, pop songs honouring Pakistan, 'Dil Dil Pakistan' and others, catchy tunes, and they imparted a carnival atmosphere. A group of boys removed their shirts and wet themselves in a fountain on the lawn, dancing. A gaggle of girls clapped hands and sang gaily. Soon, the guards began herding everybody back, back inside Pakistan. The show was over. We walked back out the archway, and towards the valve, the sound of the songs receding.

Even now I shudder at the mesh of emotions at that scene at the border on March twenty-third. The faces of some wore a disturbed look. Some looked distraught. Some chanted. Some looked fragile, shattered, tears in eyes. Some looked plain entertained. Some, like Mr Ansari, were furious, furious with the jingoism the ceremony was designed to generate. Saad and I discussed things with passionate angst. It was a confusing time. Two buses made their way past the returning masses against the setting sun, replica-blue sleeves waving out as they drove by. They waved out and the Pakistanis waved back, spontaneously, heartily. It was a Delhi Transport Corporation bus: it was Tuesday, India's turn. The following day VVS played.

# Acknowledgements

Deep thanks to Osman, Saad, and their families, Sonny, Sambit, Ram, Peter, Samar, Ehte, Mr Lele, Nishant, Shakeel bhai, Leslie, Bib, Hunter, Mangu, Gulu, Sharmeen Obaid, Shoaib Hasan, the Hashmis, Davinder Sandhu, Yuki, Pakistan Sports, Moonis, Pallosingh, Thakur, Poops, Sonali, Ma, Bay and, mostly, Shruti.

# Illustrations

Plate section:
1-3, 5 (Lahore spectators), 6, 7: Sanjoy Ghosh/*Outlook*
4 (Scene from the Samjhauta Express), 5 (Outside Gaddafi Stadium),
9-16: Gopal
4 Advertisement: courtesy Northern Railways
8: Scott Barbour/Getty Images
Map: Shuchi Thakur
Illustrations: Shreya Debi
Cover pictures: Sanjoy Ghosh, Gopal
Cover illustration and design: Moonis Ijlal

# Scorecards & Statistics

Courtesy Cricinfo.com

# First ODI, National Stadium, Karachi, 13 March 2004

Toss Pakistan

India won by 5 runs

Man of the Match Inzamam-ul-Haq

| INDIA | | R | M | B | 4/6 | |
|---|---|---|---|---|---|---|
| V Sehwag | b Naved-ul-Hasan | 79 | 85 | 57 | 14 | 1 |
| SR Tendulkar | c Naved-ul-Hasan b Shoaib Akhtar | 28 | 49 | 35 | 4 | 1 |
| SC Ganguly* | c&b Naved-ul-Hasan | 45 | 82 | 47 | 3 | 2 |
| R Dravid† | b Shoaib Akhtar | 99 | 127 | 104 | 8 | 0 |
| Yuvraj Singh | c Yasir Hameed b Naved-ul-Hasan | 3 | 11 | 9 | 0 | 0 |
| M Kaif | lbw b M Sami | 46 | 72 | 56 | 4 | 0 |
| HK Badani | not out | 8 | 14 | 5 | 1 | 0 |
| Z Khan | b M Sami | 0 | 3 | 2 | 0 | 0 |
| M Kartik | not out | 3 | 6 | 5 | 0 | 0 |
| L Balaji | | | | | | |
| A Nehra | | | | | | |
| Extras | (b 1, lb 7, w 10, nb 20) | 38 | | | | |
| Total | (7 wickets, 50 ov, 228 mins) | 349 | | | | |

1-69 (Tendulkar, 8.6 ov), 2-142 (Sehwag, 14.2 ov), 3-214 (Ganguly, 26.2 ov),
4-220 (Yuvraj Singh, 28.4 ov), 5-338 (Dravid, 47.5 ov), 6-344 (Kaif, 48.3 ov),
7-344 (Khan, 48.5 ov)

| | o | m | r | w | |
|---|---|---|---|---|---|
| Shoaib Akhtar | 10 | 0 | 55 | 2 | (3nb, 6w) |
| M Sami | 10 | 0 | 74 | 2 | (5nb, 3w) |
| Naved-ul-Hasan | 10 | 0 | 73 | 3 | (7nb) |
| Abdul Razzaq | 9 | 0 | 83 | 0 | (4nb) |
| Shoaib Malik | 10 | 0 | 50 | 0 | (1nb) |
| Yasir Hameed | 1 | 0 | 6 | 0 | |

| PAKISTAN | | R | M | B | 4/6 | |
|---|---|---|---|---|---|---|
| Yasir Hameed | b Balaji | 7 | 26 | 13 | 0 | 0 |
| Imran Farhat | c Dravid b Khan | 24 | 34 | 29 | 4 | 0 |
| Yousuf Youhana | c sub (IK Pathan) b Sehwag | 73 | 98 | 68 | 5 | 4 |
| Inzamam-ul-Haq* | c Dravid b Kartik | 122 | 154 | 102 | 12 | 2 |
| Younis Khan | b Kartik | 46 | 75 | 48 | 4 | 1 |
| Abdul Razzaq | b Khan | 27 | 22 | 16 | 2 | 1 |
| Moin Khan† | c Khan b Nehra | 16 | 35 | 17 | 0 | 0 |
| Shoaib Malik | c Kaif b Khan | 7 | 15 | 5 | 0 | 0 |
| Naved-ul-Hasan | not out | 3 | 8 | 4 | 0 | 0 |
| Mohammad Sami | | | | | | |
| Shoaib Akhtar | | | | | | |
| Extras | (lb 10, w 7, nb 2) | 19 | | | | |
| Total | (8 wickets, 50 ov, 238 mins) | 344 | | | | |

1-32 (Yasir Hameed, 6.2 ov), 2-34 (Imran Farhat, 7.4 ov), 3-169 (Yousuf Youhana, 27.4 ov),
4-278 (Inzamam-ul-Haq, 42.1 ov), 5-305 (Younis Khan, 44.5 ov),
6-322 (Abdul Razzaq, 46.4 ov), 7-340 (Shoaib Malik, 48.5 ov), 8-344 (Moin Khan, 49.6 ov)

| | o | m | r | w | |
|---|---|---|---|---|---|
| Balaji | 10 | 1 | 56 | 1 | (1w) |
| Khan | 10 | 0 | 66 | 3 | (2nb, 2w) |
| Nehra | 10 | 0 | 58 | 1 | (1w) |
| Kartik | 10 | 0 | 74 | 2 | (3w) |
| Ganguly | 1 | 0 | 14 | 0 | |
| Tendulkar | 3 | 0 | 34 | 0 | |
| Sehwag | 6 | 0 | 32 | 1 | |

Umpires: Nadeem Ghauri (P) and SJA Taufel (A); Asad Rauf (P); Match Referee: RS Madugalle (SL)

## Second ODI, Pindi Cricket Stadium, Rawalpindi, 16 March 2004 (D/N)

Toss Pakistan                                                          Pakistan won by 12 runs

| PAKISTAN | | R | M | B | 4/6 |
|---|---|---|---|---|---|
| Yasir Hameed | run out (Nehra/Yuvraj Singh) | 86 | 145 | 108 | 9 1 |
| Shahid Afridi | b Yuvraj Singh | 80 | 92 | 58 | 10 4 |
| Yousuf Youhana | b Yuvraj Singh | 24 | 30 | 26 | 2 0 |
| Inzamam-ul-Haq* | b Nehra | 29 | 31 | 34 | 1 1 |
| Younis Khan | c Dravid b Nehra | 28 | 37 | 28 | 1 0 |
| Moin Khan† | lbw b Nehra | 0 | 1 | 1 | 0 0 |
| Shoaib Malik | not out | 30 | 42 | 28 | 2 0 |
| Abdul Razzaq | not out | 31 | 16 | 18 | 4 0 |
| Shabbir Ahmed | | | | | |
| Mohammad Sami | | | | | |
| Shoaib Akhtar | | | | | |
| Extras | (lb 6, w 14, nb 1) | 21 | | | |
| Total | (6 wickets, 50 ov) | 329 | | | |

1-138 (Shahid Afridi, 18.2 ov), 2-191 (Yousuf Youhana, 28.6 ov)
3-225 (Yasir Hameed, 34.6 ov), 4-249 (Inzamam-ul-Haq, 39.1 ov)
5-249 (Moin Khan, 39.2 ov), 6-284 (Younis Khan, 45.5 ov)

| | o | m | r | w | |
|---|---|---|---|---|---|
| Balaji | 6 | 0 | 47 | 0 | (4w) |
| Khan | 7 | 0 | 72 | 0 | (2w) |
| Nehra | 10 | 0 | 44 | 3 | |
| Sehwag | 5 | 0 | 39 | 0 | (1nb) |
| Yuvraj Singh | 10 | 1 | 41 | 2 | (1w) |
| Powar | 6 | 0 | 35 | 0 | (1w) |
| Tendulkar | 6 | 0 | 45 | 0 | (2w) |

Man of the Match SR Tendulkar

| INDIA | | R | M | B | 4/6 |
|---|---|---|---|---|---|
| V Sehwag | b Shoaib Akhtar | 26 | 35 | 21 | 4 0 |
| SR Tendulkar | c Abdul Razzaq b Shoaib Malik | 141 | 173 | 135 | 17 1 |
| VVS Laxman | lbw b M Sami | 4 | 17 | 7 | 0 0 |
| SC Ganguly* | st Moin Khan b Shahid Afridi | 15 | 55 | 38 | 1 0 |
| R Dravid† | b M Sami | 36 | 74 | 45 | 2 0 |
| Yuvraj Singh | c Shabbir Ahmed b Shahid Afridi | 19 | 30 | 20 | 2 0 |
| M Kaif | c Shoaib Malik b Shoaib Akhtar | 7 | 18 | 9 | 0 0 |
| RR Powar | not out | 18 | 21 | 11 | 3 0 |
| Z Khan | lbw b Shoaib Akhtar | 0 | 1 | 1 | 0 0 |
| L Balaji | run out (Yousuf Youhana/M Sami) | 14 | 12 | 10 | 3 0 |
| A Nehra | b M Sami | 0 | 1 | 1 | 0 0 |
| Extras | (b 2, lb 22, w 6, nb 7) | 37 | | | |
| Total | (all out, 48.4 ov) | 317 | | | |

1-56 (Sehwag, 8.1 ov), 2-71 (Laxman, 11.4 ov), 3-140 (Ganguly, 23.5 ov),
4-245 (Tendulkar, 38.4 ov), 5-260 (Dravid, 41.5 ov), 6-282 (Yuvraj Singh, 44.5 ov),
7-284 (Kaif, 45.3 ov), 8-284 (Khan, 45.4 ov), 9-314 (Balaji, 48.1 ov), 10-317 (Nehra, 48.4 ov)

| | o | m | r | w | |
|---|---|---|---|---|---|
| Shoaib Akhtar | 9 | 1 | 49 | 3 | (1nb) |
| Shabbir Ahmed | 9 | 0 | 65 | 0 | |
| M Sami | 9.4 | 1 | 41 | 3 | (3nb, 4w) |
| Shoaib Malik | 10 | 0 | 59 | 1 | (1w) |
| Shahid Afridi | 8 | 0 | 57 | 2 | (2nb) |
| Abdul Razzaq | 3 | 0 | 22 | 0 | |

Umpires: Asad Rauf (P) and SJA Taufel (A); Zamir Haider (P); Match Referee: RS Madugalle (SL)

# Third ODI, Arbab Niaz Stadium, Peshawar, 19 March 2004

Toss Pakistan

Pakistan won by 4 wickets

Man of the Match Yasir Hameed

## INDIA

| | | | R | M | B | 4/6 |
|---|---|---|---|---|---|---|
| V Sehwag | c Shahid Afridi | b Shabbir Ahmed | 13 | 29 | 18 | 3 0 |
| SR Tendulkar | c Moin Khan | b Shabbir Ahmed | 0 | 7 | 5 | 0 0 |
| VVS Laxman | | b Shabbir Ahmed | 3 | 33 | 20 | 0 0 |
| R Dravid† | c Moin Khan | b Shoaib Malik | 33 | 106 | 86 | 4 0 |
| SC Ganguly* | c Moin Khan | b Abdul Razzaq | 39 | 64 | 41 | 5 1 |
| Yuvraj Singh | c Yousuf Youhana | b M Sami | 65 | 99 | 76 | 7 1 |
| M Kaif | lbw | b Abdul Razzaq | 1 | 4 | 4 | 0 0 |
| RR Powar | lbw | b Shoaib Malik | 14 | 19 | 18 | 2 0 |
| IK Pathan | | b Shoaib Akhtar | 16 | 26 | 21 | 0 1 |
| L Balaji | not out | | 21 | 21 | 12 | 3 1 |
| Z Khan | not out | | 6 | 3 | 3 | 1 0 |
| Extras | (b 1, lb 5, w 23, nb 4) | | 33 | | | |
| Total | (9 wickets, 50 ov, 210 mins) | | 244 | | | |

1-8 (Tendulkar, 1.3 ov), 2-30 (Sehwag, 5.5 ov), 3-37 (Laxman, 7.5 ov),
4-105 (Ganguly, 23.1 ov), 5-139 (Dravid, 32.2 ov), 6-140 (Kaif, 33.1 ov),
7-167 (Powar, 38.4 ov), 8-198 (Pathan, 46.1 ov), 9-237 (Yuvraj Singh, 49.2 ov)

| | o | m | r | w | |
|---|---|---|---|---|---|
| Shoaib Akhtar | 10 | 0 | 50 | 1 | (2w) |
| Shabbir Ahmed | 10 | 0 | 33 | 3 | (3nb, 10w) |
| M Sami | 10 | 0 | 71 | 1 | (1nb, 5w) |
| Abdul Razzaq | 10 | 1 | 44 | 2 | (1w) |
| Shoaib Malik | 10 | 0 | 40 | 2 | (1w) |

## PAKISTAN

| | | | R | M | B | 4/6 |
|---|---|---|---|---|---|---|
| Yasir Hameed | c Yuvraj Singh | b Pathan | 98 | 154 | 116 | 14 0 |
| Shahid Afridi | | b Pathan | 6 | 8 | 5 | 1 0 |
| Yousuf Youhana | c Laxman | b Pathan | 2 | 19 | 11 | 0 0 |
| Younis Khan | run out (Balaji) | | 18 | 21 | 16 | 3 0 |
| Shoaib Malik | c Sehwag | | 2 | 13 | 10 | 0 0 |
| Inzamam-ul-Haq* | lbw | b Tendulkar | 28 | 72 | 40 | 1 1 |
| Abdul Razzaq | not out | | 53 | 72 | 52 | 7 0 |
| Moin Khan | not out | b Khan | 22 | 55 | 34 | 1 0 |
| Shabbir Ahmed | | | | | | |
| Mohammad Sami | | | | | | |
| Shoaib Akhtar | | | | | | |
| Extras | (lb 11, w 7) | | 18 | | | |
| Total | (6 wickets, 47.2 ov, 210 mins) | | 247 | | | |

1-14 (Shahid Afridi, 2.1 ov), 2-29 (Yousuf Youhana, 6.4 ov), 3-55 (Younis Khan, 11.5 ov),
4-65 (Shoaib Malik, 14.3 ov), 5-156 (Inzamam-ul-Haq, 31.4 ov),
6-173 (Yasir Hameed, 34.5 ov)

| | o | m | r | w |
|---|---|---|---|---|
| Pathan | 10 | 0 | 58 | 3 |
| Balaji | 9.2 | 0 | 41 | 1 |
| Khan | 9 | 0 | 56 | 1 |
| Ganguly | 6 | 0 | 24 | 0 |
| Powar | 4 | 0 | 17 | 0 |
| Tendulkar | 8 | 1 | 31 | 1 |
| Yuvraj Singh | 1 | 0 | 9 | 0 |

Umpires: Nadeem Ghauri (P) and DR Shepherd (Eng); Asad Rauf (P); Match Referee: RS Madugalle (SL)

323

# Fourth ODI, Gaddafi Stadium, Lahore, 21 March 2004 (D/N)

Toss Pakistan

India won by 5 wickets

Man of the Match Inzamam-ul-Haq

| PAKISTAN | | | R | M | B | 4/6 |
|---|---|---|---|---|---|---|
| Yasir Hameed | st Dravid | b Kartik | 45 | 93 | 68 | 5 0 |
| Shahid Afridi | c Yuvraj Singh | b Pathan | 3 | 10 | 10 | 0 0 |
| Yousuf Youhana | lbw | b Pathan | 9 | 28 | 19 | 1 0 |
| Inzamam-ul-Haq* | | b Balaji | 123 | 160 | 121 | 9 4 |
| Younis Khan | c Pathan | b Kartik | 36 | 69 | 48 | 1 0 |
| Abdul Razzaq | c Kaif | b Tendulkar | 32 | 48 | 24 | 2 1 |
| Moin Khan† | | b Balaji | 0 | 1 | 2 | 0 0 |
| Shoaib Malik | c Kaif | b Khan | 13 | 13 | 8 | 2 0 |
| Shoaib Akhtar | | b Khan | 2 | 6 | 4 | 0 0 |
| Mohammad Sami | not out | | 0 | 4 | 0 | 0 0 |
| Shabbir Ahmed | not out | | 0 | 1 | 1 | 0 0 |
| Extras | (b 10, lb 9, w 6, nb 5) | | 30 | | | |
| Total | (9 wickets, 50 ov, 221 mins) | | 293 | | | |

1-8 (Shahid Afridi, 2.2 ov), 2-39 (Yousuf Youhana, 8.6 ov), 3-89 (Yasir Hameed, 20.6 ov), 4-194 (Younis Khan, 38.6 ov), 5-264 (Inzamam-ul-Haq, 46.4 ov), 6-264 (Moin Khan, 46.6 ov), 7-283 (Abdul Razzaq, 48.4 ov), 8-290 (Shoaib Malik, 49.2 ov), 9-292 (Shoaib Akhtar, 49.5 ov)

| | o | m | r | w | |
|---|---|---|---|---|---|
| Pathan | 10 | 1 | 53 | 2 | (1nb, 3w) |
| Balaji | 10 | 0 | 64 | 2 | |
| Khan | 10 | 0 | 43 | 2 | (2nb, 1w) |
| Kartik | 10 | 1 | 48 | 2 | (2nb) |
| Tendulkar | 8 | 0 | 48 | 1 | (2w) |
| Yuvraj Singh | 2 | 0 | 18 | 0 | |

| INDIA | | | R | M | B | 4/6 |
|---|---|---|---|---|---|---|
| V Sehwag | c Younis Khan | b M Sami | 26 | 53 | 29 | 5 0 |
| SR Tendulkar | c Moin Khan | b Shoaib Akhtar | 7 | 22 | 13 | 1 0 |
| VVS Laxman | | b Shoaib Akhtar | 20 | 23 | 18 | 4 0 |
| SC Ganguly* | c Moin Khan | b Abdul Razzaq | 21 | 23 | 15 | 2 1 |
| R Dravid† | not out | | 76 | 141 | 92 | 9 0 |
| Yuvraj Singh | c Yousuf Youhana | b M Sami | 36 | 44 | 35 | 5 0 |
| M Kaif | not out | | 71 | 79 | 77 | 8 0 |
| M Kartik | | | | | | |
| IK Pathan | | | | | | |
| L Balaji | | | | | | |
| Z Khan | | | | | | |
| Extras | (lb 9, w 19, nb 9) | | 37 | | | |
| Total | (5 wickets, 45 ov, 195 mins) | | 294 | | | |

1-34 (Tendulkar, 4.1 ov), 2-69 (Laxman, 8.4 ov), 3-75 (Sehwag, 9.6 ov), 4-94 (Ganguly, 12.6 ov), 5-162 (Yuvraj Singh, 23.4 ov)

| | o | m | r | w | |
|---|---|---|---|---|---|
| Shoaib Akhtar | 9 | 1 | 63 | 2 | (6w) |
| Shabbir Ahmed | 7 | 0 | 62 | 0 | (5nb, 1w) |
| M Sami | 10 | 0 | 50 | 2 | (3w) |
| Abdul Razzaq | 7 | 0 | 42 | 1 | (3nb) |
| Shoaib Malik | 7 | 0 | 38 | 0 | |
| Shahid Afridi | 5 | 0 | 30 | 0 | (1nb, 1w) |

Umpires: Asad Rauf (P) and SJA Taufel (A); Nadeem Ghauri (P); Match Referee: RS Madugalle (SL)

324

# Fifth ODI, Gaddafi Stadium, Lahore, 24 March 2004 (D/N)

**Toss Pakistan**                                                    **India won by 40 runs**

Man of the Match VVS Laxman; Man of the Series Inzamam-ul-Haq

## INDIA

| | | | R | M | B | 4/6 |
|---|---|---|---|---|---|---|
| V Sehwag | c Moin Khan | b Shabbir Ahmed | 20 | 26 | 22 | 4 0 |
| SR Tendulkar | c Moin Khan | b M Sami | 37 | 60 | 48 | 7 0 |
| VVS Laxman | c M Sami | b Shoaib Malik | 107 | 158 | 104 | 11 0 |
| SC Ganguly* | c Moin Khan | b Shoaib Akhtar | 45 | 69 | 64 | 5 0 |
| R Dravid† | | b M Sami | 4 | 18 | 10 | 0 0 |
| Yuvraj Singh | c Inzamam-ul-Haq | b Shabbir Ahmed | 18 | 22 | 19 | 2 0 |
| M Kaif | c Taufeeq Umar | b M Sami | 16 | 27 | 20 | 0 0 |
| IK Pathan | not out | | 20 | 23 | 12 | 3 0 |
| L Balaji | not out | | 10 | 9 | 6 | 0 1 |
| M Kartik | | | | | | |
| Z Khan | | | | | | |
| Extras | (b 2, lb 4, w 5, nb 5) | | 16 | | | |
| **Total** | **(7 wickets, 50 ov, 209 mins)** | | **293** | | | |

1-34 (Sehwag, 5.6 ov), 2-79 (Tendulkar, 14.1 ov), 3-171 (Ganguly, 32.4 ov),
4-183 (Dravid, 36.1 ov), 5-227 (Yuvraj Singh, 42.1 ov), 6-253 (Laxman, 45.5 ov),
7-276 (Kaif, 48.3 ov)

| | o | m | r | w | |
|---|---|---|---|---|---|
| Shoaib Akhtar | 10 | 1 | 47 | | |
| Shabbir Ahmed | 10 | 1 | 56 | 2 | (3nb, 1w) |
| M Sami | 10 | 1 | 63 | 3 | (1nb, 2w) |
| Abdul Razzaq | 10 | 0 | 54 | 0 | |
| Shoaib Malik | 10 | 0 | 67 | 1 | (1nb, 1w) |

## PAKISTAN

| | | | R | M | B | 4/6 |
|---|---|---|---|---|---|---|
| Yasir Hameed | | b Balaji | 2 | 7 | 5 | 0 0 |
| Taufeeq Umar | | b Pathan | 18 | 29 | 17 | 3 0 |
| Yousuf Youhana | lbw | b Pathan | 1 | 5 | 7 | 0 0 |
| Inzamam-ul-Haq* | c Tendulkar | b Kartik | 38 | 85 | 51 | 5 0 |
| Younis Khan | c Yuvraj Singh | b Pathan | 12 | 31 | 20 | 2 0 |
| Shoaib Malik | c Kaif | b Sehwag | 65 | 115 | 89 | 3 1 |
| Abdul Razzaq | c Sehwag | b Balaji | 5 | 12 | 9 | 0 0 |
| Moin Khan† | | b Balaji | 72 | 100 | 71 | 5 1 |
| Mohammad Sami | | b Khan | 23 | 26 | 17 | 0 1 |
| Shoaib Akhtar | run out (Yuvraj Singh) | | 2 | 3 | 2 | 0 0 |
| Shabbir Ahmed | not out | | 1 | 4 | 2 | 0 0 |
| Extras | (b 2, lb 5, w 4, nb 3) | | 14 | | | |
| **Total** | **(all out, 47.5 ov, 213 mins)** | | **253** | | | |

1-8 (Yasir Hameed, 1.4 ov), 2-9 (Yousuf Youhana, 2.5 ov), 3-25 (Taufeeq Umar, 6.1 ov),
4-58 (Younis Khan, 12.1 ov), 5-87 (Inzamam, 20.4 ov), 6-96 (Abdul Razzaq, 23.6 ov), 7-195 (Shoaib
Malik, 40.5 ov), 8-248 (M Sami, 46.3 ov), 9-250 (Shoaib Akhtar, 46.5 ov), 10-253 (Moin Khan, 47.5 ov)

| | o | m | r | w | |
|---|---|---|---|---|---|
| Pathan | 10 | 1 | 32 | 3 | (4w) |
| Balaji | 9.5 | 0 | 62 | 3 | (2nb) |
| Khan | 9 | 0 | 54 | 1 | (1nb) |
| Kartik | 10 | 0 | 42 | 1 | |
| Tendulkar | 5 | 0 | 27 | 0 | |
| Sehwag | 4 | 0 | 29 | 1 | |

Umpires: Nadeem Ghauri (P) and DR Shepherd (Eng); Zamir Haider (P); Match Referee: RS Madugalle (SL)

325

# First Test, Multan Cricket Stadium, Multan, 28 March-1 April 2004

India won by an innings and 52 runs

Toss India

| Day 1 Ind 356-2 | Day 2 Ind 675-5d, Pak 42-0 | Day 3 Pak 364-6 | Day 4 Pak 407 and 207-9 |
|---|---|---|---|
| Sehwag 228*, Tendulkar 60* | Imran Farhat 17*, Taufeeq Umar 20* | Abdul Razzaq 47* | Yousuf Youhana 107*, Shabbir Ahmed 0* |

Man of the Match V Sehwag

| INDIA | | R | M | B | 4/6 |
|---|---|---|---|---|---|
| A Chopra | c Farhat b Saqlain | 42 | 163 | 121 | 5 0 |
| V Sehwag | c Taufeeq b Sami | 309 | 531 | 375 | 39 6 |
| R Dravid* | c Yasir b Sami | 6 | 12 | 10 | 1 0 |
| SR Tendulkar | not out | 194 | 493 | 348 | 21 0 |
| VVS Laxman | run out (Youhana/Moin Khan) | 29 | 66 | 58 | 0 0 |
| Yuvraj Singh | c & b Farhat | 59 | 71 | 66 | 8 0 |
| PA Patel† | | | | | |
| A Kumble | | | | | |
| Z Khan | | | | | |
| L Balaji | | | | | |
| IK Pathan | | | | | |
| Extras | (b 8, lb 20, w 1, nb 7) | 36 | | | |
| Total | (5 wkts dec, 161.5 ov, 671 mins) | 675 | | | |

1-160 (Chopra, 39.4 ov), 2-173 (Dravid, 42.2 ov),
3-509 (Sehwag, 126.1 ov) 4-565 (Laxman, 143.1 ov),
5-675 (Y Singh, 161.5 ov)

| | o | m | r | w | |
|---|---|---|---|---|---|
| Shoaib Akhtar | 32 | 4 | 119 | 0 | |
| M Sami | 34 | 4 | 110 | 2 | (1nb) |
| Shabbir Ahmed | 31 | 6 | 122 | 0 | (1nb, 1w) |
| Saqlain Mushtaq | 43 | 4 | 204 | 1 | (5nb) |
| Abdul Razzaq | 15 | 3 | 61 | 0 | |
| Imran Farhat | 6.5 | 0 | 31 | 1 | |

326

## PAKISTAN

| | | | R | M | B | 4/6 |
|---|---|---|---|---|---|---|
| Imran Farhat | lbw | b Balaji | 38 | 118 | 83 | 6 0 |
| Taufeeq Umar | c Dravid | b Pathan | 23 | 95 | 79 | 4 0 |
| Yasir Hameed | c Patel | b Pathan | 91 | 194 | 151 | 14 0 |
| Inzamam-ul-Haq* | c Chopra | b Kumble | 77 | 153 | 118 | 13 0 |
| Yousuf Youhana | c Patel | b Khan | 35 | 105 | 75 | 5 0 |
| Abdul Razzaq | c Patel | b Pathan | 47 | 140 | 109 | 6 0 |
| Moin Khan† | | b Tendulkar | 17 | 51 | 31 | 3 0 |
| Saqlain Mushtaq | c Khan | b Pathan | 5 | 14 | 6 | 1 0 |
| Mohammad Sami | | b Kumble | 15 | 78 | 60 | 1 0 |
| Shoaib Akhtar | | c & b Tendulkar | 0 | 2 | 2 | 0 0 |
| Shabbir Ahmed | not out | | 19 | 61 | 54 | 1 0 |
| Extras | (b 4, lb 26, nb 10) | | 40 | | | |
| Total | (all out, 126.3 ov, 510 mins) | | 407 | | | |

1-58 (Taufeeq Umar, 23.6 ov), 2-73 (Imran Farhat, 28.2 ov), 3-233 (Inzamam-ul-Haq, 67.6 ov), 4-243 (Yasir Hameed, 72.3 ov), 5-321 (Yousuf Youhana, 93.4 ov), 6-364 (Moin Khan, 105.6 ov), 7-364 (Abdul Razzaq, 106.1 ov), 8-371 (Saqlain Mushtaq, 108.5 ov), 9-371 (Shoaib Akhtar, 109.2 ov), 10-407 (M Sami, 126.3 ov)

| | o | m | r | w | |
|---|---|---|---|---|---|
| Khan | 23 | 6 | 76 | 1 | (3nb) |
| Pathan | 28 | 5 | 100 | 4 | |
| Kumble | 39.3 | 12 | 100 | 2 | (1nb) |
| Balaji | 20 | 4 | 54 | 1 | (3nb) |
| Sehwag | 2 | 0 | 11 | 0 | (1nb) |
| Tendulkar | 14 | 1 | 36 | 2 | (1nb) |

## (following on)

| | | | R | M | B | 4/6 |
|---|---|---|---|---|---|---|
| Imran Farhat | c Patel | b Kumble | 24 | 68 | 54 | 4 0 |
| Taufeeq Umar | lbw | b Kumble | 9 | 79 | 60 | 1 0 |
| Yasir Hameed | c Sehwag | b Yuvraj Singh | 23 | 61 | 49 | 3 0 |
| Inzamam-ul-Haq* | run out (Yuvraj Singh) | | 0 | 4 | 1 | 0 0 |
| Yousuf Youhana | c Dravid | b Pathan | 112 | 219 | 164 | 16 2 |
| Abdul Razzaq | c Chopra | b Kumble | 22 | 45 | 49 | 3 0 |
| Moin Khan† | lbw | b Pathan | 5 | 14 | 15 | 1 0 |
| Saqlain Mushtaq | (9) lbw | b Kumble | 0 | 15 | 12 | 0 0 |
| Mohammad Sami | (8) lbw | b Kumble | 0 | 27 | 17 | 0 0 |
| Shoaib Akhtar | c Laxman | b Kumble | 4 | 54 | 42 | 1 0 |
| Shabbir Ahmed | not out | | 0 | 13 | 1 | 0 0 |
| Extras | (b 4, lb 5, w 1, nb 2, pen 5) | | 17 | | | |
| Total | (all out, 77 overs, 304 mins) | | 216 | | | |

1-33 (Imran Farhat, 17.1 ov), 2-44 (Taufeeq Umar, 19.5 ov), 3-44 (Inzamam-ul-Haq, 20.3 ov), 4-75 (Yasir Hameed, 32.2 ov), 5-106 (Abdul Razzaq, 45.2 ov), 6-113 (Moin Khan, 48.6 ov), 7-124 (M Sami, 55.2 ov), 8-136 (Saqlain Mushtaq, 59.2 ov), 9-206 (Shoaib Akhtar, 73.6 ov), 10-216 (Yousuf Youhana, 76.6 ov)

| | o | m | r | w | |
|---|---|---|---|---|---|
| Pathan | 21 | 12 | 26 | 2 | |
| Balaji | 11 | 3 | 48 | 0 | (2nb, 1w) |
| Kumble | 30 | 10 | 72 | 6 | |
| Sehwag | 3 | 0 | 8 | 0 | |
| Yuvraj Singh | 6 | 1 | 25 | 1 | |
| Tendulkar | 6 | 2 | 23 | 0 | |

Umpires: DR Shepherd (Eng); SJA Taufel (A); Asad Rauf (P); Match Referee: RS Madugalle (SL)

# Second Test, Gaddafi Stadium, Lahore, 5-8 April 2004

Toss India

Pakistan won by 9 wickets

Man of the Match Umar Gul

| Day 1 Ind 287 & Pak 61-1 | Day 2 Pak 355-3 | Day 3 Pak 489 & Ind 149-5 |
|---|---|---|
| Farhat 25*, Yasir 4* | Inzamam 118*, Youhana 62* | Sehwag 86*, Patel 13* |

## INDIA

| INDIA | | | R | M | B | 4 | 6 |
|---|---|---|---|---|---|---|---|
| A Chopra | lbw | b Sami | 4 | 10 | 7 | 1 | 0 |
| V Sehwag | c Akmal | b Gul | 39 | 66 | 43 | 6 | 1 |
| R Dravid* | c Inzamam | b Gul | 33 | 123 | 72 | 6 | 0 |
| SR Tendulkar | lbw | b Gul | 2 | 10 | 6 | 0 | 0 |
| VVS Laxman | c Taufeeq | b Gul | 11 | 28 | 21 | 2 | 0 |
| Yuvraj Singh | c Farhat | b Kaneria | 112 | 197 | 129 | 15 | 2 |
| PA Patel† | lbw | b Gul | 0 | 7 | 2 | 0 | 0 |
| AB Agarkar | c Akmal | b Shoaib | 2 | 14 | 7 | 0 | 0 |
| IK Pathan | c & b Kaneria | | 49 | 104 | 80 | 7 | 1 |
| L Balaji | c Akmal | b Sami | 0 | 6 | 6 | 0 | 0 |
| A Kumble | not out | | 6 | 34 | 20 | 1 | 0 |
| Extras | (b 6, lb 8, w 6, nb 9) | | 29 | | | | |
| Total | (all out, 64.1 ov, 303 mins) | | 287 | | | | |

1-5 (Chopra, 1.6 ov) 2-69 (Sehwag, 12.5 ov) 3-75 (Tendulkar, 14.5 ov) 4-94 (Laxman, 20.4 ov) 5-125 (Dravid, 26.5 ov) 6-127 (Patel, 28.2 ov) 7-147 (Agarkar, 31.2 ov) 8-264 (Pathan, 56.2 ov) 9-265 (Balaji, 57.4 ov) 10-287 (Y Singh, 64.1 ov)

| | o | m | r | w | |
|---|---|---|---|---|---|
| Shoaib | 16 | 4 | 69 | 1 | |
| Sami | 23 | 1 | 117 | 2 | (4nb, 2w) |
| Gul | 12 | 2 | 31 | 5 | (4nb) |
| Kaneria | 13.1 | 1 | 56 | 2 | |

| | | | R | M | B | 4 | 6 |
|---|---|---|---|---|---|---|---|
| A Chopra | lbw | b Shoaib | 5 | 31 | 27 | 1 | 0 |
| V Sehwag | c Akmal | b Shoaib | 90 | 214 | 134 | 14 | 0 |
| R Dravid* | run out (Farhat) | | 0 | 3 | 0 | 0 | 0 |
| SR Tendulkar | lbw | b Sami | 8 | 17 | 11 | 1 | 0 |
| VVS Laxman | b Gul | | 13 | 44 | 27 | 2 | 0 |
| Yuvraj Singh | b Sami | | 12 | 24 | 19 | 2 | 0 |
| PA Patel† | not out | | 62 | 172 | 107 | 10 | 0 |
| AB Agarkar | (9) c Taufeeq | b Kaneria | 36 | 64 | 49 | 8 | 0 |
| IK Pathan | (8) c Taufeeq | b Shoaib | 0 | 4 | 4 | 0 | 0 |
| L Balaji | (11) lbw | b Kaneria | 0 | 1 | 1 | 0 | 0 |
| A Kumble | (10) st Akmal | b Kaneria | 0 | 8 | 3 | 0 | 0 |
| Extras | (lb 8, w 1, nb 6) | | 15 | | | | |
| Total | (all out, 62.4 ov) | | 241 | | | | |

1-15 (Chopra, 6.6 ov) 2-15 (Dravid, 7.2 ov) 3-43 (Tendulkar, 11.1 ov) 4-88 (Laxman, 20.4 ov) 5-105 (Y Singh, 25.2 ov) 6-160 (Sehwag, 46.1 ov) 7-160 (Pathan, 46.5 ov) 8-235 (Agarkar, 60.6 ov) 9-241 (Kumble, 62.3 ov) 10-241 (Balaji, 62.4 ov)

| | o | m | r | w | |
|---|---|---|---|---|---|
| Shoaib | 17 | 4 | 62 | 3 | (1nb, 1w) |
| Sami | 26 | 6 | 92 | 2 | (1nb) |
| Gul | 13 | 1 | 65 | 1 | (4nb) |
| Kaneria | 6.4 | 2 | 14 | 3 | |

328

| PAKISTAN | | | R | M | B | 4/6 | | | | R | M | B | 4/6 |
|---|---|---|---|---|---|---|---|---|---|---|---|---|---|
| Imran Farhat | c Patel | b Balaji | 101 | 266 | 204 | 14 0 | c Singh | b Balaji | | 9 | 12 | 11 | 1 0 |
| Taufeeq Umar | | b Balaji | 24 | 71 | 52 | 4 0 | not out | | | 14 | 28 | 20 | 3 0 |
| Yasir Hameed | c Dravid | b Agarkar | 19 | 77 | 51 | 2 0 | not out | | | 16 | 15 | 12 | 3 0 |
| Inzamam-ul-Haq* | lbw | b Pathan | 118 | 323 | 243 | 14 0 | | | | | | | |
| Yousuf Youhana | c Patel | b Balaji | 72 | 218 | 153 | 13 0 | | | | | | | |
| Asim Kamal | c Patel | b Kumble | 73 | 189 | 141 | 7 3 | | | | | | | |
| Kamran Akmal† | lbw | b Pathan | 5 | 21 | 12 | 1 0 | | | | | | | |
| Mohammad Sami | | b Pathan | 2 | 9 | 5 | 0 0 | | | | | | | |
| Shoaib Akhtar | c Singh | b Kumble | 19 | 89 | 75 | 1 0 | | | | | | | |
| Umar Gul | hit wicket | b Kumble | 14 | 43 | 34 | 3 0 | | | | | | | |
| Danish Kaneria | not out | | 0 | 11 | 3 | 0 0 | | | | | | | |
| Extras | (b4, lb18, w 4, nb16) | | 42 | | | | (nb 1) | | | 1 | | | |
| Total | (all out, 160.1 ov, 663 mins) | | 489 | | | | (1 wicket, 7 ov, 28 mins) | | | 40-1 | | | |

1-47 (Taufeeq Umar, 16.6 ov)    2-95 (Yasir Hameed, 36.3 ov)
3-205 (Imran Farhat, 64.2 ov)    4-356 (Inzamam, 113.6 ov)
5-366 (Yousuf Youhana, 116.3 ov)    6-379 (Kamran Akmal, 121.2 ov)
7-386 (M Sami, 123.1 ov)    8-432 (Shoaib Akhtar, 146.4 ov)
9-470 (Umar Gul, 157.6 ov)    10-489 (Asim Kamal, 160.1 ov)

1-15 (Imran Farhat, 3.2 ov)

| | o | m | r | w | |
|---|---|---|---|---|---|
| Pathan | 44 | 14 | 107 | 3 | (5nb, 1w) |
| Balaji | 33 | 11 | 81 | 3 | (2nb, 2w) |
| Agarkar | 23 | 5 | 80 | 1 | (1nb) |
| Kumble | 44.1 | 5 | 146 | 2 | (1nb, 1w) |
| Tendulkar | 12 | 1 | 38 | 1 | (2nb) |
| Singh | 3 | 0 | 7 | 0 | |
| Sehwag | 1 | 0 | 8 | 0 | (1nb) |

| | o | m | r | w | |
|---|---|---|---|---|---|
| Pathan | 4 | 0 | 25 | 0 | |
| Balaji | 3 | 0 | 15 | 1 | (1nb) |

Umpires: SA Bucknor (WI); SJA Taufel (A); N Ghauri (P); Match Referee: RS Madugalle (SL)

329

# Third Test, Pindi Cricket Stadium, Lahore, 13-16 April 2004

India won by an innings and 131 runs

Toss India

| Day 1 Pak 224, Ind 23-1 | Day 2 Ind 342-4 | Day 3 Ind 600, Pak 49-2 | Man of the Match R Dravid; Man of the Series V Sehwag |
|---|---|---|---|
| Patel 13*, Dravid 10* | Dravid 134*, Ganguly 53* | Yasir Hameed 8*, Kamran Akmal 10* | |

## PAKISTAN — First Innings

| Batsman | Dismissal | R | M | B | 4 | 6 |
|---|---|---|---|---|---|---|
| Imran Farhat | lbw b Nehra | 16 | 51 | 39 | 3 | 0 |
| Taufeeq Umar | lbw b Balaji | 9 | 45 | 32 | 2 | 0 |
| Yasir Hameed | c Laxman b Pathan | 26 | 51 | 38 | 4 | 0 |
| Inzamam-ul-Haq* | c Patel b Nehra | 15 | 51 | 28 | 2 | 0 |
| Yousuf Youhana | b Pathan | 13 | 55 | 37 | 2 | 0 |
| Asim Kamal | lbw b Balaji | 21 | 63 | 46 | 4 | 0 |
| Kamran Akmal† | c Laxman b Balaji | 17 | 42 | 28 | 4 | 0 |
| Mohammad Sami | run out (Pathan) | 49 | 154 | 122 | 7 | 0 |
| Shoaib Akhtar | b Balaji | 0 | 1 | 2 | 0 | 0 |
| Fazl-e-Akbar | lbw b Kumble | 25 | 98 | 55 | 4 | 0 |
| Danish Kaneria | not out | 4 | 24 | 13 | 1 | 0 |
| Extras | (b 14, lb 5, w 7, nb 3) | 29 | | | | |
| **Total** | (all out, 72.5 ov, 322 mins) | **224** | | | | |

1-34 (Taufeeq Umar, 10.5 ov), 2-34 (Imran Farhat, 11.6 ov), 3-77 (Yasir Hameed, 22.2 ov), 4-77 (Inzamam-ul-Haq, 23.3 ov), 5-110 (Yousuf Youhana, 34.5 ov), 6-120 (Asim Kamal, 37.4 ov), 7-137 (Kamran Akmal, 43.4 ov), 8-137 (Shoaib Akhtar, 43.6 ov), 9-207 (Fazl-e-Akbar, 66.1 ov), 10-224 (M Sami, 72.5 ov)

| | O | M | R | W | |
|---|---|---|---|---|---|
| Pathan | 22 | 7 | 49 | 2 | (2nb, 1w) |
| Balaji | 19 | 4 | 63 | 4 | (1nb, 3w) |
| Nehra | 21 | 4 | 60 | 2 | (3w) |
| Ganguly | 2 | 0 | 9 | 0 | |
| Kumble | 8.5 | 2 | 24 | 1 | |

## PAKISTAN — Second Innings

| Batsman | Dismissal | R | M | B | 4 | 6 |
|---|---|---|---|---|---|---|
| Imran Farhat | c Sehwag b Balaji | 3 | 41 | 25 | 0 | 0 |
| Taufeeq Umar | lbw b Pathan | 13 | 48 | 34 | 2 | 0 |
| Yasir Hameed | c Patel b Nehra | 20 | 70 | 39 | 4 | 0 |
| Inzamam-ul-Haq* | c Patel b Balaji | 9 | 39 | 28 | 1 | 0 |
| Yousuf Youhana (5) | c & b Kumble | 48 | 88 | 61 | 9 | 0 |
| Asim Kamal (6) | not out | 60 | 135 | 90 | 13 | 0 |
| Kamran Akmal† (7) | b Balaji | 23 | 31 | 29 | 5 | 0 |
| Mohammad Sami (4) | c Ganguly b Tendulkar | 0 | 10 | 1 | 0 | 0 |
| Shoaib Akhtar | c Dravid b Kumble | 28 | 20 | 14 | 4 | 2 |
| Fazl-e-Akbar | c Nehra b Kumble | 12 | 17 | 10 | 3 | 0 |
| Danish Kaneria | c Pathan b Kumble | 0 | 4 | 2 | 0 | 0 |
| Extras | (b 5, lb 11, w 2, nb 11) | 29 | | | | |
| **Total** | (all out, 54 ov, 255 mins) | **245** | | | | |

1-30 (Imran Farhat, 9.2 ov), 2-34 (Taufeeq Umar, 10.1 ov), 3-64 (Kamran Akmal, 17.3 ov), 4-90 (Yasir Hameed, 24.2 ov), 5-94 (Inzamam-ul-Haq, 25.5 ov), 6-175 (Yousuf Youhana, 42.6 ov), 7-179 (M Sami, 44.1 ov), 8-221 (Shoaib Akhtar, 48.3 ov), 9-244 (Danish Kaneria, 53.6 ov), 10-245 (Fazl-e-Akbar, 52.6 ov)

| | O | M | R | W | |
|---|---|---|---|---|---|
| Pathan | 15 | 6 | 35 | 1 | (4nb, 1w) |
| Balaji | 20 | 2 | 108 | 3 | (2nb, 1w) |
| Kumble | 8 | 2 | 47 | 4 | (1nb) |
| Nehra | 6 | 2 | 20 | 1 | |
| Ganguly | 4 | 0 | 18 | 0 | (2nb) |
| Tendulkar | 1 | 0 | 1 | 1 | |

| INDIA | | | R | M | B | 4/6 |
|---|---|---|---|---|---|---|
| V Sehwag | c Yasir | b Shoaib | 0 | 1 | 1 | 0 0 |
| PA Patelt | c Akmal | b Fazl-e-Akbar | 69 | 203 | 141 | 10 0 |
| R Dravid | | b Farhat | 270 | 740 | 495 | 34 1 |
| SR Tendulkar | c Akmal | b Shoaib | 1 | 6 | 3 | 0 0 |
| VVS Laxman | | b Shoaib | 71 | 153 | 99 | 12 0 |
| SC Ganguly* | run out (sub Nazir) | | 77 | 175 | 128 | 12 0 |
| Yuvraj Singh | lbw | b M Sami | 47 | 121 | 119 | 7 0 |
| IK Pathan | c Fazl-e-Akbar | b Kaneria | 15 | 40 | 35 | 2 0 |
| A Kumble | st Akmal | b Kaneria | 9 | 27 | 28 | 0 1 |
| L Balaji | c sub (Malik) | b Farhat | 11 | 18 | 6 | 1 1 |
| A Nehra | not out | | 1 | 7 | 9 | 0 0 |
| Extras | (b 11, lb 12, w 6) | | 29 | | | |
| Total | (all out, 177.2 overs, 750 mins) | | 600 | | | |

1-0 (Sehwag, 0.1 ov)            2-129 (Patel, 48.1 ov),
3-130 (Tendulkar, 49.1 ov)    4-261 (Laxman, 83.6 ov),
5-392 (Ganguly, 124.1 ov)     6-490 (Y Singh, 153.6 ov),
7-537 (Pathan, 164.4 ov)       8-572 (Kumble, 172.4 ov),
9-593 (Dravid, 175.2 ov)       10-600 (Balaji, 177.2 ov)

| | o | m | r | w |
|---|---|---|---|---|
| Shoaib Akhtar | 21.2 | 7 | 47 | 3 |
| Fazl-e-Akbar | 40.4 | 3 | 162 | 1 |
| Danish Kaneria | 62 | 4 | 178 | 2 (1w) |
| M Sami | 40 | 11 | 116 | 1 (1w) |
| Imran Farhat | 12.2 | 1 | 69 | 2 |
| Yasir Hameed | 1 | 0 | 5 | 0 |

Umpires: RE Koertzen (SA), DR Shepherd (Eng); Zamir Haider (P); Match Referee: RS Madugalle (SL)

331

# ODI Series Averages: India

**Batting and Fielding**

| Name | Mat | I | NO | Runs | HS | Ave | SR | 100 | 50 | Ct | St |
|------|-----|---|----|------|-----|------|--------|-----|-----|-----|-----|
| HK Badani | 1 | 1 | 1 | 8 | 8* | - | 160.00 | - | - | - | - |
| L Balaji | 5 | 3 | 2 | 45 | 21* | 45.00 | 160.71 | - | - | - | - |
| R Dravid | 5 | 5 | 1 | 248 | 99 | 62.00 | 73.59 | - | 2 | 3 | 1 |
| SC Ganguly | 5 | 5 | 0 | 165 | 45 | 33.00 | 80.48 | - | - | - | - |
| M Kaif | 5 | 5 | 1 | 141 | 71* | 35.25 | 84.93 | - | 1 | 4 | - |
| M Kartik | 3 | 1 | 1 | 3 | 3* | - | 60.00 | - | - | - | - |
| Z Khan | 5 | 3 | 1 | 6 | 6* | 3.00 | 100.00 | - | - | 1 | - |
| VVS Laxman | 4 | 4 | 0 | 134 | 107 | 33.50 | 89.93 | 1 | - | 1 | - |
| A Nehra | 2 | 1 | 0 | 0 | 0 | 0.00 | 0.00 | - | - | - | - |
| IK Pathan | 3 | 2 | 1 | 36 | 20* | 36.00 | 109.09 | - | - | 1 | - |
| RR Powar | 2 | 2 | 1 | 32 | 18* | 32.00 | 110.34 | - | - | - | - |
| V Sehwag | 5 | 5 | 0 | 164 | 79 | 32.80 | 111.56 | - | 1 | 2 | - |
| Yuvraj Singh | 5 | 5 | 0 | 141 | 65 | 28.20 | 88.67 | - | 1 | 3 | - |
| SR Tendulkar | 5 | 5 | 0 | 213 | 141 | 42.60 | 90.25 | 1 | - | 1 | - |

**Bowling**

| Name | Mat | O | M | R | W | Ave | Best | 5 | 10 | SR | Econ |
|------|-----|------|---|-----|---|-------|------|---|-----|------|------|
| L Balaji | 5 | 45.1 | 1 | 270 | 6 | 45.00 | 3-62 | - | - | 45.1 | 5.97 |
| SC Ganguly | 5 | 7 | 0 | 38 | 0 | - | - | - | - | - | 5.42 |
| M Kartik | 3 | 30 | 1 | 164 | 5 | 32.80 | 2-48 | - | - | 36.0 | 5.46 |
| Z Khan | 5 | 45 | 0 | 291 | 7 | 41.57 | 3-66 | - | - | 38.5 | 6.46 |
| A Nehra | 2 | 20 | 0 | 102 | 4 | 25.50 | 3-44 | - | - | 30.0 | 5.10 |
| IK Pathan | 3 | 30 | 3 | 143 | 8 | 17.87 | 3-32 | - | - | 22.5 | 4.76 |
| RR Powar | 2 | 10 | 0 | 52 | 0 | - | - | - | - | - | 5.20 |
| V Sehwag | 5 | 15 | 0 | 100 | 2 | 50.00 | 1-29 | - | - | 45.0 | 6.66 |
| Yuvraj Singh | 5 | 13 | 1 | 68 | 2 | 34.00 | 2-41 | - | - | 39.0 | 5.23 |
| SR Tendulkar | 5 | 30 | 1 | 185 | 2 | 92.50 | 1-31 | - | - | 90.0 | 6.16 |

* Also in ODI squad: Parthiv Patel, Amit Bhandari (third, fourth & fifth ODIs)

**Coach** John Wright
**Manager** Ratnakar Shetty
**Physio** Andrew Leipus
**Trainer** Greg le Roux
**Computer Analyst** S Ramakrishnan
**Media Manager** Amrit Mathur

# ODI Series Averages: Pakistan

**Batting and Fielding**

| Name | Mat | I | NO | Runs | HS | Ave | SR | 100 | 50 | Ct | St |
|------|-----|---|-----|------|-----|-------|--------|-----|-----|-----|-----|
| Abdul Razzaq | 5 | 5 | 2 | 148 | 53* | 49.33 | 124.36 | - | 1 | 1 | - |
| Imran Farhat | 1 | 1 | 0 | 24 | 24 | 24.00 | 82.75 | - | - | - | - |
| Inzamam-ul-Haq | 5 | 5 | 0 | 340 | 123 | 68.00 | 97.70 | 2 | - | 1 | - |
| Mohammad Sami | 5 | 2 | 1 | 23 | 23 | 23.00 | 135.29 | - | - | 1 | - |
| Moin Khan | 5 | 5 | 1 | 110 | 72 | 27.50 | 88.00 | - | 1 | 8 | 1 |
| Naved-ul-Hasan | 1 | 1 | 1 | 3 | 3* | | 75.00 | - | - | 2 | - |
| Shabbir Ahmed | 4 | 2 | 2 | 1 | 1* | - | 33.33 | - | - | 1 | - |
| Shahid Afridi | 3 | 3 | 0 | 89 | 80 | 29.66 | 121.91 | - | 1 | 1 | - |
| Shoaib Akhtar | 5 | 2 | 0 | 4 | 2 | 2.00 | 66.66 | - | - | - | - |
| Shoaib Malik | 5 | 5 | 1 | 117 | 65 | 29.25 | 83.57 | - | 1 | 1 | - |
| Taufeeq Umar | 1 | 1 | 0 | 18 | 18 | 18.00 | 105.88 | - | - | 1 | - |
| Yasir Hameed | 5 | 5 | 0 | 238 | 98 | 47.60 | 76.77 | - | 2 | 1 | - |
| Younis Khan | 5 | 5 | 0 | 140 | 46 | 28.00 | 87.50 | - | - | 1 | - |
| Yousuf Youhana | 5 | 5 | 0 | 109 | 73 | 21.80 | 83.20 | - | 1 | 2 | - |

**Bowling**

| Name | Mat | O | M | R | W | Ave | Best | 5 | 10 | SR | Econ |
|------|-----|-----|---|-----|----|-------|------|-----|-----|------|------|
| Shahid Afridi | 3 | 13 | 0 | 87 | 2 | 43.50 | 2-57 | - | - | 39.0 | 6.69 |
| Shabbir Ahmed | 4 | 36 | 1 | 216 | 5 | 43.20 | 3-33 | - | - | 43.2 | 6.00 |
| Shoaib Akhtar | 5 | 48 | 3 | 264 | 9 | 29.33 | 3-49 | - | - | 32.0 | 5.50 |
| Yasir Hameed | 5 | 1 | 0 | 6 | 0 | - | - | - | - | - | 6.00 |
| Naved-ul-Hasan | 1 | 10 | 0 | 73 | 3 | 24.33 | 3-73 | - | - | 20.0 | 7.30 |
| Shoaib Malik | 5 | 47 | 0 | 254 | 4 | 63.50 | 2-40 | - | - | 70.5 | 5.40 |
| Abdul Razzaq | 5 | 39 | 1 | 245 | 3 | 81.66 | 2-44 | - | - | 78.0 | 6.28 |
| Mohammad Sami | 5 | 49.4 | 2 | 299 | 11 | 27.18 | 3-41 | - | - | 27.0 | 6.02 |

*Also in ODI squad: Saqlain Mushtaq, Rao Iftikhar Anjum (first & second ODIs), Misbah-ul-Haq (first & second ODIs), Taufeeq Umar (third, fourth & fifth ODIs)

**Coach** Javed Miandad
**Manager** Haroon Rashid
**Doctors/Trainers** Dr Riaz Ahmed, Dr Taufeeq Razzak

# Test Series Averages: India

**Batting and Fielding**

| Name | Mat | I | NO | Runs | HS | Ave | SR | 100 | 50 | Ct | St |
|---|---|---|---|---|---|---|---|---|---|---|---|
| AB Agarkar | 1 | 2 | 0 | 38 | 36 | 19.00 | 67.85 | - | - | - | - |
| L Balaji | 3 | 3 | 0 | 11 | 11 | 3.66 | 84.61 | - | - | - | - |
| A Chopra | 2 | 3 | 0 | 51 | 42 | 17.00 | 32.90 | - | - | 2 | - |
| R Dravid | 3 | 4 | 0 | 309 | 270 | 77.25 | 53.55 | 1 | - | 4 | - |
| SC Ganguly | 1 | 1 | 0 | 77 | 77 | 77.00 | 60.15 | - | 1 | 1 | - |
| Z Khan | 1 | 0 | - | - | - | - | - | - | - | 1 | - |
| A Kumble | 3 | 3 | 1 | 15 | 9 | 7.50 | 29.41 | - | - | 1 | - |
| VVS Laxman | 3 | 4 | 0 | 124 | 71 | 31.00 | 60.48 | - | 1 | 3 | - |
| A Nehra | 1 | 1 | 1 | 1 | 1* | - | 11.11 | - | - | 1 | - |
| PA Patel | 3 | 3 | 1 | 131 | 69 | 65.50 | 52.40 | - | 2 | 10 | - |
| IK Pathan | 3 | 3 | 0 | 64 | 49 | 21.33 | 53.78 | - | - | 1 | - |
| V Sehwag | 3 | 4 | 0 | 438 | 309 | 109.50 | 79.20 | 1 | 1 | 2 | - |
| Yuvraj Singh | 3 | 4 | 0 | 230 | 112 | 57.50 | 69.06 | 1 | 1 | 2 | - |
| SR Tendulkar | 3 | 4 | 1 | 205 | 194* | 68.33 | 55.70 | 1 | - | 1 | - |

**Bowling**

| Name | Mat | O | M | R | W | Ave | Best | 5 | 10 | SR | Econ |
|---|---|---|---|---|---|---|---|---|---|---|---|
| AB Agarkar | 1 | 23 | 5 | 80 | 1 | 80.00 | 1-80 | - | - | 138.0 | 3.47 |
| L Balaji | 3 | 106 | 24 | 369 | 12 | 30.75 | 4-63 | - | - | 53.0 | 3.48 |
| SC Ganguly | 1 | 6 | 0 | 27 | 0 | - | - | - | - | - | 4.50 |
| Z Khan | 1 | 23 | 6 | 76 | 1 | 76.00 | 1-76 | - | - | 138.0 | 3.30 |
| A Kumble | 3 | 130.3 | 31 | 389 | 15 | 25.93 | 6-72 | 1 | - | 52.2 | 2.98 |
| A Nehra | 1 | 27 | 6 | 80 | 3 | 26.66 | 2-60 | - | - | 54.0 | 2.96 |
| IK Pathan | 3 | 134 | 44 | 342 | 12 | 28.50 | 4-100 | - | - | 67.0 | 2.55 |
| V Sehwag | 3 | 6 | 0 | 27 | 0 | - | - | - | - | - | 4.50 |
| Yuvraj Singh | 3 | 9 | 1 | 32 | 1 | 32.00 | 1-25 | - | - | 54.0 | 3.55 |
| SR Tendulkar | 3 | 33 | 4 | 98 | 4 | 24.50 | 2-36 | - | - | 49.5 | 2.96 |

*Also in Test squad: Murali Kartik, Mohammad Kaif (second & third Tests)

**Coach** John Wright
**Manager** Ratnakar Shetty
**Physio** Andrew Leipus
**Trainer** Greg le Roux
**Computer Analyst** S Ramakrishnan
**Media Manager** Amrit Mathur

# Test Series Averages: Pakistan

**Batting and Fielding**

| Name | Mat | I | NO | Runs | HS | Ave | SR | 100 | 50 | Ct | St |
|------|-----|---|----|----|-----|-----|-----|-----|-----|-----|-----|
| Abdul Razzaq | 1 | 2 | 0 | 69 | 47 | 34.50 | 43.67 | - | - | - | - |
| Asim Kamal | 2 | 3 | 1 | 154 | 73 | 77.00 | 55.59 | - | 2 | - | - |
| Danish Kaneria | 2 | 3 | 2 | 4 | 4* | 4.00 | 22.22 | - | - | 1 | - |
| Fazl-e-Akbar | 1 | 2 | 0 | 37 | 25 | 18.50 | 56.92 | - | - | 1 | - |
| Imran Farhat | 3 | 6 | 0 | 191 | 101 | 31.83 | 45.91 | 1 | - | 3 | - |
| Inzamam-ul-Haq | 3 | 5 | 0 | 219 | 118 | 43.80 | 52.39 | 1 | 1 | 1 | - |
| Kamran Akmal | 2 | 3 | 0 | 45 | 23 | 15.00 | 65.21 | - | - | 7 | 2 |
| Mohammad Sami | 3 | 5 | 0 | 66 | 49 | 13.20 | 32.19 | - | - | - | - |
| Moin Khan | 1 | 2 | 0 | 22 | 17 | 11.00 | 47.82 | - | - | - | - |
| Saqlain Mushtaq | 1 | 2 | 0 | 5 | 5 | 2.50 | 27.77 | - | - | - | - |
| Shabbir Ahmed | 1 | 2 | 2 | 19 | 19* | - | 34.54 | - | - | - | - |
| Shoaib Akhtar | 3 | 5 | 0 | 51 | 28 | 10.20 | 37.77 | - | - | - | - |
| Taufeeq Umar | 3 | 6 | 1 | 92 | 24 | 18.40 | 33.21 | - | - | 4 | - |
| Umar Gul | 1 | 1 | 0 | 14 | 14 | 14.00 | 41.17 | - | - | - | - |
| Yasir Hameed | 3 | 6 | 1 | 195 | 91 | 39.00 | 57.35 | - | 1 | 2 | - |
| Yousuf Youhana | 3 | 5 | 0 | 280 | 112 | 56.00 | 57.14 | 1 | 1 | - | - |

**Bowling**

| Name | Mat | O | M | R | W | Ave | Best | 5 | 10 | SR | Econ |
|------|-----|---|---|---|---|-----|------|---|-----|-----|------|
| Abdul Razzaq | 1 | 15 | 3 | 61 | 0 | - | - | - | - | - | 4.06 |
| Danish Kaneria | 2 | 81.5 | 7 | 248 | 7 | 35.42 | 3-14 | - | - | 70.1 | 3.03 |
| Fazl-e-Akbar | 1 | 40.4 | 3 | 162 | 1 | 162.00 | 1-162 | - | - | 244.0 | 3.98 |
| Imran Farhat | 3 | 19.1 | 1 | 100 | 3 | 33.33 | 2-69 | - | - | 38.3 | 5.21 |
| Mohammad Sami | 3 | 123 | 22 | 435 | 7 | 62.14 | 2-92 | - | - | 105.4 | 3.53 |
| Saqlain Mushtaq | 1 | 43 | 4 | 204 | 1 | 204.00 | 1-204 | - | - | 258.0 | 4.74 |
| Shabbir Ahmed | 1 | 31 | 6 | 122 | 0 | - | - | - | - | - | 3.93 |
| Shoaib Akhtar | 3 | 86.2 | 16 | 297 | 7 | 42.42 | 3-47 | - | - | 74.0 | 3.44 |
| Umar Gul | 1 | 25 | 3 | 96 | 6 | 16.00 | 5-31 | 1 | - | 25.0 | 3.84 |
| Yasir Hameed | 3 | 1 | 0 | 5 | 0 | - | - | - | - | - | 5.00 |

*Also in Test squad: Misbah-ul-Haq, Imran Nazir (second & third Tests), Naved-ul-Hasan (third Test), Iftikhar Anjum (third Test), Abdur Rauf (third Test)

**Coach** Javed Miandad
**Manager** Haroon Rashid
**Doctors/Trainers** Dr Riaz Ahmed, Dr Taufeeq Razzak

# Index

# Index

# Index

# Index

# *Index*

# Index

# *Index*

# Index

# Index